DIPLOMACY AT THE BRINK

★★★★★★★★★★★★★★★★★★★★★★★★★★★★★★★★★★★

DIPLOMACY
AT THE BRINK

★★★★★★★★★★★★★★★★★★★★★★★★★★★★★★★★★★★

Eisenhower, Churchill, and Eden
in the Cold War

DAVID M. WATRY

LOUISIANA STATE UNIVERSITY PRESS
BATON ROUGE

Published by Louisiana State University Press
Copyright © 2014 by Louisiana State University Press
All rights reserved
Manufactured in the United States of America
First printing

DESIGNER: Michelle A. Neustrom
TYPEFACE: Whitman
PRINTER AND BINDER: Maple Press

LIBRARY OF CONGRESS CATALOGING-IN-PUBLICATION DATA

Watry, David M., 1958–
    Diplomacy at the brink : Eisenhower, Churchill, and Eden in the Cold War /
David M. Watry.
        pages cm
    Includes bibliographical references and index.
    ISBN 978-0-8071-5718-3 (cloth : alk. paper) — ISBN 978-0-8071-5719-0
(pdf) — ISBN 978-0-8071-5720-6 (epub) — ISBN 978-0-8071-5721-3 (mobi)
    1. United States—Foreign relations—Great Britain. 2. Great Britain—Foreign
relations—United States. 3. Eisenhower, Dwight D. (Dwight David), 1890–1969.
4. Churchill, Winston, 1874–1965. 5. Eden, Anthony, Earl of Avon, 1897–1977.
6. United States—Foreign relations—1953–1961. 7. Great Britain—Foreign relations—1945–1964. 8. Cold War—Diplomatic history. I. Title.
    E183.8.G7W277 2014
    327.73041—dc23

                                                          2014009824

CONTENTS

Illustrations follow page 48.

ACKNOWLEDGMENTS

Many people have helped me in the preparation of this book. I want to recognize the many significant contributions from my family: my mother, Ruth Watry; my sisters, Debra Weidenfeller and Dianne Bilbrey; my brothers-in-law, Don Weidenfeller and Karl Bilbrey; and my nieces and nephews, Ross Nichols, Michael Weidenfeller, Rachel Weidenfeller, and Erin Nichols. This book is dedicated to the memory of my dad, Earl Watry, who passed away while I researched this book. He, in many ways, inspired me to do this book.

I wish to personally thank and acknowledge Dr. Joyce S. Goldberg for her support, encouragement, and direction. I will be forever in her debt and grateful for her expertise, passion, patience, and understanding. I also wish to thank Dr. Kenneth R. Philp and Dr. Stanley H. Palmer. Their critiques, evaluations, and arguments made my book a much more polished product than it would have been without their significant help. Finally, I also valued the many suggestions made by my good friend Ted Babcock.

A special word of thanks goes to Chris Abraham, Archivist, and Kathy Struss, Audiovisual Archivist, Dwight D. Eisenhower Library; Almarie Ehlers, Conference Coordinator, Churchill College, Cambridge; Caroline Herbert, Archives Assistant, Churchill Archives Centre, Cambridge; Allen Packwood, Director, Churchill Archives Centre, Cambridge; Claire Nicholas, Administrative Assistant, Woodbrooke Quaker Study Centre, Birmingham; Jenny Childs, Archivist–Special Collections, University of Birmingham; Colin Harris, Superintendent–Special Collections, Bodleian Library, Oxford; and Amanda K. Hawk, Assistant for Public Services, Seeley G. Mudd Manuscript Library, Princeton. I would also like to thank Louisiana

State University Press for publishing my manuscript, in particular Senior Acquisitions Editor Alisa A. Plant for believing in this project and working with me to make this happen. I would like to thank Dr. Chris Tudda for suggesting additional primary research, which made the manuscript even stronger. I would like to also thank Susan Murray for her brilliant and meticulous copyediting. Any mistakes in this book are completely my own.

The spelling of names has been modernized in a limited number of instances; for example, the spellings Mao Zedong and Zhou Enlai are used rather than earlier, alternative spellings. When necessary for clarity, grammar and punctuation were altered in archival material.

My appreciation goes to those who gave me permission to access valuable papers and documents, including Duncan Sandys, who gave me permission to access the Sandys Papers; and the late Baroness Soames (Mary Churchill Soames), who gave me permission, in a handwritten note, to review her late husband's papers. Let me express my deep gratitude to the Countess of Avon (Clarissa Churchill Eden) for allowing me to review her late husband's papers. The Avon Papers were absolutely essential for the writing of my book.

DIPLOMACY AT THE BRINK

CHAPTER 1

INTRODUCTION

Few historians have discussed the significant differences among Dwight D. Eisenhower, Winston Churchill, and Anthony Eden during the Cold War. John Lukacs, an eminent Hungarian-born American historian well known for his admiration of Winston Churchill, observed that "in none of the numerous biographies of Eisenhower is there a substantial description of how this seemingly simple (though in reality rather complex) military man, with his easygoing and liberal reputation, shed his pro-Russian and sometimes pro-Democratic opinions to become a rigid anti-Communist, a Republican, and eventually even a self-styled conservative." Lukacs's analysis is insightful. Eisenhower did shed his pro-Russian and pro-Democratic opinions, and his eventual transformation to a right-wing ideologue, particularly in foreign affairs, can only be fully understood in the context of his transatlantic relationships with Churchill and Eden.[1]

In studying the relationship between Eisenhower and Churchill, one can easily see the tremendous ideological differences between them in dealing with the many international crises of the 1950s. During the Cold War, the roles of Eisenhower and Churchill essentially reversed from what they had been during the Second World War. Eisenhower no longer reported to Churchill; now Churchill reported to him. Eisenhower advocated a hard line on the Soviet Union, while Churchill advocated a détente with the Soviet Union, a complete reversal of their positions at the end of the Second World War. Eisenhower's new conservatism rejected détente and called for the rollback of Communism throughout the world. U.S. foreign policy turned out to be diametrically opposed to Churchill's foreign policy of détente. The United States and Great Britain could no longer count on each other for mutual support in foreign affairs. Eisenhower firmly rejected Churchill's call for a grand and global Anglo-American alliance. Promised collective security through the North Atlantic Treaty Organization (NATO) and the Southeast Asia Treaty Organization (SEATO) broke down under the heavy weight of the ideological differences between them.

The "special relationship" between the United States and Great Britain continually deteriorated throughout Eisenhower's first administration. Differing visions of the Communist threat in Korea, Indochina, and Quemoy and Matsu led to a fracturing of the transatlantic alliance. Cognizant of the problems of British and French colonialism, Eisenhower decided on a policy of anti-Communism and anticolonialism in the Far East, North Africa, and the Middle East. He deliberately put his policies of anti-Communism and anticolonialism ahead of helping Western allies in his global fight against Communism. Ironically, this split in the transatlantic alliance undoubtedly benefited the Soviet Union.

Shaking up the political and military establishment in Washington by rejecting Paul Nitze's National Security Council Paper 68 (NSC-68), Eisenhower opposed a massive buildup of the U.S. military because it placed far too heavy a financial burden on the United States. He quickly moved to replace it with the more economical "New Look" defense policy, intended to assure the military and the public "more bang for the buck." George F. Kennan's reactive containment policy led to a disastrous and hugely unpopular stalemate in Korea. Eisenhower scrapped Kennan's policy in favor of a far more ambitious and risky but potentially more successful policy of "brinksmanship." Eisenhower worried about perceptions of the United States losing or retreating in the Cold War, while Churchill sought to negotiate with the Communists in deals that might prove to be mutually beneficial.[2]

Unlike President Harry Truman, who had lectured about the need to save the United States from Communism, Eisenhower discoursed about the "long-term" needs of the United States and about saving "the American way of life." Furthermore, he understood the vital importance of maintaining the health of the economy in providing for an essential military defense. Truman's inert and torpid foreign policy in his second term had too often relied on standard military strategies. Eisenhower preferred a nuanced, pro-active, covert, and even "hidden hand" foreign policy in order to defeat the Communists by outplaying them at their own subversive game.[3]

This new brand of Republican foreign policy resurrected the "Old Right" ideas of General Douglas MacArthur, Senator Robert A. Taft, and former president Herbert Hoover. Eisenhower's political advisers, who in the 1960s often wrote admiringly of MacArthur's military plan to end the Korean War, stand in stark contrast to the historians of the 1970s, 1980s, and 1990s, who have all but ignored MacArthur or gone so far as to trivialize his nuclear threats to end the Korean War. Yet, a close reading of Eisenhower's memoirs and his National Security Council meetings in the first term shows the powerful influence of MacArthur's military thinking on him, particularly when he faced a myriad of military problems in the Far East.[4]

The former isolationist Senator Robert A. Taft of Ohio also encouraged Eisenhower to adopt an extreme right-wing global foreign policy. He now argued against American isolationism in favor of a policy based in part on the nineteenth-century beliefs of Admiral Alfred Thayer Mahan. Taft's and Mahan's ideas would become the basis of Eisenhower's New Look, with military emphasis on the air force and the navy over army ground troops. Taft strove to reduce military expenditures, exemplified by large numbers of American ground troops in Europe, while at the same time expanding the power and scope of the American military, specifically through the strategic use of the navy, air force, and atomic power. Eisenhower and Taft had previously disagreed on the importance of collective security agreements, the main reason for Eisenhower's candidacy for the Republican nomination in 1952. After the election, however, he dramatically adopted Taft's ideas about U.S. foreign relations, as written into the Republican platform by John Foster Dulles. The Republican platform, with its underlying unilateralism, harkened back to the nineteenth century, which would ultimately undermine and destroy the "special relationship."[5]

A fervent supporter of Robert Taft in 1952, former President Herbert Hoover called for the United States to implement a "Gibraltar" defense of the Western Hemisphere. Eisenhower's actions in Guatemala in 1954, and later in Cuba, demonstrated his serious disregard for international laws, organizations, and especially Western allies whenever he perceived a Communist threat in the Western Hemisphere. Eisenhower, like Theodore Roosevelt, acted as the policeman of the Western Hemisphere. The influence of conservative Republicans on hemispheric defense can most readily be seen in Guatemala, where he moved swiftly and unilaterally to overthrow the government of Jacobo Arbenz despite British objections to his covert plans. Nevertheless, Eisenhower fully expected Churchill and Eden to help him quash a UN investigation of his illegal activities in overthrowing the democratically elected Arbenz.[6]

Secretary of State John Foster Dulles deserves special recognition for orchestrating Eisenhower's very deceptive foreign policy. His many speeches demonstrated his credentials and his influence as a hard-core cold warrior in the battle against Communism, even as his critics maintained that he offered few or very simple solutions to highly complex global problems. In his own article in *Life*, entitled "A Policy of Boldness," Dulles proposed that American foreign policy should be active rather than reactive. He endorsed the liberation of the satellite countries and the rollback of Communism in Eastern Europe. Dulles backed a new strategy to attack the Communist threat that included the possibility of "massive retaliation."[7]

Many American historians have disapproved of Dulles because of the huge gulf between his idealistic speeches and his actual policies. Still, they have admired Eisenhower for avoiding unnecessary military action. Historian Robert A. Divine contended, "Yet in the aftermath of Vietnam, it can be argued that a president who avoids hasty military action and refrains from extensive involvement in the internal affairs of other nations deserves praise rather than scorn." He has completely misconstrued the Eisenhower years. Eisenhower not only engaged in numerous covert military actions and threats, but he was also heavily involved in manipulating the internal affairs of other nations, both hostile and friendly.[8]

A closer review of the archival record makes abundantly clear that Eisenhower and Dulles worked as a team while promoting a profoundly far-right Republican foreign policy agenda that did directly interfere in the internal affairs of other nations. The two men regularly conferred on the possible use of nuclear weapons in Korea, Indochina, and on the Chinese mainland. In Operation Everready, they plotted with Churchill a possible military ouster of Syngman Rhee in South Korea, shortly before the North Korean government signed an armistice. They actively sustained the highly unpopular and authoritarian Diem regime in South Vietnam. Eisenhower and Dulles, through the CIA, aggressively arranged the overthrow of Prime Minister Mohammed Mossadegh in Iran and President Jacobo Arbenz in Guatemala. They also planned covert political and military operations against Communist-influenced governments in Egypt and Syria. They not only initiated the overthrow of hostile dictators, but together they also swayed the internal affairs of Western allies. The president and secretary of state covertly supported those members of the British cabinet, such as Harold Macmillan and R. A. Butler, who sought Anthony Eden's removal as prime minister in 1956. This powerful and ideologically driven U.S. diplomacy could never be made compatible with Britain's balance-of-power diplomacy.[9]

British historian John Charmley has correctly asserted that British and American national interests diverged greatly in the 1950s. He maintained that Churchill's subservience to the United States actually caused serious harm to British interests. Nonetheless, it would be Eden's lack of subservience to the United States that would eventually lead to the complete unraveling of the British Empire, particularly in the Middle East. The great harm to British interests would occur, for the most part, under Eden and his successors. Churchill sought accommodation with Eisenhower, which became increasingly difficult with the growing ideological differences and the diverging national interests. He had hoped for "détente" with the new Soviet leadership after Stalin's death, while Eisenhower saw the new Soviet leadership, guided by the same Communist ideology, as differing little from Stalin's leadership. Churchill believed in personal diplomacy and the power of summits to create new agendas. He also defended the concept of colonialism, insisting it had helped civilize and democratize Third World countries. This put Churchill in direct conflict with Eisenhower, who promoted national independence movements.[10]

Unlike Eden, Churchill understood Great Britain's growing economic weakness in its relation to the United States. This recognition of financial frailty severely handicapped British diplomatic initiatives throughout his premiership. British historian Alan P. Dobson contended that the special economic relationship between America and the United Kingdom began deteriorating as early as 1952, while Robin Edmonds asserted that mutual hostility toward the Soviet Union guaranteed the continuance of the "special relationship." Nevertheless, this relationship radically deteriorated in

1952 with the election of Eisenhower, who purposely demoted the Anglo-American alliance and completely rebuffed Churchill's proposal of a grand alliance.[11]

Military considerations also played an important role in the transatlantic alliance. Helen Leigh-Phippard looked closely at the importance of military aid in defining the relationship between the United States and Great Britain. She thought the "special relationship" between the two countries really began collapsing with the end of the Korean War. Similarly, British historian R. B. Manderson-Jones has examined the importance of the political, economic, and military differences between the Americans and the British on the future of western Europe. The minor differences in Europe proved far less important than the momentous differences between the two countries in the Middle East and the Far East. In the 1980s, Fraser J. Harbutt carefully scrutinized the importance of Churchill's Iron Curtain speech as a cause of the Cold War and explained how Churchill alerted America to the growing Soviet threat. Timothy J. Botti concluded that the nuclear arms relationship between the Americans and British evolved slowly and painfully, eventually leading to a full partnership. In spite of these detailed analyses, it remains quite clear that the British in the 1950s moved from being an equal partner to a junior partner in the Anglo-American relationship.[12]

Great Britain's political, economic, and military power around the world slowly dissipated in the early 1950s. Historian Chi-Kwan Mark has perceptively asserted that "Britain's Cold War strategy was predicated on its postwar military and economic weaknesses, so that diplomacy would be the main instrument to preserve its influence in great power status in the world." Britain's policy toward China revolved around defending its vital interests in Hong Kong. The British incessantly urged military restraint with regard to China. The United States used Hong Kong as an intelligence base but did not consider it essential in fighting the Cold War. Nevertheless, Churchill and Eden took every opportunity to avoid any possibility of war with China.[13]

The Middle East in the early 1950s stood largely as a British sphere of influence. Great Britain, more than any other Western country, protected Arab nations from Soviet subversion through the Baghdad Pact signed in 1955. Eden's justification for the British invasion of Egypt in 1956 rested on his deep-seated conviction that Nasser was a Soviet agent. In his biography of Eden, David Dutton summarized his entire career in reference to Egypt: "The ghost of Suez was still stalking Eden as he was getting ready for the end and wondering about the verdict of history. In his mind his whole proud career had been scarred by a decision which misfired for a lack of American co-operation." This astonishing analysis concerned an experienced politician who had been told rather bluntly by Eisenhower that the United States would not support a British military invasion of Suez.[14]

Over time, Eisenhower and Dulles became more and more critical of British diplomacy, particularly as Prime Minister Eden executed it. Dutton further explained: "The Secretary [Dulles] was convinced that the British throughout the world were a rapidly declining power. He was convinced they no longer had any basic will to meet big international responsibilities, that they were trying to put as good a face on it as possible, but that you could not count on the British to carry on in any responsible way, or, indeed, form an effective bulwark with us against anything." American policy makers constantly voiced their concerns and fears about the reliability of their British allies in combating the real dangers of Communism in the Middle East.[15]

Moreover, Eisenhower fiercely campaigned against British and French colonialism in northern Africa and the Middle East. He defended a new and growing nationalism and anticolonialism in the Middle East and Africa as a safeguard against any possible inroads by the Soviets. The internal political strife of the Middle East led sadly to the complete unraveling of the transatlantic alliance. The Soviets gradually gained tremendous influence in Egypt and Syria. The growing American and British rift over colonialism actually encouraged further Soviet subversion in the Middle East.[16]

On the crisis in Suez, Alan P. Dobson wrote: "When the shooting started several things determined Eisenhower's response. He was angry that he had not been consulted and that the invasion took place on the eve of the US presidential election. He feared this type of gunboat diplomacy would tarnish the US reputation in the Third World unless he came out against it." Eisenhower not only did not like the timing of the British invasion of Suez, but he also felt personally double-crossed by Eden. Eden failed to anticipate or understand Eisenhower's cold-blooded hostility to British military action in Egypt.[17]

In a stunning response to the British military invasion of Suez, President Eisenhower forced a sterling crisis on Great Britain, which led to the cancellation of their invasion of Egypt. He used Britain's internal economic and monetary weakness to crush British and French military adventurism in the Suez. Now it was Eden who felt betrayed. His chancellor of the Exchequer, Harold Macmillan, begged for help from the United States to stop the sterling crisis and avert a British economic catastrophe: "In the meantime it would be tragic and as I have said, a major victory for the communists—if we were to allow what has happened to result in an economic disaster for the free world. We can prevent it, but only if we act together and act speedily. That is why I most earnestly ask your help." Eisenhower had it in his power to destroy the British economy, and he wanted to make sure the British knew it.[18]

After all of the Anglo-American intrigue during the Suez Crisis, the Soviets actively conspired to make further inroads in the Middle East. A State Department telegram from Moscow dated November 14, 1956, informed Dulles of a Soviet central committee session on November 2, 1956. This telegram specifically stated: "The Middle East will be the focus of Soviet efforts in near future. Shepilov and Zhukov were exponents of view that the Middle East represents a vital link which can be severed to cut the West off from the East. Distraction of Western position in Middle East will open Africa to Soviet influence, and will permit denial to the West of strategic bases, vital communications lines, raw materials, and markets." Eisenhower justifiably feared the increasing influence of the Soviet Union in the Middle East, but ironically this growing Soviet influence stemmed directly from the rupture in the Anglo-American alliance.[19]

This new radical American "brinksmanship" policy extended well beyond political enemies, such as the Communists, to the British, who by drastic miscalculation had become trapped in the middle of the ideological war between the United States and the Soviet Union. Eisenhower's unilateralism went so far as to not only ignore old friends but, when necessary, to annihilate them. British fears of a "Fortress America" or a new isolationism based on U.S. unilateralism had been totally corroborated.

Most American historians still cling to the long-standing myth of a benevolent and passive President Dwight D. Eisenhower who merely sought a middle path between Old Guard Republicans and liberal Democrats. In chapter 2, a closer inspection of public speeches and the internal records of Eisenhower, Dulles, Churchill, and Eden reveals instead a president to the far right of the Old Guard Republicans, deeply involved in a very perilous foreign policy. Ending the Korean War has often been cited as an example of Eisenhower's moderation. Eisenhower actually threatened China with nuclear weapons. Historians ignore the reality of his threatening Syngman Rhee with a military coup. The British, with the important exception of Winston Churchill, seemed genuinely shocked by the real possibility of an expanded war with China occurring at the same times as a military coup in South Korea. Chapter 3 demonstrates that Eisenhower's extreme radicalism in the Far East went well beyond anything that General Douglas MacArthur, former president Herbert Hoover, and Senator Robert Taft ever advocated or promoted. He initiated a new revolutionary American diplomacy called "brinksmanship," a foreign policy that met the consistent and unyielding opposition of the British in the Far East throughout the 1950s. Eisenhower's atomic diplomacy and militarism came into direct conflict with British diplomatic efforts, as discussed in chapter 4. Eisenhower, behind the scenes, tried to end the Geneva Conference of 1954. Chapter 5 describes the British and the Americans cooperating, for the most part, in the crushing of democratically elected governments in Iran and Guatemala. Chapter 6 documents the British and the Americans reversing roles, with Eisenhower opposing British military intervention in the Suez, and chapter 7 analyzes the incredible economic, political, diplomatic, and psychological pressure Eisenhower brought to bear to end the Suez Crisis and overthrow British prime minister Anthony Eden.

The Eisenhower administration's foreign relations in the first term were never moderate and were, in fact, guided by the ideology of the Old Right. The so called "special relationship" between the United States and Great Britain, so carefully and firmly established by Franklin D. Roosevelt and Winston Churchill during the years of the Second World War, was ultimately destroyed, along with the British Empire, by the inability of Winston Churchill and Anthony Eden to fully grapple with the radical nature of Eisenhower's diplomacy.

CHAPTER 2

CONSERVATIVE IDEOLOGY
AND BRINKSMANSHIP

T he transatlantic relationship between Eisenhower and Churchill
steadily disintegrated between 1953 and 1955, a trend clearly dis-
cerned from both their public speeches and their private correspondence. Their serious political differences had much to do with their
opposing views of how to deal with the Soviet Union. While espousing
high idealism in statements about foreign policy, Eisenhower deeply distrusted the Soviet regime and refused to engage in real negotiations with
the Communists. Churchill took the opposite position and, despite his
mistrust, favored an open dialogue with the Soviets in the hope of reaching agreements of mutual interest. In addition, the Eisenhower-Churchill
relationship broke down over serious disagreements about Indochina,
Quemoy and Matsu, China, regional alliances, the use of atomic weapons, the doctrine of peaceful coexistence, and American unilateralism.
Over time, these differences did not dissipate but magnified, and they became more complicated by ideological arguments over Communism and
colonialism.[1]

The first Republican president of the United States in twenty years,
Dwight D. Eisenhower represented a truly radical break from the past,
especially in foreign affairs. He totally rejected Truman's European-based
diplomacy, which had reflexively backed British colonial interests in the
Third World. Instead, he favored a global-oriented foreign policy expressing new ideas of brinksmanship and anticolonialism to combat the Communist threat, not just as a European problem, but as a worldwide danger.
Eisenhower waged an all-out ideological war on the men in the Kremlin
in order to stop an international Marxist revolution.

Still, Eisenhower did not appear to be any kind of radical. He presented himself as a moderate Republican who accepted New Deal legislation and who gave careful consideration to Democratic proposals in the domestic arena. Indeed, Eisenhower the domestic president can best be described as a centrist. In dealing with foreign affairs, however, he demonstrated, contrary to most public perceptions and historical consensus, that he was a die-hard right-wing Republican.[2]

In his inaugural address in January 1953, Eisenhower spoke in Manichaean tones about foreign policy. In the battle between good and evil there could be no compromise. He spoke of Communism's malignant spirit and suggested that the fight against it had a transcendent meaning. In outlining the principles that would guide his presidency, Eisenhower affirmed his absolute repugnance to resorting to war as a tool for achieving diplomatic objectives. Yet, he also abhorred appeasement and spoke eloquently about his intent to defend the nation's honor and security. Eisenhower denounced any type of U.S. imperialism, espoused the concept of regional alliances, and defended the efforts of the United Nations to solve the problems of the world. Many of these high ideals would be challenged in the first years of the Eisenhower administration.[3]

In a national broadcast shortly after the inauguration, John Foster Dulles also reassured Americans that Eisenhower's foreign policy would be guided by "enlightened self-interest." He expressed his full concurrence with Eisenhower about the nature of the Cold War and warned: "We have to pay close attention to what is going on in the rest of the world. And the reason for that is that we have enemies who are plotting our destruction. These enemies are the Russian Communists and their allies in other countries." Dulles repudiated negotiations with Soviet leaders. If the Soviets were plotting the destruction of the United States, how could they be trusted? There could be no good-faith negotiations with the leaders of the Soviet Union. Still, he reiterated Eisenhower's denunciation of war and specifically argued against any type of preventative war with the Soviet Union. Dulles, it appeared, planned to fight the Soviets ideologically and rhetorically.[4]

After his inauguration, Eisenhower deliberately downgraded the "special relationship" with Great Britain because he dreaded being tied politically to British colonialism. As he wrote in his diary: "No such special relationship can be maintained or even suggested, publicly. In public relationship all nations are sovereign and equal." Eisenhower quietly dispensed with Churchill's proposed plan for a grand Anglo-American global alliance, preferring instead to support Third World nationalist movements if they proved to be anti-Communist. Churchill faced a new American government that no longer sanctioned or safeguarded his colonial interests and seemed completely indifferent and possibly hostile to the long-term interests of the British Empire.[5]

While the new Eisenhower administration seemed appropriately preoccupied with the problems of Korea and the Far East, Churchill's government dealt with the complex problems of the Middle East, specifically Iran and Egypt. The United States, unlike Great Britain, had no major interest in Iranian oil, but Eisenhower did fear the possibility of Iran falling out of the Western orbit. The balance of power in the Middle East would be affected catastrophically by Iranian oil falling under the control of the Soviet Union. British foreign secretary Anthony Eden, objecting to this American point of view, maintained that Iran should not be categorized as being in the hands of East or West; rather, he believed that Iran fell into the large category of unaligned nations. In a meeting with Eisenhower and Dulles, Eden said that he "thought it unlikely that Mossadegh would link himself up with the West. But he was just as reluctant to join the East. Persia wished to stay in the middle. This had been Persia's policy for two thousand years and he did not think it was likely to change now." Eden, who had majored in Oriental studies at Oxford, directly challenged Eisenhower and Dulles on their black-and-white view of the world. However, they viewed Iran strictly in terms of Cold War politics, while Churchill and Eden viewed it mainly in terms of British oil and prestige.[6]

After Stalin's death in March 1953, Churchill became increasingly hopeful about the possibility of détente with the new Soviet leadership. As a student of history, he knew that with the death of Stalin, leaders in the Kremlin might seek political and economic reforms. The West, Churchill argued, should support political and economic reforms in the Soviet Union that could be of mutual interest: "It has been well said that the most dangerous moment for evil governments is when they begin to reform." Much more than Eisenhower, Dulles, or even Eden, he thought Stalin's death created the possibility for real change in the Soviet Union, and so he began an enthusiastic public campaign promoting détente with the Soviet Union.[7]

Meanwhile, the most ideologically driven U.S. secretary of state, John Foster Dulles, prepared his all-out Cold War against the Soviet Union. As early as 1960, historians and journalists acknowledged real differences between the British and the Americans. The British treated the Soviets like their predecessors had treated the Russians under the czar. Dulles rejected this business-as-usual approach to the Soviets. He believed that Soviet expansionism and Communist ideology meant that a business-as-usual approach to diplomacy would not work. This fundamental distinction between the Americans and the British, noted even before the Eisenhower administration had left office, corroborated the differences in their perception of the ideological threat posed by the Soviet Union. Dulles persevered in his all-out ideological war against the Soviet Union, while the British, particularly Anthony Eden, continued their pragmatic balance-of-power approach.[8]

Dulles's unpopularity and the press's antagonism to him could be blamed on his intense anti-Communist ideology. His anti-Marxist, dense, legalistic rhetoric hardly appealed to the left-leaning or liberal historians of the past thirty years, or even to many others. Dulles tenaciously persisted in seeing the world in terms of good and evil, with the Communists obviously in league with the devil. He has often been wrongly blamed as the man responsible for this American policy of extreme ideological hostility to the Soviet Union. The man who actually initiated America's foreign policy often hid behind the scenes, while Dulles publicly played the role of "bad cop" to Eisenhower's "good cop." No one should doubt Eisenhower's control of the show behind the scenes as he played the public role of peacemaker.[9]

In a memorable speech to the American Society of Newspaper Editors on April 16, 1953, Eisenhower, in keeping with Churchill's new spirit of détente, made a remarkably conciliatory speech aimed at the Soviet Union calling for peaceful acts rather than rhetoric as the measuring stick of relations between the two countries. The Cold War had drained both sides financially and had left the people of the world frightened of nuclear war. In a now famous passage, Eisenhower declared, "Every gun that is made, every warship launched, every rocket fired signifies, in the final sense, a theft from those who hunger and are not fed, those who are cold and not clothed." Even as a social and political conservative, he stressed the importance of having a social conscience about the poor.[10]

As a military man, Eisenhower pointed out how excessive military spending robbed the poor of the necessities of life. He called for further reductions in the military budget by indicating: "The cost of one modern heavy bomber is this: A modern brick school in more than 30 cities. It is: Some 50 miles of concrete highway. We pay for a single fighter plane with a half million bushels of wheat. We pay for a single destroyer with new homes that could have housed more than 8000 people." The military-industrial complex could destroy America's basic economic infrastructure and the American way of life. Eisenhower reached out to the Soviets using solid economic and consumer arguments in making his case for international peace. He stated, in concrete terms, how both countries could economically benefit from a reduction in military spending. Eisenhower's speech should have been the beginning of a policy of détente between East and West. Churchill fully supported Eisenhower's speech: "Your speech about Russia was well received here by all parties."[11]

The Soviets, however, reacted unenthusiastically in their review of Eisenhower's speech in *Pravda*, implying that the new Soviet leadership would not change either its foreign policy or its Communist ideology. Eisenhower's attempt at détente ended with both sides viewing the other with suspicion. This created the political atmosphere for brinksmanship. William Strang, British permanent under-secretary of state, thought the piece in Pravda could be considered civil, but it seemed mostly unenthusiastic and distrustful. His analysis suggested that the Kremlin, after Stalin's death, did not intend to open itself up to this new spirit of détente. Strang told Churchill that the Soviets reacted negatively to Eisenhower's initiative, concluding: "The general effect is that the Soviet government will require further and more concrete proof that United States policy has become genuinely 'peace loving' before they can fully cooperate with the United States." The Soviets required concrete and positive actions from the United States, but instead saw nothing but the hostile speeches of John Foster Dulles. Unlike both Eisenhower and Churchill, they did not need to cater to consumer needs or the political and economic demands of their citizens.[12]

Undeterred, Churchill looked forward to visiting Moscow in the near future, well aware that Eisenhower and his British cabinet disapproved of such a meeting. His private secretary John Colville wrote: "Lord S [Salisbury] says he found Eisenhower violently Russophobe, greatly more so than Dulles, and that he believes the President to be personally responsible for the policy of useless pinpricks and harassing tactics the U.S. is following against Russia in Europe and the Far East." Salisbury correctly noticed that Eisenhower, not Dulles, instigated this new militantly anti-Communist foreign policy.[13]

The New Look defense policy initially presumed a far greater role for regional military alliances. In relying on military alliances, the United States would be able to cut back on the cost of its military industrial complex. In a national radio broadcast on April 29, 1953, Dulles, urging the Europeans to improve the quality of their fighting force rather than enlarge it, scolded them: "We must remember that in a world of toughness it is a lot better to be compact and hard than it is to be big and soft." He urged the Europeans to adopt the American model of reducing military expenditures while at the same time improving their overall military posture: "We sought economic health which would be consistent with military strength. We did not want our military strength to be a carrier of economic disease." He thought far enough ahead to realize that a military buildup in Europe might cause an economic collapse that could later rebound economically on the United States.[14]

Actively encouraging the Europeans to slowly develop their own defenses through NATO and depending on regional alliances, Eisenhower linked U.S. national security to a reduction in military expenditures. In a press conference on April 30, 1953, he proposed to cut $8.5 billion from the military budget in 1954 and introduced his New Look defense policy. Meanwhile, Churchill continued to press for a meeting with the top leaders in the Kremlin. In a letter to Eisenhower, he reflected on the need for action, openly worrying about Eisenhower's extremely negative attitude: "I find it difficult to believe that we shall gain anything by an attitude of pure negation and your message to me certainly does not show much hope." Churchill expressed his annoyance with both Eisenhower's attitude and his lack of action in dealing with the Soviet Union in a positive way.[15]

British hopes for détente depended on cooperation from both Eisenhower and Dulles. Churchill uttered his hope for détente with the Soviet

Union even as Dulles spoke cautiously and counseled against a Soviet trap. Dulles thought Churchill gave people false hope about the nature of the Soviet regime. He charged that Churchill's efforts to achieve peace would result only in an illusion of peace rather than a reality. The Soviets could not be trusted because ultimately they sought the downfall of the West. The prime minister and secretary of state could not have been further apart or have had a more different point of view. Where Churchill saw opportunity, Dulles saw danger. They would never reach an understanding on any type of negotiations with the Soviets.[16]

British foreign secretary Anthony Eden and Dulles had not only policy differences, but personality differences as well. As early as the 1960s, Richard Goold-Adams wrote: "They have been described as 'the Roundhead and the Cavalier,' with differences as profound as those between the two elements in the English Civil War. There was much that was Cromwellian about Dulles, and his disdain for Eden as well as Eden's complete distrust of him brought to an end the whole wartime era of Anglo-American partnership, with effects that can be felt to this day." Dulles appeared to the world as the Puritan, while Eden looked like a debonair Cavalier. As a Puritan, Dulles understood the world in moral terms of black and white. As a Cavalier, Eden viewed the world in many different colors. Policy differences aggravated real personality differences between them. Profound ideological distinctions went beyond mere policy and personality differences. Unquestionably, each one's entirely different outlook on the world, and how to order it, substantiated the shocking differences between the two men. Dulles refused to trust the Soviets, while Churchill and Eden held out the hope of finding mutual interests between East and West, despite the ideological hostility.[17]

Presenting his own assessment of global politics in a speech to the British House of Commons on May 11, 1953, Churchill looked forward to an armistice that would end the hostilities in Korea. He wanted the Korean War to go away because it served as a distraction from the real Cold War existing in Europe. In Egypt, Churchill discussed removing many of the eighty thousand British troops in the area of the Suez Canal: "Naturally, we do not wish to keep indefinitely 80,000 men at a cost of, it might be, over 50 million pounds a year discharging the duty which has largely fallen upon us, and on us alone." As a proponent of colonialism, Churchill recognized the high cost of maintaining the British military base at Suez. British control of the canal established a difficult situation for the latest Egyptian government. He expressed his hope for new talks on the Suez Canal. He also made clear to the Soviets his opposition to the British sacrificing West Germany in any peace negotiation. In his speech to the House, Churchill depicted the French position in Indochina as steadily worsening. He spoke with open contempt of France's inability to send sufficient troops to Indochina. Churchill blamed France's lack of a national service for the insufficient French troops in Indochina. He also reminded the House of Commons of the changed attitude in the Kremlin since the death of Stalin and proposed a conference of leading powers. In his proposed closed-door conference, the leaders of the world might be able to find areas of mutual agreement. Churchill feared the West might become divided and become increasingly unwilling to bear the high cost of defense. He had implicitly and publicly criticized Eisenhower's cost-saving New Look defense proposal.[18]

Paradoxically, Foreign Secretary Eden disagreed with Churchill's sanguine assessment of relations with the Soviets following Stalin's death. The British prime minister and foreign secretary fundamentally diverged on what should be the British policy toward the Soviet Union. Eden envisioned no change in Soviet foreign policy: "I did not share the optimism of those who saw in this event an easement of the world's problems. The permanent challenge of communism transcends personalities, however powerful." He did agree with Churchill about the Soviets seeking a lessening of tensions with the West, while trying to avoid unnecessary Stalinist provocations. Churchill and Eden, however, did worry about John Foster Dulles's speeches and the further possibility of Republican isolationism.[19]

The past spokesman for American isolationism, Senator Robert A. Taft (R-Ohio), maintained that U.S. foreign policy should be firmly dedicated to preventing Communist aggression, even though, in a speech delivered before the National Conference of Christians and Jews in Cincinnati, Ohio, on May 26, 1953, he insisted that American soldiers had no role to play in Asia: "I have never felt that we should send American soldiers to the continent of Asia, which, of course, includes China proper and Indochina, simply because we are so out-numbered in fighting a land war on the continent of Asia it would bring about complete exhaustion even if we were able to win." His speech echoed the enormous skepticism already expressed by Churchill on French Indochina. Taft and Churchill fundamentally agreed on the futility of fighting land wars in the jungles of Asia.[20]

Upset that England and France might show themselves to be merely fair-weather friends, Taft charged: "It seems clear that Mr. Churchill and the French administration would be willing to assign that zone of influence gladly and abandon the Poles, the Czechs, the Hungarians, and the Rumanians to the tender mercies of Soviet Russia in return for some cutting of armaments, freer trade and promises to behave in the future." The western Europeans might sacrifice the Eastern Europeans for what might amount to empty promises made by the Soviets. Fearing that America's allies, particularly the British, could not be trusted, Taft proposed American unilateralism. If the Soviets could not be trusted, neither could U.S. allies, even the British. While he vociferously communicated his distrust of Churchill personally and the British generally, the underlying premise of his proposed military budget cuts and Eisenhower's New Look defense posture still depended on regional military alliances, including with the British. The Republicans proposed a schizophrenic foreign policy based on American unilateralism. The policy depended on these untrustworthy allies in regional alliances in order to reduce the U.S. military budget.[21]

Most important, Churchill and Eden really dreaded the dangers they foresaw to Anglo-American relations with the rise of Republican isolationism and unilateralism. Churchill wrote Eisenhower on May 29, 1953: "I am so glad to read just now your remarks about Taft's speech. I look back with dark memories to all that followed inch by inch upon the United States' withdrawal from the League of Nations over 30 years ago. Thank God you are at the helm." He genuinely believed that Taft had endorsed U.S. isolationism. Taft, in his speech, had wanted to discard the United Nations in the peace negotiations in Korea. Eisenhower, in a press conference, thoroughly rejected Taft's position. Although he had, on this occasion, disagreed with Taft on the importance of the UN in the negotiations of the Korean armistice, his foreign policy had already drifted decidedly to the right of Taft.[22]

While the British remained concerned about Republican isolationism, Dulles remained anxious about perceived American isolationism in Europe. In a memorandum to the president on June 5, 1953, Dulles wrote:

"Obviously, consequences other than a truly united approach to world problems would be grave. In the United States, they would give an impetus to isolationism. Among our NATO allies . . . the incipient tendency on the part of Churchill toward a position of 'mediation' between the United States and the USSR could find extensive support." For his part, he expressed considerable unease that the Europeans might perceive the United States as isolationist and that this would ultimately split the Western alliance, allowing Churchill to act as mediator in the disputes between East and West. Churchill, acting as a mediator, would undoubtedly undermine American ideological and moral arguments against the Soviets. Dulles wanted to wage an all-out ideological war against Communism. In fact, many Europeans voiced a deep concern about Dulles's rhetoric. They were also concerned about Republicans reducing foreign-aid programs and military expenditures. Republican cost cutting only confirmed the worst fears of the Europeans about the new Republican administration.[23]

In addition, Eisenhower and Dulles experienced bitter frustration with Churchill's political positions in Egypt. In negotiating for a British military base deal at Suez, Churchill made no real concessions to the Egyptian government. Eisenhower frequently pressed the British to be more flexible in their negotiations with the Egyptians, and, in deference to his British ally, he had discontinued providing arms to the new Egyptian government. Nevertheless, Churchill and the British Foreign Office increasingly complained about a lack of American cooperation in keeping a British base at Suez. These British complaints about Egypt grated on the nerves of Secretary of State Dulles, who claimed: "Churchill's message of support spoke of far-reaching concessions on his part, which we fail to identify; implies that we should have joined in the Cairo discussions whether the Egyptians liked it or not; mentions the United States bases in England 'not even established by treaty' in manner which may contain a veiled threat." Churchill had truly annoyed Dulles with his nonexistent concessions, his insistence on American involvement in Egyptian affairs, and the veiled or not-so-veiled threats about American bases in England. Churchill aggravated Eisenhower with his diplomatic tactics. Eisenhower did not like to be pushed around on Egypt, even by his good friend Winston Churchill, who, in deference to his age and his service in the Second World War, was usually granted a lot of leeway.[24]

Yet, the transatlantic alliance slowly began fracturing under the intense pressure of the Cold War. Churchill and Eisenhower continued to wrangle about Iran and Egypt. Eisenhower's aggressive anti-Communist stance in Iran made him appear indifferent to British national and economic interests. Egypt proved even more contentious. Eisenhower actively pursued the friendship of the new Egyptian government. The British, particularly Churchill, became alienated when the United States offered to provide economic and military assistance to the Egyptians, with Churchill stating: "If at the present time the United States indicated divergence from us in spite of the measure of agreement we had reached after making so many concessions, we should not think we had been treated fairly by our great Ally, with whom we are working in so many parts of the globe for the causes which we both espouse." He suggested a political trade-off, with the British receiving the support of the United States in Egypt for British support in Asia. Eisenhower, however, preferred to have Egypt as a dependable anti-Communist ally in the Middle East, while Churchill seemed more concerned with protecting the last vestiges of British colonialism by holding on to the British military base at Suez.[25]

Battling each other vigorously over how to handle Egypt, Churchill sought Eisenhower's assistance and, for the most part, only received his cold shoulder. Norwegian historian Tore T. Petersen has perceptively observed: "While listening politely to Churchill, Eisenhower afterwards noted in his diary that the plea for Anglo-American unity is nothing but a ploy to gain support for the British predicament in the Middle East. He thought Churchill's ideas old-fashioned and paternalistic." Eisenhower did not sympathize with British colonialism in Egypt[26]

An increasing concern about American isolationism had crossed the Atlantic and challenged the new Republican administration. Dulles, knowing the Europeans feared a Republican administration as possibly isolationist, wrote: "Our policies do involve considerably reduced U.S. expenditures abroad, and the Congress, primarily the Republicans, are cutting back that program. This seems, to foreigners, to confirm their fears that U.S. policy is moving toward 'isolationism.'" The Europeans perceived American unilateralism as a new type of isolationism. Indeed, just before the Bermuda Conference of 1953, Dulles believed the United States and Great Britain might not even share a common approach to world problems. He genuinely feared that a break in the Anglo-American relationship would promote isolationism in the United States. American isolationism might lead to Churchill's role as mediator between the United States and the Soviet Union; destroying a united Western alliance. Any British role as a mediator between East and West tended to widen Anglo-American disunity and incur even more political disagreements.[27]

After lunching with Churchill on July 24, John Colville, Churchill's private secretary, wrote: "Still wrapped up with the possibility of bringing something off with the Russians and with the idea of meeting Malenkov face to face. [He is] very disappointed in Eisenhower, whom he thinks both weak and stupid." Churchill's growing unhappiness resulted from Eisenhower's rigid anti-Communist ideology concerning the Soviets and his absolute refusal to have a summit meeting with them. The time to resolve the differences between them had been planned for the Bermuda Conference, a conference originally planned for summer, but postponed due to Churchill's stroke in June 1953.[28]

Meeting in Bermuda in December 1953, Eisenhower and Churchill tried to hammer out an agreement about the world situation and resolve the outstanding issues between their two countries. The first order of business at the Bermuda Conference involved the possibility of North Korean violations of the Korean armistice. In the event of any breach of the armistice by the North Koreans, Eisenhower promised nuclear retaliation on North Korean military targets. Churchill quickly agreed to the American proposal and mentioned that he could tell the Parliament that he been fully consulted in advance of such an attack. On December 4, 1953, in a conversation with Prime Minister Churchill, the president indicated: "We would expect to strike back with atomic weapons at military targets. We would not expect to bomb cities but would attack areas that were directly supporting the aggression. The Prime Minister said that he quite accepted this and that the President's statement put him in a position to say to the Parliament that he had been consulted in advance and had agreed." They seemed to be in total agreement on the necessity of using nuclear weapons on the North Koreans in the event that North Korea repudiated the existing armistice. Churchill signaled a green light for American use of nuclear weapons in Korea. Eisenhower then demanded British nonrecognition of Communist China. Although Churchill sympathized with Eisenhower's request, he responded that unfortunately recognition "had now become established fact which would be difficult to alter." The British Labor government had already recognized the Communist government of China on January 6, 1950. The United States could not expect a reversal of this decision.[29]

The next day Churchill reneged, presumably under serious pressure from Eden, on his prior agreement to allow Eisenhower to use nuclear weapons in North Korea in the event of an attack or breakdown in the armistice: "There followed a lengthy discussion of the effect of a resumption of hostilities in Korea. Sir Winston referred to his public utterances in this respect but twice during the ensuing discussions mentioned that Mr. Eden was more fully informed and that he did not wish anything he said in this area to be considered a commitment until Mr. Eden was brought into the talks." Apparently, the foreign secretary had reminded the prime minister that the British government did not approve of the use of nuclear weapons in Korea for the fear of expanding the war to China and the Soviet Union.[30]

Imploring the Americans and the French at this three-party Bermuda Conference to become more flexible in their dealings with the new Soviet regime, Churchill argued against finding deception in every Soviet tactical move. To make his own point, Eisenhower responded in an undiplomatic manner with a rather crude depiction of the Soviet Union as a prostitute:

> If we understood that under this dress was the same old girl, if we understood that despite bath, perfume or lace, it was the same old girl on that basis then we might explore all that Sir Winston had said if we might apply the positive methods of which M. Bidault had spoken. Perhaps we could pull the old girl off the main street and put her on a back alley. He did not want to approach this problem on the basis that there had been any change in the Soviet policy of destroying the Capitalist free world by all means, by force, by deceit or by lies. This was their long term purpose. From their writings it was clear there had been no change since Lenin.[31]

Colville wrote, "To end on a note of dignity, when Eden asked when the next meeting should be, the President acidly replied, 'I don't know. Mine is with a whisky and soda'—and got up to leave the room." If Churchill thought he could easily persuade Eisenhower or Dulles to change their minds on a possible détente with the Soviet Union, he learned the hard way this would not be possible.[32]

On December 5, Eisenhower once again emphasized his willingness to respond to North Korean provocations with atomic weapons. The discussion on nuclear weapons with the Americans deeply troubled both Churchill and Eden. The British genuinely feared the possibility of nuclear war. The Americans and the British fundamentally differed on the nature of atomic weapons and warfare. The British naturally assumed that the use of atomic weapons should and would be actively discouraged. Eisenhower viewed the atomic bomb as nothing more than a new and improved conventional weapon. Churchill worried about the possibility of a Soviet nuclear strike against London. Nevertheless, Eisenhower reserved to himself the right to use nuclear weapons: "The only part of the discussion that led to opposition (this from Winston) was the assertion that in the event of renewed attack, we would feel free to use the atomic bomb against military targets, whenever military advantage dictated such use. This awakened in Winston many fears which he voiced again and again." Eisenhower also absolutely repudiated any summit with Soviet leaders. Churchill mistakenly held Dulles responsible, not Eisenhower, as the terrible culprit, who behind the scenes destroyed the Bermuda Conference.[33]

Dissenting from Churchill's concept of a major summit between the Big Three Powers, Dulles argued vigorously against negotiations with the Soviets. Churchill wondered if Dulles secretly controlled Eisenhower and all of the subsequent meetings in Bermuda. Lord Moran, Churchill's physician, quoted him as saying about Dulles: "Ten years ago I could have dealt with him. Even as it is I have not been defeated by this bastard. I have been humiliated by my own decay." Churchill's health and energy had been steadily deteriorating since his stroke the previous summer, yet he showed no eagerness to hand over the prime ministership to Anthony Eden.[34]

Shortly after the Bermuda Conference, Eisenhower addressed the General Assembly of the United Nations on December 8, 1953, on the importance of the development of atomic power for peaceful purposes. He proposed peaceful uses of nuclear energy and urged a transformation of the world's thinking about atomic power. Eisenhower planned on helping the developing countries of the Third World through atomic energy. He publicly represented and embodied American idealism to developing nations, but behind closed doors, he made clear his support for the United States' production of more nuclear weapons.[35]

Even as Eisenhower delivered his positive message to the United Nations, at a North Atlantic Council meeting in Paris on December 14, 1953, Secretary Dulles talked about how the United States might be forced into an "agonizing reappraisal" of its position in Europe: "If, however, the European Defense Community should not become effective; if France and Germany remain apart, so that they would again be potential enemies, then indeed there would be grave doubt whether Continental Europe could be made a place of safety. That would compel an agonizing reappraisal of basic United States policy." He pressed for European unity to combat the Soviet threat and to fend off the Soviet Union's subversion of the Western alliance. Dulles wanted the Europeans to support the North Atlantic Treaty Organization and the European Defense Community in order to provide for a realistic defense framework for the Atlantic community. Dulles's unfortunate attempt at promoting transatlantic unity through public threat and intimidation seriously backfired.[36]

This "agonizing reappraisal" caused Churchill to react on December 22, 1953, with an extremely caustic letter to Eisenhower about Egypt. He fumed about the Egyptian base issue appearing inconsequential to the Americans, although it remained very important to the British, warning: "Whether you take sides against us in Egypt or not will not affect the support which we have thought it right to give you over China. It will, however, make it more difficult for Anthony and me to help you in the Far East if we have to do it in the face, not only of Socialist opinion, but of general feeling of indignation throughout the country." Churchill had raised a dangerous linkage: American help in the Middle East in exchange for British help in the Far East.[37]

Another troubling issue for the Anglo-American relationship involved Britain's diplomatic recognition and relation with the Chinese government. Vice President Richard M. Nixon strenuously objected to any nation's recognition of China: "All attempts to bring an aggressive Communist China into the family of nations must be stopped with all means at America's disposal." All of Southeast Asia could fall into the hands of the

Communists. China should be considered an outlaw nation. Meanwhile, the British continued to expand their commercial relations with the Chinese. Nixon's views mirrored Eisenhower's extremely negative outlook toward the Chinese Communists, which can be seen in the Eisenhower-Churchill correspondence in 1954 and 1955. Economic trade relations between China and Great Britain greatly exacerbated the serious political problems in the Anglo-American relationship.[38]

In his State of the Union address in 1954, President Eisenhower proposed taking the initiative in the Cold War. He promised an activist U.S. foreign policy not merely reacting to the Communists, but actually taking the initiative and implementing policies favorable to the free world. Unlike Truman, he planned to control the destiny of the United States through a proactive foreign policy, not limited in its actions. Eisenhower's foreign policy called for action by promoting freedom, the American economy, and the security of the people of the United States. Protecting the freedom of the American people meant stopping Communism worldwide. He would also strengthen the economy by cutting the military budget and protect the rights of individual citizens. Eisenhower, in 1954, contrasted his successful foreign policy with the failed policies of the past.[39]

The radically conservative philosophy of Senator Robert A. Taft in foreign affairs had come to the forefront and been completely adopted by the president. Eisenhower forcefully conveyed his strong belief in a global Communist conspiracy to undermine the freedom of people all over the world. Although publicly he maintained the value of collective security to reduce this Communist threat, privately Eisenhower's belief in collective security had dramatically diminished. Transatlantic cooperation in Korea and Iran in 1953 rapidly disappeared in places like Indochina and Quemoy and Matsu in 1954.[40]

In a broadcast to the nation on February 24, 1954, Dulles highlighted the value of moral principles as the ultimate weapon in America's diplomatic arsenal. He made the case against any cynical conduct of foreign affairs, a not-so-subtle jab at British balance-of-power diplomacy. Dulles trusted moral principles, as had Woodrow Wilson, and promoted American values reflecting Eisenhower's idealism: "Our ultimate reliance is not dollars, is not guided missiles, is not weapons of mass destruction. The ultimate weapon is moral principle." He imagined an American foreign policy guided by unchanging moral principles rather than one merely promoting U.S. corporations abroad. Dulles affirmed Asia's right not to be sacrificed in order to provide more financial security for western Europe. He repudiated Eden's diplomacy in the Far East as merely a cynical exercise in a balance-of-power game.[41]

British ambassador to the United States Sir Roger Makins took great offense at Dulles's fire-and-brimstone rhetoric. In response to an inquiry about a possible Churchill speech in the United States, he suggested to Colville that the "Prime Minister might say something about the historical approach to international problems (Americans tend to an *a priori* approach). This might lead to some reflections on the unwisdom of taking up inflexible or dogmatic positions in international affairs; on the meaning and purpose of negotiation; and on the need for patience, restraint, and tolerance." Makins instinctively defended the concept of balance-of-power diplomacy and the need to have allies in the fight against Communism. American idealism and rhetoric had led to an inflexibility in diplomacy. Furthermore, Dulles's absolute refusal to negotiate with the Soviets increasingly irritated the British Foreign Office. Makins hoped that Churchill could set the Americans straight on how to conduct foreign affairs: "The main trouble with the American people at the moment is fear, fear of themselves and their new responsibilities, fear above all of what is vaguely and loosely called communism. To these fears is added lack of confidence in their government." To Makins, the Republicans' fear of Communism looked exceedingly irrational.[42]

Disdaining any type of McCarthyism, Eisenhower made the point of championing fiscal responsibility as a way of strengthening the country against the foreign threat of Communism. Eisenhower publicly scorned Republicans who advocated increasing military spending while promising tax cuts for all. He opposed all forms of government irresponsibility that would lead to inflation or leave our children and grandchildren massive debts to pay. This type of generational theft amounted to bad economics and poor social planning. A powerful economy and a balanced budget could provide for a vital defense, and this could only be done through fiscal responsibility. Eisenhower courageously and consistently resisted all Republican calls for more tax cuts and instead supported extensive spending cuts in military expenditures in order to balance the federal budget. Fiscal responsibility and a sound economy would lead to a stronger nation.[43]

Nevertheless, the French were failing in Indochina. In a telephone conversation between Dulles and Admiral Radford on March 24, 1954, "Radford said we must stop being optimistic about the situation. The Secretary said he talked with the President—we must stop pleading etc. and we must have policy of our own even if France falls down. We could lose Europe, Asia, and Africa all at once if we don't watch out." In March 29, 1954, speech, Dulles proclaimed: "We shall not however be disposed to give Communist China what it wants from us merely to buy its promises of future good behavior." Behind the scenes, in a meeting with congressional leaders in late March, Eisenhower warned them that he might have to take military measures in order to save Dien Bien Phu. In contrast to Eisenhower's more restrained statements in public, Dulles gave a speech to the House Foreign Affairs Committee on April 4, 1954, declaring: "This basic incompatibility of communism with freedom drives them always to seek to expand their area of control. This is not merely due to a lust for power but a genuine fear of freedom." The Communists must destroy freedom in order to exist. Freedom and Communism could not peacefully coexist since they are by their very nature antithetical to each other. Dulles believed that the Soviets acted out of both fear and ideology. He put a much higher priority than did Churchill and Eden on holding the line on Communism in the Far East. In the spring of 1954, Eisenhower famously promulgated the "domino theory," stating that all of the countries of Southeast Asia could eventually fall to the Communists like a row of dominoes.[44]

CHAPTER 3

BRINKSMANSHIP AND
THE FAR EAST

Massachusetts senator John F. Kennedy shared the profound British skepticism about the deteriorating military situation in Indochina. In a speech to the Senate on April 6, 1954, he cautioned his fellow senators, "But to pour money, material, and men into the jungles of Indochina without at least a remote prospect of victory would be dangerously futile and self-destructive." Kennedy believed that only the people of Indochina— the people of Cambodia, Laos, and Vietnam—could win their freedom from the Communists. The United States should aid the free peoples of Indochina in their quest for freedom from the French and the Communists. His concerns mirrored those of the late Senator Taft, who had died in July 1953. Kennedy continued with his gloomy assessment: "I am frankly of the belief that no amount of American military assistance in Indochina can conquer an enemy which is everywhere and at the same time nowhere, an enemy of the people which has the sympathy and covert support of the people." There could be no simple way to win a war or even to measure political success in Southeast Asia. In order to stop the dominoes from falling, one must be able to define success and measure it. He accused Dean Rusk, the former assistant secretary of state for Far Eastern affairs, and other U.S. officials of having lied about the French granting freedoms in Indochina. Only through making Cambodia, Laos, and Vietnam politically independent, completely devoid of French colonialism, could the people of Indochina achieve true freedom.[1]

In April 1954, Dulles travelled to London to discuss with both Churchill and Eden the multifaceted problems facing Indochina. He optimistically reported to Eisenhower about the British moving away from their previous position of no action before the Geneva Conference: "The British are extremely fearful of becoming involved with ground forces in Indochina, and they do not share the view of our military that the loss of northern Vietnam would automatically carry with it the loss of the entire area." Churchill and Eden considered the Geneva Conference an excellent opportunity to negotiate a peace agreement. The British and the Americans dramatically disagreed on Eisenhower's domino theory.[2]

In a letter to Dulles on April 23, 1954, Eisenhower vented his extreme displeasure with what he perceived to be as British military intransigence on Indochina: "I do suggest that you make sure the British government fully appreciates the gravity of the situation and the great danger of French collapse in the region. The British must not be able to merely shut their eyes and later plead blindness as an alibi for failing to propose a positive program." Churchill's refusal to go militarily into French Indochina undoubtedly annoyed Eisenhower. Eisenhower then sent Admiral Arthur W. Radford, chairman of the Joint Chiefs, to London to dispute the British military chiefs' and Churchill's views on the futility of fighting a war in Indochina.[3]

Parting company with the United States on the meaning of collective security in Southeast Asia, the British prepared to accept collective security in Southeast Asia, excluding Indochina. Dulles understood that Eden had already agreed to a form of collective security for all of Southeast Asia, including Indochina. Eden then proposed, after the Geneva Conference, that the southern portion of Vietnam might be included in the defense of Southeast Asia. Dulles wrote: "I asked Mr. Eden where we stood on our joint communiqué of April 13. He said that they were not prepared to examine the possibility of a collective defense which might commit them to fight in Indochina. It was definite that they were not prepared to fight in Indochina, and they were not willing to have any conversations which assumed that as a premise. The area which they are prepared to help defend would have to exclude Indochina." The British might fight for Malaya, Hong Kong, or Singapore, but not for Cambodia, Laos, or Vietnam. They made clear their unwillingness to fight in French Indochina. Having felt betrayed by Eden's explanation of the April 13 communiqué, Dulles explored the possibility of a broader understanding of the communiqué: "Mr. Eden said that subsequent study had already brought them to the conclusion that this was unacceptable if it involved their fighting, but if there was a peaceful settlement at Geneva which partitioned Indochina, then they might be prepared to include the non-communist portion in the defense area." Dulles instinctively distrusted Eden and felt double-crossed by what he regarded as his shifting positions on the defense of Indochina.[4]

Eisenhower proposed a joint military action in Indochina, while Churchill remained exceedingly circumspect about any kind of military commitment in the Far East. The question of whether Eisenhower would save Dien Bien Phu came up in the early spring of 1954, well before the Geneva Conference. As a result of congressional action, the Eisenhower administration needed British concurrence to support a military rescue of French forces at Dien Bien Phu. Churchill and the British cabinet promptly rejected Eisenhower's request for joint military intervention until negotiations at the Geneva Conference had been completely exhausted, ensuring a tragic ending for the surrounded French military garrison. After the French surrender at Dien Bien Phu, Dulles gave a nationally televised address on May 7, 1954, calling for a collective defense of Southeast Asia. Churchill poured cold water over Dulles's proposal in a speech to the House of Commons on May 17, 1954, by suggesting that the collective defense of Southeast Asia must be examined after the Geneva Conference. He gave Eden his marching orders to obtain a cease-fire settlement and end the French Indochina War through negotiation. Churchill categorically refused to be trapped, even by Eisenhower, in an unwinnable war in French Indochina.[5]

As convoluted as the problems of Indochina appeared to be, Eisenhower showed even greater concern about the possibility of an endless series of wars in the larger area of Southeast Asia. He very seriously considered striking China as the supreme instigator of the turmoil. Eden had been noticeably distressed over the hawkish statements coming from Admiral Radford: "I said that I assumed they had not forgotten the Russo-Chinese alliance. It was possible that if we went into Indo-China we should find ourselves fighting Vietnam as well as Vietminh, and in addition heading for a world war." The British used the Sino-Soviet Treaty as almost a guarantee that no military action could be taken against the Chinese Communists.[6]

The president, on the other hand, sensed that the Sino-Soviet Treaty might not always be in the national interest of the Soviet Union, particularly if the United States attacked China. He mentioned, on a number of occasions, that a war with China might not inevitably lead to a war with the Soviet Union. Eden wrote: "Admiral Radford replied that he had never thought that the Chinese would intervene in Indo-China, nor had they the necessary resources available. If they attempted air action, we could eliminate this by bombing the Chinese airfields, which were very vulnerable." Radford echoed the American military's extreme hubris about fighting a war in Southeast Asia, which Eden thought utter nonsense in the light of the Sino-Soviet Treaty.[7]

Eden described Churchill's unfavorable reaction to an American proposal for the rescue of the French at Dien Bien Phu: "Sir Winston summed up the position by saying that what we were being asked to do was to assist in misleading Congress into approving a military operation, which would in itself be ineffective, and might well bring the world to the verge of a major war." Churchill wanted to avoid a major war in the Far East even as Eisenhower actively strategized with the National Security Council about the possibility of completely eliminating all potential Chinese threats and a possible war with the Soviet Union. Churchill and Eden believed Eisenhower would use a rescue military operation at Dien Bien Phu as a pretext for a military attack against China, leading to a global war. Eisenhower perceived Dien Bien Phu as a military problem that needed a military solution. The British totally rejected the American proposal.[8]

Learning of Eisenhower's anger over the British rejection of armed intervention, Eden advised Churchill: "It is probably inevitable that the Americans should feel a little sore just now. They will get over it." Unhappily for Eden, they did not get over it, nor did they forget his failure to support their position. Nevertheless, Churchill remained steadfastly opposed to British military intervention in French Indochina, bluntly telling Admiral Radford: "The British people would not be easily influenced by what happened in the distant jungles of Southeast Asia; but they did know that there was a powerful U.S. base in East Anglia and that war with China, who could invoke the Sino-Russian Pact, might mean an assault by hydrogen bombs on these islands." He would not risk the destruction of Great Britain over what he identified as French colonial failures in Indochina. He clearly viewed Indochina, like India, as a European colonial matter rather than the central focus of the Cold War and certainly not worth endangering his country through the real threat of a global nuclear war. Churchill's great dream of a global Anglo-American partnership became more and more a horrible nightmare.[9]

Recognizing the growing differences on policy between the United States and Great Britain, Eisenhower anguished over the idea of the Communists taking military advantage from the political division in the West. The Geneva Conference could be a cover for extensive military planning and training by the Communists. Writing despondently to Churchill on April 28, 1954, he stated: "Likewise, I am deeply concerned by the seemingly wide differences in the conclusions developed in our respective governments, especially as these conclusions relate to such events as the war in Indochina and the impending conference in Geneva." Eisenhower wanted to know why they were coming up with "drastically differing answers to problems involving the same set of facts." Ideologically speaking, they grew further and further apart, coming up with tremendously different conclusions.[10]

The national interests of the United States and Great Britain came into conflict because of British colonialism. Dulles deeply resented that U.S. foreign policy appeared to be dictated by the colonial interests of our allies as opposed to our own national interests and our own tradition of anticolonialism. He morosely wrote to Eisenhower: "I said the United States was eager to beat the communists at their own game and to sponsor nationalism in the independent colonial areas, which was in accordance with our historic tradition, but that we were restrained from doing so by a desire to cooperate with Britain and France in Asia, in north Africa and in the Near and Middle East." Dulles somberly concluded: "This, however, did not seem to be paying any dividends because when the chips were down there was no cohesion between us. Here at Geneva we were presenting a pathetic spectacle of drifting without any agreed policy or purpose." Despite all of their difficult negotiations, Dulles and Eden remained divided in Geneva. The British sought a diplomatic solution at Geneva, while the Americans prepared for what they assumed would be an inevitable military conflict.[11]

Churchill, realizing how transatlantic relations with the United States had become gravely strained over Indochina, began to rebuild his relationship with both Eisenhower and Dulles. While Dulles may have no longer favored direct U.S. armed intervention in Indochina, he did support the idea that the French must be forced to recognize the independence movements within Indochina. Dulles advocated a grand strategy of collective security for all of Southeast Asia, an organization similar to NATO, while Eisenhower, for his part, just wanted a greater show of Western unity in the Far East.[12]

Looking forward to the Anglo-American summit in Washington in June 1954, the two leaders, Eisenhower and Churchill, remained surprisingly enthusiastic. Churchill, however, recognized that the Dulles-Eden relationship had seriously deteriorated. Eden had quarreled violently with Dulles at Geneva, shouting, "The trouble with you, Foster, is that you want World War III." Churchill mildly reprimanded Eden for not showing Dulles sufficient respect while negotiating at Geneva: "The time has come when Anglo-American relations require strengthening. I am all for developing friendship with Russia, perhaps at the expense of China but we must never let there be any doubt about which side we are on." Eden had become far too friendly with the Russians and the Chinese, while ignoring the Americans, with the possible exception of Under Secretary of State Walter Bedell Smith. Churchill, unlike Eden, wisely recognized the importance of keeping on the good side of Eisenhower.[13]

Meanwhile, Dulles became increasingly irritated with Eden in trying to work out a collective security agreement for the Far East. The secretary of state wanted to defeat the Communists by their own methods. He supported independence movements in the colonial areas of Asia, but felt markedly restrained by British and French colonialism. British ambassador Roger Makins predicted troubling times ahead, especially if there could be no agreement at the Geneva Conference: "I think, however, that we are approaching another dangerous corner. From here it seems to me likely, if not perhaps the most likely development that the French may come forward with a plan involving increased military effort in Indochina, provided the Americans will intervene directly." The British resisted seeking a military solution to a problem that should and could be solved diplomatically. Makins put even more pressure on Eden to come up with a peace treaty in Geneva.[14]

Thinking that Eisenhower really desired an unsuccessful diplomatic outcome at the Geneva Conference, Eden wrote rather dejectedly to the prime minister: "I am becoming increasingly troubled at the international position which may develop about the time of our visit to the United States. . . . There is also only too much evidence here that the main American concern is not now, if it ever has been, for the success of the conference, but with preparations for intervention." If the Americans did not trust the British, undoubtedly the British did not trust the Americans, particularly about American military planning for Indochina. Eden worked desperately to achieve his peace agreement in Geneva in order to avoid a major war in Indochina.[15]

Afraid of a long guerrilla war in French Indochina, Eden engaged in serious negotiations with the Communists at Geneva. While in theory, Eisenhower may have had no problem with negotiations, he could never quite trust any agreement made with Communists. Eisenhower assumed that any agreement at Geneva would be preconditioned on commitments that the Communists would take very lightly, while giving them the time to take advantage of any future military situation. Eden decided that none of the Americans comprehended the British position, with the possible exception of Under Secretary of State Walter Bedell Smith.[16]

As Dulles had originally feared, the British foreign secretary had become, in principle, an intermediary between East and West, a difficult and unenviable position in which he had put himself. As an intermediary, Eden could no longer be considered a true Western ally. In a sense, the Communist strategy to divide the Americans from the British had been successful. Eden's relationship with Dulles deteriorated precipitously.[17]

Moreover, Eisenhower encouraged an abrupt termination of the Geneva Conference because he feared the Communists had already used the negotiations solely to advance their own military position. Eden wrote: "Bedell Smith showed me a telegram from President Eisenhower advising him to do everything in his power to bring to the Conference to an end as rapidly as possible, on the grounds that the communists were only spinning things out to suit their own military purposes. This implied that to keep hostilities going would help the French and their allies. I was sure that the reverse was the truth." Eisenhower clearly preferred terminating the Geneva Conference, which would end any chance for a peaceful settlement of the political disputes in Asia. Washington and London plainly were working at cross-purposes.[18]

In Washington, British ambassador Roger Makins became increasingly concerned about John Foster Dulles's dark mood and the growing differences between London and Washington in Geneva. Makins warned Eden of Dulles's pessimism about Anglo-American relations. Dulles slowly realized the basic incompatibility of British and French colonialism with America's traditional anticolonialism. In addition, national and economic interests also greatly diverged. The Anglo-American relationship steadily unraveled. Makins thought Dulles saw the two countries moving in far different directions. The Washington summit risked the real possibility that these major differences would be highlighted by the press and show a real division in the transatlantic alliance:

> On colonialism, Dulles's line was that the United States had weakened her leadership and her mission in the world by supporting or appearing to support, British and French policies in the Middle East and North Africa, thus risking the charge of being an imperialist power. Egypt and Saudi Arabia provided the examples. Some way must be found of re-establishing the American moral position on the issue of colonialism and taking the initiative rather than remaining on the defensive. Dulles seems to have been particularly affected by Zhou Enlai's attacks at Geneva.[19]

He then communicated an incredibly foreboding and Cassandra-like warning to Eden that Dulles planned to reclaim America's traditional anticolonialism, regardless of British colonialism in the Far East and the Middle East, in furthering non-Communist nationalist movements.[20]

In a follow-up letter to Eden, Makins cautioned that the real breakdown in relations between the United States and Great Britain would occur not in the Far East, but in the Middle East. In a truly perceptive analysis of Eisenhower's foreign policy, Makins deduced: "America will not go isolationist, we shall hear more of the traditional attitudes; self-determination in colonial areas, hemispheric solidarity, especially in South America, peripheral defense in this context reliance on selected friends (including ourselves) rather than on united action. We may find ourselves having to deal with a powerful, nationalistic and frustrated America." He unmistakably knew that American foreign policy would be increasingly unilateral rather than isolationist.[21]

The ambassador described flawlessly the new radical Republican foreign policy emanating from Washington. Self-determination in colonial areas could only be viewed as an attack on British and French colonialism. Hemispheric defense meant that the British needed to stay out of the Western Hemisphere, as in the case of Guatemala. A peripheral defense implied less reliance on regional military alliances and more on unilateral military action by the United States. Makins had cleverly deciphered Eisenhower's "hidden hand" foreign policy.

On June 27, 1954, Churchill pressed the Americans once again on the possibility of his meeting with the Soviets prior to a Three Power meeting. Dulles repeated to the prime minister his warning about the potential dangers of such a meeting, particularly if nothing positive resulted. Churchill confronted a powerful adversary in Dulles. After the Washington conference, he ruminated on the incredible strength of the United States: "We do not yet realize her immeasurable power. She could conquer Russia without any help. In a month the Kremlin would be unable to move troops. The Americans would become enraged and violent. I know them very well. They might decide to go it alone. That was what Dulles meant when he talked about an agonizing reappraisal of policy." Churchill correctly recognized the United States as the sole superpower in the world in the mid-1950s. America could claim superpower status politically, economically, and militarily, while not needing the Europeans to defeat the Soviet Union. The Americans did not need allies, unlike the British or the French. They could go it alone.[22]

Two days later, Dulles had breakfast with former president Herbert Hoover, who frequently expressed his doubts about the reliability of Western allies: "Mr. Hoover spoke in general terms about our foreign policy, emphasizing that, in his opinion, military alliances were of no dependability and that the only strength on which we could rely was our own. He felt with the development of atomic weapons, it was inevitable that England and Western European countries would be neutral." America's power combined with this new Republican ideology put all military alliances into question, including NATO and SEATO. Like Douglas MacArthur and the rest of the Old Right, Hoover intuitively distrusted regional military alliances and collective security arrangements. The British and the French could not be depended on or trusted for important military action in Asia.[23]

At the same time, Churchill remained confident enough about his personal relationship with Eisenhower to send an exploratory message in July 1954 to Soviet foreign minister Vyacheslav Molotov about the possibility of a Three Power meeting. He then wrote Eisenhower about his proposal and received a bristling reply filled with sarcasm: "You did not let any grass grow under your feet, when you left here I had thought, obviously erroneously, that you were undecided about this matter, and that when you had cleared your mind I would receive some notice." Eisenhower may have been more offended by Churchill's failure to consult with him than by the actual message sent to the Soviets. The worst thing for any leader is being caught by surprise. Eisenhower, obviously upset with Churchill's proposal, still wished that something good might come of his letter.[24]

Nonetheless, in a speech to the Lions International Convention in New York on July 9, 1954, the minority leader of the House of Representatives, Massachusetts Republican Joseph W. Martin Jr., asserted that freedom and Communism could not coexist. He attacked the entire notion of this new concept called "peaceful coexistence." In a free society, "a man's word is his bond," Martin said. "Yet today there are forces loose in the world whose sole aim is the substitution of misrepresentation for truth, suspicion for trust and heresy for faith. These forces can be identified very simply. They constitute the world communist conspiracy." Communism represented a philosophy hostile to truth and morals, a philosophy based on an amoral view of human life. An American committed to truth and justice could not be indifferent to the dangers of Communism. Negotiations and compromises with Communists amounted to a surrender to evil, a view most prominently promoted by Eisenhower and rejected by Churchill.[25]

Still, this new concept called "peaceful coexistence," an innovative phrase used by Anthony Eden, now had a new champion in Winston Churchill. Churchill made the significant point of telling the House of Commons how President Eisenhower had declared his own faith in peaceful coexistence between Communist and non-Communist nations. He also decided, as had Eisenhower, that this did not mean, in any sense, any type of appeasement or any acceptance of Communist subversion. Still, surely with Dulles in mind, Churchill incisively pointed out the considerable ideological difference between peaceful coexistence and a policy of forced rollback: "What a vast ideological gulf there is between the idea of peaceful coexistence vigilantly safeguarded and forcibly extirpating the communist fallacy and heresy." He skillfully pointed out the intellectual and moral inconsistency of supporting peaceful coexistence while at the same time secretly planning military operations and guerilla actions against Communists. Churchill's public attack on forced rollback continued to illustrate deep ideological divisions between the British and the Americans.[26]

The Geneva Conference of 1954 divided Vietnam temporarily into two parts, with the Communists consolidating power in the north and a U.S.-supported government trying to organize in the south. South Vietnam needed popular support in its efforts to defeat Communism. French colonialism had ended, and Dulles expected the newly independent countries of Cambodia, Laos, and South Vietnam to provide the best defense against Chinese Communist insurgents.[27]

Directly challenging Eisenhower's brinksmanship foreign policy, on July 30, 1954, General Matthew B. Ridgway, chief of staff of the U.S. Army, voiced his sober concerns about the overall costs of any new land war in Asia: "The effects of full scale war in this era affect all aspects of national life, not only while the war is in progress but for years, even decades, after." The chief of staff knew that another American war in Asia, after Korea, would be catastrophic. Too many people refused to take into full account the terrible effects of war, particularly the aftermath. Wounded and handicapped soldiers would need decades of health care. Ridgway, in a wholly insubordinate speech, came out robustly against any policy of military brinksmanship. He blasted brinksmanship as both "immoral and dangerous." Ridgway sternly warned against a policy of bluff, which should be especially avoided if we could not back up our military threats. He protested against fighting another land war in Asia and doubted the ability of the U.S. Navy and Air Force to win a war on their own. Ridgway made the British case against Eisenhower's brinksmanship policies by pointing out the necessity of ground troops. In any Asian war, American troops would inevitably be outnumbered. His dovish views contrasted rather sharply with the views of Admiral Radford. Ultimately, Ridgway knew that U.S.

ground troops would be required and swallowed up by the enemy in a hopeless military quagmire.[28]

Ridgway had criticized brinksmanship, and he would continue to attack Eisenhower's New Look defense policies as an "all or nothing" approach. Eisenhower, who wanted the New Look in order to save money on military expenditures, stated: That's the trouble with Ridgway. He's talking theory—I'm trying to talk sound sense." Eisenhower was very critical of Ridgway and would not reappoint him as the army's chief of staff in 1955. Still, many Americans began supporting a stronger U.S. presence in the Far East to defend the freedom of these newly independent Asian countries. The Communists too often perceived brinksmanship as mere bluff and the Americans as paper tigers. Brinksmanship at some point would require the American military to do something, if nothing more than to prove that brinksmanship was not all bluff. Robert T. Oliver, journalist and Asian specialist, on September 7, 1954, confirmed: "At the time I was in Geneva, attending the conference on Korea and Indochina, and it was very apparent to us there that the communists were not in the least disturbed by what they confidently interpreted as a bluff. They pushed ahead both with their political demands and with their military attacks in Indochina as though our bold talk were nothing but the buzzing of so many mosquitoes." He accurately articulated the great weakness of brinksmanship. The British, on the other hand, correctly believed that Eisenhower meant exactly what he said and believed that the war in Indochina should be internationalized and vastly expanded.[29]

After the signing of the Geneva Peace Agreements in July 1954, in a speech to the Conservative Party Conference in Blackpool, England, on October 7, 1954, Eden vigorously defended the importance of the Geneva peace accords and the fundamental principles of British foreign policy. He argued for strengthening the Anglo-American partnership and pronounced the Geneva Peace Agreements as just and equitable. Eden paid tribute to the United States and John Foster Dulles. He could afford to be publicly magnanimous to Secretary Dulles after having successfully achieved peace in Geneva. Eden, however, also recognized that the Geneva peace accords did require constant vigilance. Forcefully defending the concepts of collective security and a balance-of-power approach to diplomacy, Eden stated: "In history we have often found ourselves in a conflict to prevent Europe falling under the domination of one power. This time I believe that by acting in advance with our friends we can avert that danger." Eden promoted the concept of collective security in the Far East. By joining the Southeast Asia Treaty Organization (SEATO), Great Britain had undertaken serious military promises and obligations that they had no intention of fulfilling. The British would never use military force to defend the countries of Indochina.[30]

At the same Conservative Party Conference, two days later, Churchill began publicly charging the United States with possibly returning to isolationism: "For America to withdraw into isolation would condemn all Europe to communist subjugation and our famous and beloved island to death and ruin." He had been scared by Dulles, fearing the United States could write off western Europe and survive in "Fortress America." He vehemently attacked the Labour Party and specifically former British cabinet member Aneurin Bevan, who, Churchill added: "one day aspires to become the leader of the Labour Party, [and] did not hesitate to tell the Americans to go it alone. One could not imagine any more fatal disaster than this evil counselor should be taken at his word on the other side of the Atlantic. There is already in the U.S. no little talk of a return to isolation, and the policy is described as Fortress America." Once more sounding the alarm, Churchill alerted the British public to the dangers of U.S. isolationism and unilateralism. Nonetheless, his own deeply Eurocentric foreign policy erroneously dismissed the vital importance of Asia in the fighting of the Cold War.[31]

In his State of the Union Address in 1955, Eisenhower directly confronted Churchill's notion that the battle between the free world and the Communist world could be or should be limited to Europe or dealt with by a mere balance-of-power approach. He offered his own comprehensive approach to the Cold War by making a powerful judgment of its very nature. He rejected the idea that the Cold War represented merely a material struggle based on economic theories, governments, or military power. Eisenhower assigned a true and transcendent meaning to the Cold War by putting it on a spiritual plane based on human nature and the reality of a spiritual world. He considered the Cold War a struggle for the soul of mankind, while British statesmen scoffed at such mystical ideas and continued their practice of power politics.[32]

According to Eisenhower, nothing less than human freedom for all mankind was at stake. The battleground for this war included not only Europe, but Asia, Africa, and South America. Eisenhower would do everything in his power to keep the United States and the world free. Less than a week later, in a not-so-oblique and unflattering reference to the British, Dulles avowed: "The struggle for peace cannot be won by pacifism or by neutralism or by weakness. These methods we have tried and they have failed. Aggression is deterred only by an evident will and capacity to fight for rights more precious than is a debasing peace." He conveyed an unmistakable message to the British, reminding them of the dangers of appeasement, particularly in the Far East. The British believed a nuclear war over Quemoy and Matsu was unthinkable. The British faulted the Americans for pursuing a unilateral "Fortress America" strategy.[33]

Thoughtfully weighing in on the apparent collapse of collective security in Asia, Douglas MacArthur, retired general of the U.S. Army, in a speech to the American Legion in Los Angeles on January 26, 1955, declared: "The situation demonstrates the inherent weakness of the theory of collective security, the chain is no stronger than its weakest link, and what is even more vital, its full power can only be utilized when all links are brought simultaneously into action. The diverse interests of allies always tend towards separation rather than unity." He subtly accused the British of being the weak link in the chain of defense against Communism in Asia. MacArthur quoted Napoleon, "Give me allies as an enemy so that I can defeat them one by one." Unfortunately, the Western allies were already much divided.[34]

In a speech to the Foreign Policy Association in New York City on February 16, 1955, Dulles asserted that too few Asians truly believed in the American commitment to the region. The United States had already accepted the Korean and Indochina armistices, which the Chinese Communists claimed as Communist successes. Americans had recently helped in the removal of National Chinese troops in the Tachens, offshore islands near the Chinese mainland. The Communists had gained additional territory and had maintained the psychological edge in the struggle for the minds and hearts of the people in the East. When and where would the United States draw the line on Communism in Southeast Asia? Dulles worried about the Communists having the psychological edge in Asia. The United States had been slowly losing ground. Dulles wanted the West to regain the psychological advantage. Freedom, not Communism, must be seen as the wave of the future.[35]

In a speech before the Executives Club in Chicago on February 18, 1955, British ambassador Roger Makins responded to what he perceived to be attacks by American policy makers on British foreign policy by defending the British case for a traditional balance-of-power approach in containing the Soviets: "If there was one phrase which made a better stick to beat the European dog with than secret diplomacy, it was power politics or the balance of power. This was commonly regarded as a sort of Machiavellian device invented either by the perfidious British or the Germans, a kind of diplomatic sleight of hand; worldly wise, devious, immoral, unscrupulous, selfish, and certainly quite un-American." The lack of morality in British balance-of-power diplomacy did seem un-American to Eisenhower and Dulles. Two centuries earlier, in his famous Farewell Address, George Washington had argued against classical European diplomacy as leading to nothing less than endless wars and financial ruin. Makins stated: "I only really wanted to suggest to you one general conclusion, and that is that wars only break out when the balance of power in the world, or some part of the world, breaks down." He criticized the United States for thinking it could go it alone in the fight against Communism. The West needed a coordinated effort to defeat Communism. Makins further observed that many Americans had a negative view of Great Britain because they perceived a deterioration of British power and opposed Britain's clinging to outmoded forms of colonialism.[36]

Makins claimed that the British Empire had changed into the British Commonwealth and that London exercised as much power through partnerships and allies as it once had through empire: "Do not underrate the formidable complex of military, economic, and moral force which the commonwealth can exert in world affairs today. . . . All reaffirmed that their countries would remain united as free and equal members of the commonwealth, freely cooperating in the pursuit of peace, liberty, and progress." The commonwealth had actually increased the political power in London. This assertion by the ambassador completely contradicted frantic British efforts to maintain colonialism in Iran, Egypt, and other parts of the world. Unlike the United States, Britain had no formal relationship with Formosa and therefore had no responsibility to defend Formosa, except possibly through the UN. Fascinatingly, Roger Makins, British ambassador to the United States, publicly challenged Eisenhower's policy on China by supporting the Chinese Communist government's legal claim to Quemoy and Matsu. The British favored sacrificing Quemoy and Matsu.[37]

Furthermore, Churchill feared the American threat to use nuclear weapons in the defense of Quemoy and Matsu might lead to a global war. In a speech to the House of Commons on March 1, 1955, he compared the Cold War to the Reformation and the Thirty Years War in the seventeenth century. Science had created weapons of mass destruction, such as the hydrogen bomb, changing the very nature of war. Churchill proposed universal disarmament, including conventional and nuclear weapons, and a reliable program for inspection. Until such a universal disarmament plan could be implemented, the British supported the Americans and their possession of nuclear weapons as a deterrent to war. The British would build their own nuclear arsenal in order to bolster the power of the free world and to increase their influence within the Western alliance. This theory of deterrence, however, did not really work with psychopaths like Hitler. Some other method would be needed in that event. Churchill presumed that the Communists could be considered rational actors in international affairs in his unwavering belief in the value of deterrence.[38]

The question of nuclear deterrence and whether the Chinese Communists could be considered rational actors on the international stage arrived in the spring 1955 within the context of the crisis over Quemoy and Matsu in the Formosa Straits. The United States had already concluded a Mutual Defense Treaty with Formosa in December 1954. Congress further authorized the president to deploy U.S. military forces to Formosa under certain circumstances, such as a direct attack by China upon Formosa or the Pescadores Islands. The treaty, however, remained deliberately vague as to whether the president had been authorized to defend the offshore islands of Quemoy and Matsu. This became the central issue between the U.S.

government and the British government when the Chinese Communists began shelling the Nationalist islands in 1955, presumably as a prelude to an overall attack on Formosa.[39]

Eisenhower defended America's right to defend Quemoy and Matsu if the real purpose of a Chinese Communist attack on those islands was a preliminary step to the taking of Formosa or the Pescadores Islands. To the British, Quemoy and Matsu belonged to the Chinese Communists. In a speech to the House of Commons on March 8, 1955, the foreign secretary advocated the Nationalists leaving Quemoy and Matsu. The Communists, in return, would promise not to attack Formosa and the Pescadores Islands. Eden's speech received bipartisan backing in the House of Commons. In his memoirs, Eisenhower scathingly wrote: "This arrangement, he [Eden] argued, could be followed by discussion of the political issues, which would produce a peaceful settlement. Such a suggestion, more wishful than realistic, in the light of our past experiences, I simply could not accept." He spurned the concept of negotiating with the Chinese Communists on the issue of Quemoy and Matsu. There was nothing to negotiate.[40]

Responding on national television and radio on the very same day, Dulles warned: "We hope that a cease-fire may be attainable. We know that friendly nations, on their own responsibility, are seeking to find substance for these hopes. Also, the United States is studying the matter in a search for peace. So far these efforts have not been rewarded by any success. The Chinese Communists seem to be determined to try to conquer Formosa." Dulles and Eisenhower saw no political or military advantages to be gained in negotiating any type of deal with the Chinese Communists. Eisenhower's pointed refusal to negotiate directly with Peking created a growing rift between the British and the Americans, as evidenced by his nuclear threats and the increasingly vitriolic nature of his correspondence with Churchill.[41]

The president informed the American people in a press conference on March 16, 1955, that he would use tactical nuclear weapons in a war in Asia, albeit limiting atomic bombing to military targets. Senate Majority Leader Lyndon B. Johnson (D-Tex.) described this possibility as an "irresponsible adventure," while Republican Senate Minority Leader William F. Knowland (R-Calif.) feared even greater appeasement of Communists.

Eisenhower wrote a letter to Churchill during the Formosa Straits crisis, "still seeking a common understanding between us on our problems in the Far East. In it I compared the aggressiveness of the Red Chinese in the Formosa Strait with that of Japanese in Manchuria and the Nazis in Europe in the 1930s. Concessions were no answer." He bitterly blamed the British for pursuing an appeasement policy in the Far East. One can only imagine Churchill's outrage at being compared to his old-time Conservative nemesis Neville Chamberlain.[42]

Adlai Stevenson, in a radio broadcast on April 11, 1955, criticized Eisenhower's foreign policy along the same lines as had the British. Eisenhower's policies meant "either another damaging and humiliating retreat, or else the hazard of war, modern war, unleashed not by necessity, not by strategic judgment, not by the honor of allies or for the defense of frontiers, but by a policy based more on political difficulties here at home than the realities of our situation in Asia." He made the British case against Eisenhower's foreign policy. Stevenson indicted Eisenhower as dangerous and even radical in his accommodation of the Republican Party's right wing.[43]

Firing back at Stevenson two weeks later on April 25, 1955, in a speech to the Associated Press in New York, Eisenhower denounced Stevenson, in general terms, by talking about "unstable men." While he condemned a "trigger happy" mentality, Eisenhower cautioned against despair and inaction: "A crisis may be fatal when, by it, unstable men are stampeded into headlong panic. Then, bereft of common sense and wise judgment, they too hastily resort to armed forces in the hope of crushing a threatening foe, although thereby they impoverish the world and may forfeit the hope for enduring peace." Eisenhower warned against despairing men trying to escape hard realities. He had intentionally and fiercely attacked Adlai Stevenson, reminding the voters of his own vast experience in foreign affairs.[44]

American foreign policy should be constructed on the basic principles of justice and cooperation. The real danger in conducting foreign affairs came from not being realistic and from not making necessary sacrifices for the common good. Eisenhower promoted the principle that free trade with other countries provided the best pathway to peace and economic prosperity. Spiritual truths and material wealth need not be in opposition. Eisenhower's proactive diplomacy favored action over inaction. This high-risk brinksmanship paid off when the Chinese Communists gradually backed down and the Formosa Straits Crisis peacefully faded away in the summer of 1955.[45]

In a subsequent address at the Geneva Conference on July 18, 1955, Soviet premier Nikolai A. Bulganin endorsed the concept of "peaceful co-existence." The Soviet Union respected all countries, regardless of the type of government. The Soviets would not interfere with the internal affairs of other governments. Bulganin happily pronounced: "We have always been in favor of peace among the peoples and of peaceful coexistence between all nations irrespective of their internal systems, irrespective of whether the state concerned is a monarchy or a republic, whether it is capitalist or socialist, because the social and economic system existing in any country is the internal affair of its people." The Soviet premier launched a Soviet peace offensive against the West by proposing maximum troop levels. The Soviet proposal offered to finally put limits on the arms race.[46]

Interpreting Bulganin's address and proposals as a Soviet attempt to divide, disarm, and ultimately conquer the West, Dulles answered in an address to the United Nations General Assembly on September 22, 1955, arguing against international Communism. He claimed it would continue to destroy freedom through subversion in the Third World. The Soviets simply could not be trusted; hence it was hard for the United States to develop good working relations with them. Dulles stated: "President Eisenhower also raised the problem of international communism. He said that for 38 years this problem has disturbed relations between other nations and the Soviet Union. It is, indeed, difficult to develop really cordial relations between governments, when one is seeking by subversion to destroy the other." He also expressed his tremendous skepticism over Soviet peace proposals and arms limitation agreements.[47]

Proving to be even tougher on Communist China, Dulles charged the Chinese with being the aggressors in Korea and having taken over Tibet. The Chinese wanted their fellow Communists to conquer Indochina. Mao Zedong had launched an unprovoked attack against the Chinese Nationalists. Dulles pronounced: "The record of this Communist regime has been an evil one. It fought the United Nations in Korea, for which it stands here branded as an aggressor. It took over Tibet by armed force. It became allied with the Communist Viet Minh in their effort to take over Indochina by armed force. Then following the Indochina armistice, it turned its military attention to the Taiwan area." He portrayed the Chinese as behind all of the evil in Korea, Indochina, and Formosa. Dulles mocked the Communists and proposed that they harmonize their peaceful words with peaceful actions.[48]

When Churchill grudgingly retired in April 1955, Eden became prime minister. His new foreign secretary, Harold Macmillan, in a speech to the Foreign Press Association in London on September 22, 1955, openly vilified Dulles's concept of brinksmanship and his defense of "massive retaliation." No one could win a nuclear war. Any reasonable man would decline to use atomic weapons since it would inevitably lead to mutually assured destruction. The threat of massive retaliation rang hollow and might instead actually instigate aggression, Macmillan argued: "First, there can be no victor in nuclear war. Secondly, since the sanction is so terrible, we must realize that men, however resolute, will shrink from using it—even against unprovoked aggression, unless they are convinced that to be conquered is worse than to be annihilated." Modern war allowed for no real winners and should be avoided at all cost, preferably through peaceful diplomacy. Modern science made the annihilation of mankind possible. One possible positive outcome, Macmillan predicted, was that no war would ever be fought.[49]

This forced Dulles to energetically defend his policy of brinksmanship in a speech before the Illinois Manufacturers' Association in Chicago on December 8, 1955. He enthusiastically endorsed brinksmanship as a tactic to discourage aggression in the Cold War. The nature of the tactics depended on the requirements of the defense of various regions. Dulles championed the concept of deterrence based on the power and influence of America's nuclear and conventional forces.[50]

Unquestionably, the most crucial difference between Eisenhower and Churchill had to do with their perceptions of Communism. Eisenhower possessed a bleak outlook with regard to negotiations with any Communist power. Churchill and Eden had a much more optimistic and positive outlook on negotiations with the Soviets and the Chinese. Eisenhower's pessimism about Communists extended to U.S. allies as well. While he expressed the necessity of preserving various regional military alliances, he had no confidence in his British ally. Eisenhower's extreme pessimism led to an unmistakable unilateralism in American foreign policy. This unilateralism, characterized by the diplomatic use of brinksmanship, heightened the tensions and dangers of the Cold War. Dulles outrageously bragged about threatening to use nuclear weapons on China during the Korean War, the Indochina War, and the crisis of Quemoy and Matsu. This kind of brinksmanship diplomacy shocked the British, who trusted in patience, pragmatism, and a global balance of power. Rolling back Communism and peaceful coexistence proved to be diametrically opposed ideas. Eisenhower and Churchill continually sparred over British colonialism. Finally, American idealism, tempered by Eisenhower's pessimism about Communism, could not be reconciled with British pragmatism. These ideological differences doomed the Anglo-American relationship.

Dulles, Churchill, Eisenhower, and Eden at the White House on June 25, 1954. At this Washington Conference, Churchill agreed to help the U.S. quash a UN investigation of the overthrow of Arbenz in Guatemala. Eden and the British Foreign Office had favored a UN investigation. (National Park Service photo. Dwight D. Eisenhower Presidential Library and Museum)

Acting British Foreign Secretary Lord Salisbury stood between Eisenhower and Dulles at the White House on July 14, 1953. Salisbury wrote Churchill on July 3, 1953, "I do not like the idea of the United States or us embarking on wars both with Rhee and the Chinese Communists. . . ." Churchill supported Eisenhower's threats against both Rhee and the Chinese Communists. (National Park Service photo. Dwight D. Eisenhower Presidential Library and Museum)

Churchill arrived in Washington, D.C., in June 1954 and was greeted by Mamie Eisenhower, Dwight D. Eisenhower, Secretary of State John Foster Dulles, and Vice President Richard M. Nixon. (National Park Service photo. Dwight D. Eisenhower Presidential Library and Museum)

Eden and Dulles met in Washington, D.C., in June 1954. Eden and Dulles disliked each other and this was exacerbated by Anglo-American differences on Indochina and Quemoy and Matsu. (National Park Service photo. Dwight D. Eisenhower Presidential Library and Museum)

British Foreign Secretary Selwyn Lloyd, Prime Minister Eden, Dulles, Eisenhower, and British Ambassador Roger Makins smiled at the cameras at the White House in early 1956, prior to the Suez Crisis. (National Park Service photo. Dwight D. Eisenhower Presidential Library and Museum)

Makins, Lloyd, Dulles, and Ambassador to Great Britain Winthrop Aldrich looked on as Eden signed a document in front of Eisenhower in the White House Cabinet Room in 1956. (National Park Service photo. Dwight D. Eisenhower Presidential Library and Museum)

An unhappy Eisenhower listened to Dulles's comments on the Suez Crisis on a television and radio broadcast from the White House on August 3, 1956. (National Park Service photo. Dwight D. Eisenhower Presidential Library and Museum)

Eisenhower invited wartime friends, including Churchill and Prime Minister Harold Macmillan, to a dinner at Winfield House in London on September 1, 1959. Anthony Eden was noticeably absent from the Winfield House dinner. (U.S. Naval Photographic Center photo. Dwight D. Eisenhower Presidential Library and Museum)

CHAPTER 4

ATOMIC BRINKSMANSHIP

Korea, Indochina, and Formosa

T
he transatlantic historical thread linking the Korean War, the Indochina War, and the crisis over Quemoy and Matsu was the constant American threat of using nuclear weapons against the Chinese Communists. Did Eisenhower seriously contemplate using atomic bombs against China? Many historians believe that he bluffed his way through three major international crises in the Far East with never a serious thought of using nuclear weapons. A closer look at American and British archives reveals an Eisenhower who not only contemplated but also planned their use if he deemed the action militarily or even politically necessary.

Eisenhower's very real threats to use nuclear weapons can be found in numerous memoranda to Dulles, the National Security Council (NSC), and the Joint Chiefs of Staff, and especially in his correspondence with Churchill. Operation Everready, the military plan to overthrow Korean president Syngman Rhee in June and July 1953, shows him as a skilled poker player who always made sure that he had "five aces" in every hand. More accurately, he constantly raised the stakes so high that other players such as Anthony Eden, Syngman Rhee, Zhou Enlai, and Mao Zedong would be forced to submit to him. John Eisenhower stated: "The Russians did not look at Ike and see a humble farm boy from sleepy turn-of-the-century Abilene, Kansas, but rather 'Wild Bill Hickok,' the gun-toting U.S. marshal from the Abilene of the earlier Wild West." Eisenhower's threats ultimately proved to be totally effective because the Soviets, the Chinese, and the British took them absolutely seriously.[1]

Great Britain and the United States substantially agreed on how to contain Communism in Europe. Nonetheless, in Korea the British tended to minimize the Communist threat. While the British government publicly supported the U.S. position in Korea, privately British officials feared the United States would expand the war to mainland China and, as a result, the Soviets would invoke the Sino-Soviet Treaty, leading to world war. When President Truman mentioned to the national press in 1950 the possibility of employing atomic bombs in Korea, Prime Minister Clement Attlee rushed to Washington to argue against their use and the wider war they would inevitably provoke. The British wanted the Korean War contained and limited to the Korean peninsula, while both Truman and General Douglas MacArthur actually discussed using atomic weapons and widening the war beyond Korea.[2]

Eisenhower blamed President Truman for the military stalemate in Korea. Eisenhower came to despise him, particularly after the 1952 campaign. His chief of staff, Sherman Adams, wrote: "In all of the six years I was with Eisenhower in the White House he made it a point to have nothing whatever to do with Truman, except for one casual nod of recognition when he encountered his predecessor at the funeral of Chief Justice Fred Vinson in 1953." Dean Acheson, Truman's secretary of state, had made a catastrophic mistake in a speech to the National Press Club on January 12, 1950, in telling the North Koreans and the Chinese that South Korea remained outside the defense perimeter of the United States. This provided an open invitation for the Communists to invade South Korea. In his "I Shall Go to Korea" speech, on October 25, 1952, Eisenhower proclaimed: "The Secretary of State announced his famous 'defense perimeter'—publicly advising our enemies that so far as nations outside this perimeter were concerned, 'no person can guarantee these areas against military attack.' Under these circumstances, it was cold comfort to the nations outside this perimeter to be reminded that they could appeal to the United Nations. These nations of course, included Korea." Eisenhower, in a vitriolic campaign speech, wholeheartedly blasted Truman and his foreign policy.[3]

After more than two years of military stalemate in Korea, President-Elect Eisenhower decided to go to Korea. Before he left for Asia, he had a conversation with British foreign secretary Anthony Eden. Eden warned Eisenhower against using nationalist Chinese troops for an invasion of mainland China. The foreign secretary noted: "The General said nothing to indicate that he had in mind the use of Chiang Kai-shek's troops. I had the impression that he was at present averse from any step which might lead to an extension of the conflict." Eden seemed relieved about Eisenhower essentially agreeing with British policies.[4]

After his trip to Korea in December 1952, Eisenhower met with retired general Douglas MacArthur, who offered his own plan to end the Korean War. MacArthur's recommendations included threatening the North Koreans with the use of atomic bombs. The mere threat of bombing, he insisted, would force the Communists to end the war. Eisenhower wrote: "The Joint Chiefs of Staff were pessimistic about the feasibility of using tactical atomic weapons on front-line positions, in view of the extensive underground fortifications which the Chinese Communists had been able to construct; but such weapons would obviously be effective for strategic targets in North Korea, Manchuria, and on the Chinese coast." Much more than the Joint Chiefs, Eisenhower, with encouragement from MacArthur, looked for the possibility of using nuclear weapons.[5]

Churchill judged the new Eisenhower administration as suffering from a serious lack of experience in foreign affairs. In a message dated January 8, 1953, he wrote Eden and R. A. Butler, chancellor of the Exchequer, that Eisenhower simply wanted a one-on-one meeting with Stalin in Stockholm. Churchill thought that Eisenhower seemed to be in far too much of a hurry to solve all of the world's problems. He urged him to slow down and take the time necessary to evaluate the world situation. Having grave concerns about the new administration and its new policies, Churchill cautioned: "I tell you all this to show you the rough weather that may well be ahead in dealing with the Republican Party who has been out of office; and I feel very sure we should not expect early favorable results. Much patience will be needed." His negative opinions of Republican Party leaders with whom he had recently met gravitated toward condescension. Once he was even heard to suggest that "he would have no more to do with Dulles whose 'great slab of a face' he disliked and distrusted." Churchill tended to blame Dulles for being the bull in the China shop and causing all of the difficult problems in the "special relationship."[6]

In his first State of the Union address, Eisenhower dramatically rescinded Truman's orders, which had the Seventh Fleet literally defending Communist China from an invasion from Formosa. The British did not approve of this announcement. Eisenhower made his thoughts clear; "The practical value of the announcement was simply this, like my visit to Korea, it put the Chinese Communists on notice that the days of stalemate were numbered; that the Korean War would either end or extend beyond Korea. It thus helped, I am convinced, to bring that war to a finish." Eisenhower's policies were designed to end the stalemate in Korea. Indeed, in a meeting of the National Security Council on February 11, 1953, "he [Eisenhower] then expressed the view that we should consider the use of tactical atomic weapons on the Kaesong area, which provided a good target for this type of weapon. In any case, the President added, we could not go on the way we were indefinitely." Eisenhower argued for the possible use of nuclear weapons in Korea.[7]

Like Churchill, Eden thought that the inexperienced Americans posed certain hazards and even dangers in relation to the Korean War. In a meeting on February 13, 1953, with French president Georges Bidault, Eden warned of the problem of a continuing stalemate in Korea: "The difficulty was that a stalemate of this kind was particularly uncongenial to the American temperament." The British minister of defense believed the Americans could militarily outmaneuver the Communists in Korea, but that such a military action would result in from thirty thousand to forty thousand American casualties. Eden understood this was unacceptable to the American people and to the Eisenhower administration, which had promised the American people a reduction in casualties. He correctly sensed Eisenhower's desperate need to end the ongoing stalemate in Korea.[8]

Although Eisenhower understood the British position on Korea, this did not stop him from threatening to use atomic weapons there or from criticizing the British for giving diplomatic recognition to the Communist Chinese government. The British legitimately feared that a wider war would inevitably lead to world war. Eisenhower intensified their anxieties by his planned actions in Korea.[9]

A more experienced diplomat than Eisenhower, Dulles tried to ameliorate British fears and preserve the transatlantic alliance. He often pushed the Communists to the brink, and he also pushed the British, particularly

Eden, to the point of frustration. In his discussion with Eden on March 9, 1953, Dulles calmly revealed the United States' goal of total disengagement from Korea. He disclosed his concern that the Korean War had been used by the Communists for propaganda purposes. South Koreans would soon substitute for Americans in the fighting, and Dulles reassured Eden that the United States had no plans to expand the war or to use Formosa in any military invasion of mainland China. The basic goal of U.S. policy remained the withdrawal of American troops from Korea. In the event of a major escalation of the war by the Americans, Eden needed to know whether the British would be consulted or merely informed of American military actions. Dulles promised Eden an active role as a consultant on the war in Korea.[10]

Eden made clear the British government's opposition to a naval blockade of China. He argued that a naval blockade would be militarily ineffective and as an act of war would lead to too many dangers: "I wished to repeat the objection of the British Government on the question of a naval blockade of China. Their principal objection was that it would be ineffective. China could receive by the Trans-Siberian Railway many times the amount of goods she was at present receiving by sea. Moreover to impose a blockade by force would be politically most dangerous since it would involve stopping communist ships and blockading Soviet-controlled ports." The British position sought to limit U.S. military actions to the Korean peninsula. Otherwise, Eden feared, China might invoke the Sino-Soviet Treaty and massively expand the war.[11]

Meanwhile, despite British objections, Eisenhower still reserved the right to use atomic bombs in Korea. Historian Timothy J. Botti has noted: "At the end of March . . . he told the NSC that he would be willing to employ atomic weapons in Korea if a 'substantial victory over the communist forces' could be achieved and the military stalemate broken. . . . But Eisenhower's commitment to resort to nuclear weapons if necessary was clear." Robert Cutler, administrative assistant to the president for national security matters, in discussing how to have a successful military campaign in Korea wrote: "He [Eisenhower] indicated that the use of atomic weapons in such a campaign should depend on military judgment as to the advantage of their use on military targets." Eisenhower prepared to use atomic bombs on military targets. Eden rejected both the use of atomic weapons and even Eisenhower's threats to use such weapons on the North Koreans and the Chinese.[12]

Nevertheless, at Eisenhower's request, Secretary of State Dulles made secret nuclear threats against North Korea and China. Historian Edward Friedman confirmed this in an important publication: "He [Eisenhower] deliberately conveyed word to the communists, including the North Koreans, Chinese, and Russians, through secret channels that, if progress toward a settlement was not made, any past limits were off as to both targets and weapons, and that, if we saw fit, we would use the atomic bomb." To add more validity to the threat, Eisenhower moved nuclear warheads to Okinawa. In May 1953, Dulles warned Indian prime minister Jawaharlal Nehru of the possibility that American military forces in Korea might resort to the use of nuclear weapons. As a leader of the neutralist movement in the Third World, Nehru appeared an ideal mediator between Washington and Peking. Dulles deliberately provided this message to Nehru hoping that he would leak it to the Chinese Communists. Whether this message ever reached the Chinese, a subject of serious debate among Cold War historians, is irrelevant. The Chinese and the Soviets knew about the president's desire to end the Korean War and his discussions about nuclear attacks with his National Security Council.[13]

The Soviets had carefully tracked the movement of U.S. nuclear missiles into the Far East. Eisenhower later decided: "They didn't want a full-scale war or an atomic attack. That kept them under some control." The Soviets knew of the American threat to use nuclear weapons. They forced Mao Zedong and Zhou Enlai to accept a reasonable armistice. McGeorge Bundy, former national security advisor under President Kennedy, added: "Dwight Eisenhower contributed even more than Harry Truman to the folklore of atomic diplomacy. He believed that it was the threat of atomic war that brought an armistice in Korea in 1953. . . . John Foster Dulles told allied statesmen in private a lurid tale of nuclear deployments made known to the Chinese." Despite Bundy's skepticism, Eisenhower certainly believed in his concept of brinksmanship.[14]

Even the threat of a nuclear attack directly contradicted British foreign policy in the Far East. Eisenhower believed atomic weapons could be used on military targets in Korea. On May 6, 1953, in a National Security Council meeting, Eisenhower again raised the issue of dropping nuclear bombs on North Korean airfields. The problem with using the atomic bomb in Korea was getting the approval of the allies. Eisenhower made no moral distinction between conventional or atomic weapons. No one should doubt that, had the North Koreans broken the armistice, he would have responded with nuclear weapons. The Korean stalemate showed the weakness of Kennan's theory of containment. Sherman Adams, Eisenhower's chief of staff, wrote: "If you are ready to stand up against a potential aggressor with an impressive deterrent of massive retaliatory power, the Dulles theory contended, the aggression was not likely to occur. This accurately summarized the basic theory of the Dulles strategy as it opposed the containment defense policy of the Truman-Acheson regime." Truman failed because he had played by rules set by the Communists and had settled for an endless stalemate. Eisenhower broke the rules and introduced the powerful threat of nuclear warfare.[15]

Another significant problem between the Americans and the British concerned the lack of serious consultation on important military operations. In a message to British ambassador Roger Makins concerning the possibility of an American military attack on Chinese targets along the Yalu River, Churchill revealed that British air vice marshal D. H. F. Barnett had leaked vital information about the United States planning to attack targets along the Yalu River:

I have just learned that United Nations Command plan major bombing attack on one or possibly two targets near Yalu River almost immediately. 2. I fear that these operations at this moment will be thought to be an attempt to spoil agreement at Panmunjom. Are they really necessary whilst things hang in the balance of negotiations? If there is no overriding military necessity I can see only harm resulting from this plan. 3. Please see Bedell Smith urgently and tell him my views. You could ask whether these operations could not be deferred. 4. For your information. This report had come to us from Air Vice Marshall Barnett in Tokyo. We have not heard of the plan directly from Washington. We do not want to compromise Barnett's relations with General Mark Clark but at the same time I have strong views on the unwisdom of this operation, of which we might well have been informed from Washington. I leave it to you how best to convey these views to General Bedell Smith.[16]

This created a difficult dilemma for British ambassador Roger Makins since confronting Bedell Smith would reveal the source, British air vice marshal Barnett. Advising Churchill against a specific warning to the president about the dangers of military operations, Ambassador Makins cautioned, "I am sure you will appreciate that it is not possible to make representations to Bedell Smith about a top secret operational matter of which we have no knowledge except through Air Marshall Barnett, without divulging the source." He subsequently received an order from Churchill to "take no action" in the matter. On May 10, eight Thunderjets struck a hydroelectric facility at Sui-ho very close to the Yalu River.[17]

In May 1953, Churchill inherited the Foreign Office from the physically incapacitated Eden. He proved to be much more flexible in dealing with the Americans than had Eden. After his death in 1965, those who had been close to him revealed how his relationship with Eden grew increasingly difficult and why Churchill had serious doubts about Eden's suitability as his political successor. The controversial diaries of Lord Moran, Churchill's personal physician, corroborated this: "'It is a great relief to have charge of F.O. instead of having to argue with Anthony.' Moran has Churchill saying in 1953, when Eden was ill, 'I can get something done.'" Churchill did help end the Korean War by dealing directly with Eisenhower from the Foreign Office. Unlike Eden, who worried about flouting international law, Churchill and Eisenhower wanted an armistice in Korea, regardless of legal niceties.[18]

The political differences between Churchill and Eden often exacerbated tensions in the transatlantic relationship. Time after time, Churchill revealed himself to be much more flexible and patient than Eden, allowing the Americans to pursue their policy of brinksmanship. Richard V. Damms wrote: "In mid-May, Eisenhower approved contingency plans to expand the war with a new ground offensive up the waist of the peninsula accompanied by tactical nuclear air strikes against Chinese air bases in Manchuria, but he remained deeply concerned about adverse allied reaction to such a scheme and the possibility of Soviet nuclear retaliation against Japanese cities." Churchill, the Sandhurst graduate and nineteenth-century military adventurer, supported this type of military scheming much more than did the legalistic Eden. On May 20, 1953, General Omar Bradley briefed the National Security Council and the president about the possible military expansion of the war beyond Korea and the necessity of using atomic bombs, if the war was expanded. Historian Evan Thomas has written: "As conceived by General J. Lawton Collins, the Army Chief of Staff, it also called for the use of mustard gas to drive the enemy from the caves into the open, where they would be targets for tactical nuclear weapons." Eisenhower's military plan to use tactical nuclear weapons and mustard gas would have left Korea ravaged for centuries.[19]

In a message to Churchill on May 23, 1953, Eisenhower declared, "I believe that a prompt public and unequivocal statement that the United Kingdom was fully consulted and fully supports the position which the United Nations Command is taking in the forthcoming Executive Sessions would assure an armistice promptly, if in fact the Communists want one on the basis acceptable to us." The British government prepared a statement on Korea for the public.[20]

Churchill and Eisenhower did fundamentally agree that South Korean president Syngman Rhee was an even bigger obstacle to peace than the Chinese Communists because of his absolute refusal to negotiate an armistice. Historian H. W. Brands wrote: "Rhee's rhetoric and subversive activity had jeopardized the safety of American troops to such a degree that the Eisenhower administration seriously considered authorizing UN commander Mark Clark to conduct a military coup, arrest Rhee, and declare martial law throughout South Korea." The Eisenhower plan to overthrow Rhee had the code name Operation Everready.[21]

On June 18, 1953, Rhee tried to sabotage the armistice negotiations by releasing twenty-five thousand North Korean POWs. He had not been authorized by the UN Command to release these prisoners, and the subject of releasing prisoners of war demanded further negotiations. Eisenhower sternly warned Rhee: "Unless you are prepared immediately and unequivocally to accept the authority of the UN Command to conduct the present hostilities and to bring them to a close, it will be necessary to effect another arrangement. Accordingly, the UN Commander in Chief has been authorized to take such steps as may become necessary in the light of your determination." Dulles also condemned Rhee's prisoner release as a "violation of the authority of the United Nations command in which the Republic of Korea had agreed." Eisenhower had, in effect, put Rhee on notice that his very position as president of the Republic of Korea stood in jeopardy. General Mark Clark had been authorized to remove Rhee, if it was deemed militarily necessary.[22]

Venting his deep frustrations to Churchill on June 19, 1953, Eisenhower wrote: "The Korean business is indeed difficult. There can be no question as to the soundness of your observation about the trouble we shall have if the war goes on and Syngman Rhee remains in his present office." His frustration with Rhee had peaked. Eisenhower and Churchill worked secretly planning for the execution of Operation Everready against Rhee, who had been overtly sabotaging the armistice talks. Churchill knew and fully approved of the American contingency plan to remove Rhee from power in South Korea. Both Eisenhower and Churchill communicated their fervent desire to have him removed.[23]

On June 21, 1953, British ambassador Roger Makins sent a long, handwritten top-secret letter to Prime Minister Churchill:

1. I saw the President this morning and gave him your message.
2. On Rhee he sympathizes with your desire but said emphatically that any change must come or appear to come from within. He felt strongly that the Western powers that had intervened in Korea to uphold freedom and democracy must not be seen to be setting up a puppet government. He had given much thought to this. He had some hope that there were elements in South Korea who understood that their country was wholly dependent on the United States for its reconstruction and future support and that they would exert influence. I asked him whether something would not be done through the South Korean army. He seemed to think the army might in fact make a move.
3. As to the additional British brigade, the President observed that this would have a gainsaying effect in the United States.
4. Finally he said he would not answer your message today but would reflect further upon it. He entirely agrees that the matter should be

kept in closest secrecy. Any hint that such a thing was under discussion could have most serious effect.

5. The President was in excellent form and very friendly.

6. I understand, very confidentially, that the President and some of his advisors have, in fact, already discussed at length ways and means of dealing with Rhee and that there are also unconfirmed indications that a military coup in Korea is being prepared.

7. The President did not raise the time factor involved in the move of British Brigade, but this may come up later. I suppose there is no possibility of bringing troops from Hong Kong garrison rather than from Egypt.[24]

Eisenhower fully consulted and informed the British about Operation Everready. At the same time, he made contingency plans for a nuclear war expanding the Korean War to mainland China. Eisenhower's plans had gone far beyond anything the Old Guard Republicans ever contemplated in pursuing an end to the Korean War.

An enthusiastic Churchill gave Eisenhower a green light on Operation Everready and any military action he might deem necessary to take against President Rhee. He sent the following message to Eisenhower on June 24, 1953: "I am holding three battalions and an artillery regiment at short notice in Hong Kong 'to reinforce Gen. Mark Clark's Army in any action that may be required of them by United Nations.' Let me know whether you would like this made public. I did not quite understand what 'gainsaying' meant, but presume you meant it would stave off adverse criticism in the United States." He passionately backed the American plan to overthrow Rhee. Churchill ordered the British military to go on standby alert and to be ready to assist the Americans.[25]

In Korea on June 25, 1953, General Mark Clark discussed with his generals when and how to replace President Rhee: "General Clark feels that the only conditions under which there might be a possibility that the Republic of Korea Army would take action to replace present Republic of Korea government would be after Rhee had been informed categorically that we intend to withdraw from Korea unless he agrees to armistice and the Republic of Korea Army is convinced that we mean business." The

Joint Chiefs' response to this was: "You are further authorized widest latitude in specific terms of armistice and handling problem ROK attitude toward armistice." Clark's reply: "I am convinced that the sooner we sign an armistice, with or without Rhee's support, the better our position will be to handle Rhee when we are not worried about a Commie attack. I will keep you advised of my plans based on further developments." This began a pattern for the Eisenhower administration, with Churchill's approval or at least acquiescence, of threatening numerous leaders of foreign countries with military coups, which will be discussed in later chapters.[26]

The British did involve themselves in mediating the differences between the Americans and the Chinese on the vexing issue of the release of POWs. Selwyn Lloyd, British minister of state, wrote Churchill on June 25, 1953: "I told the High Commissioner that I hope Mr. Nehru would make clear to the Chinese the danger of them taking up a fixed position on this matter. Probably it would be impossible to recapture the prisoners. If, therefore, this was insisted on as a condition precedent to an armistice it might very well mean that Syngman Rhee had his way and there would be no armistice." By this time the Chinese Communists wanted an armistice as much as the Americans did. Clearly, the Americans and the British worked very closely together to bring about the armistice in Korea.[27]

Responding to Churchill's offer of military help with a message from the president two days later, Dulles wrote: "The President asked me to thank you for your private and personal message received today. He particularly welcomes the spirit prompting point 3. We are inclined to feel that it would be better not to make this public just now." Dulles seemed to be happy about the spirit of transatlantic cooperation between the British and the Americans, and in a follow-up message the president personally thanked the prime minister.[28]

Meanwhile, Eisenhower sent Walter S. Robertson, assistant secretary of state for Far Eastern affairs, to Korea to try to convince Rhee to support an armistice plan. If Rhee cooperated, he would be promised a mutual defense treaty and billions of dollars in both military and economic aid. However, as historian Clay Blair has written: "If that failed, they would try a gigantic bluff. They would rescind those offers and threaten to withdraw all American forces from the peninsula, leaving South Korea to its fate. If the bluff also failed, they were prepared to stage a coup d'etat [Operation

Everready], replacing Rhee with a more amenable South Korean leader." Robertson's job was to convince Rhee to cooperate and sign an armistice.[29]

Deputy Secretary of Defense Roger Kyes wrote to General Clark: "Within broad latitude already given you there may be possibility of quietly and adroitly creating impression among Rhee and ROK leaders that UNC is preparing to withdraw if ROK attitudes remained unchanged. Such measures should speak for themselves rather than require making of overt statements to Rhee and ROK leaders." Officially, there would be no threats made against Rhee, but unofficially our actions would speak louder than our words. Rhee's regime remained under the cloud of a military threat from the UN Command. Eisenhower absolutely refused to allow Rhee to sabotage the Korean armistice talks. If Rhee had done anything more to damage the United Nations Command or undermine the U.S. diplomatic effort to obtain an armistice, he would have been removed from power through Operation Everready.[30]

The newly appointed acting British foreign secretary, Lord Salisbury, reflected the views of the British Foreign Office, writing a rather stern cautionary note to Churchill about the incredible dangers of a military coup in South Korea occurring at the same time the Korean War might be expanded into China. On July 3, 1953, he wrote: "I do not at all like the idea of the United States or us embarking on wars both with Rhee and the Chinese Communists, and greatly hope that things will not come to that. It would be likely to cause bewilderment to those whose sons are fighting in Korea and also to earnest supporters of the United Nations." Lord Salisbury's extraordinary letter to Churchill confirmed Eisenhower's activities, with the active cooperation of Churchill, in preparing to embark on wars with both Mao Zedong and Syngman Rhee at the same time in July 1953.[31]

The Eisenhower administration had gone far beyond anything the Far Right had ever advocated. Churchill had definitely gone out on a limb for the Americans with no support coming from the British Foreign Office, including Lord Salisbury, whom he had just appointed acting foreign secretary to temporarily replace Eden. Rhee undoubtedly felt the heat of the pressure coming from the American military. Assistant Secretary of State for Far Eastern Affairs Robertson reported: "He raged that the military were trying to cause dissension among his troops and that these broadcasts were attempts to intimidate and frighten him with threats." Robertson further observed: "He said, 'I have some face too, and if I go out to people announcing agreement on President Eisenhower's and Secretary of State's program they will think it is because of these threats by military.'" Under enormous military and psychological pressure from Eisenhower, Rhee finally capitulated and agreed to cooperate with UN forces on a Korean armistice on July 8, 1953. Rhee's anxiety concerning the possibility of a future attack from North Korea had been overcome by reassurances from the Americans of continued support. They would strive for a mutual defense treaty, the unification of Korea, and the eventual removal of Chinese troops from North Korea.[32]

Ironically, the key to peace in Korea had been getting Rhee's cooperation on an armistice. Historian Stephen Ambrose has written: "In Seoul, meanwhile, Walter Robertson and General Clark were conferring daily with Rhee, threatening him with an American pullout if he did not cooperate in the armistice, promising him virtually unlimited American aid if he did. Rhee resisted the pressure, helped by reports from the States that seemed to indicate a near revolt by Republican senators against their own administration." Eisenhower massively increased the psychological pressure on Rhee through the constant threat of a political or military coup.[33]

Historians have too often failed to view Eisenhower's threat of an American pullout or the promise of unlimited American aid to South Korea as a radical break from the past. Nor do they even acknowledge the stark and incredible reality that behind the scenes Eisenhower had plainly threatened Rhee with a political or military coup. In his diary on July 24, 1953, Eisenhower complained: "Rhee has been such an unsatisfactory ally that it is difficult indeed to avoid excoriating him in the strongest of terms." Eisenhower exceeded the belligerency of the Old Guard Republicans, such as MacArthur, Taft, and Hoover, in threatening and planning nuclear war with China and at the same time bullying Rhee by means of a possible military coup. No longer inhibited by Eden's opposition in the British Foreign Office, Churchill wholeheartedly endorsed Eisenhower's radical proposals. Eisenhower then put the maximum pressure on both the North Koreans and the South Koreans in order to achieve his goal of peace and stability in Korea. The success of Eisenhower's Korean policy strengthened and solidified his growing belief in brinksmanship.[34]

INDOCHINA

In his memoirs, Anthony Eden noted: "On January 12, 1954, after proclaiming the doctrine of instant retaliation, Mr. Dulles gave warning that Chinese intervention would have 'grave consequences which might not be confined to Indochina.'" Dulles threatened the Chinese leadership with the possibility of massive retaliation. If the Chinese Communists intervened in Indochina, the United States reserved the right to retaliate against China. Many historians have wrongly labeled Dulles as "the real hawk at Dienbienphu." Great Britain's interests and concerns in Indochina proved to be considerably less than those of the United States. Churchill viewed Indochina as merely a problem of French colonialism. He scoffed at Eisenhower's domino theory. Historian Alan P. Dobson has argued: "One might see a contrast between British pragmatism and US moralistic idealism taking shape here. In any case, the substance of the differences noted above was at the heart of the difficulties they had in coordinating policies." The difficult problems between Eisenhower and Churchill on Indochina stemmed from deep ideological differences about the nature of the Communist threat.[35]

In a National Security Council meeting on January 8, 1954, Eisenhower said there "was just no sense in even talking about United States forces replacing the French in Indochina. . . . This war in Indochina would absorb our troops by divisions!" There would be no more Koreas under Eisenhower. Nevertheless, Eisenhower strongly believed in aiding the French in Indochina, plainly stating: "My God, we must not lose Asia—we've got to look the thing right in the face." Eisenhower needed to come up with a plan to save Indochina.[36]

On March 29, 1954, in response to the French call for help to defend Dien Bien Phu, Dulles offered United Action, a Western alliance to intervene militarily in Vietnam. In his memoirs, Richard M. Nixon wrote: "In Washington the Joint Chiefs of Staff, under their Chairman, Admiral Arthur Radford, devised a plan, known as Operation Vulture, for using three small tactical atomic bombs to destroy Vietminh positions and relieve the garrison." Eisenhower planned on using nuclear weapons to rescue Dien Bien Phu.[37]

On April 4, 1954, at 8:20 PM, in the upstairs study at the White House Eisenhower had agreed with Dulles and Radford on a plan to send American forces to Indochina under certain strict conditions. It was to be, first and most important, a joint action with the British, including Australian and New Zealand troops, and, if possible, participating units from such Far Eastern countries as the Philippines and Thailand so that the forces would have Asiatic representation. Secondly, the French would have to continue to fight in Indochina and bear a full share of responsibility until the war was over. Eisenhower was also concerned that American intervention in Indochina might be interpreted as a protection of French colonialism. He added a condition that would guarantee future independence to the Indo-Chinese states of Vietnam, Laos, and Cambodia.[38]

The U.S. Congress, in consultation with Eisenhower and Dulles, conditioned American participation in any military action in Vietnam on British involvement. Indochina would not be another Korea in which the United States supplied 90 percent of the manpower. On April 7, 1954, Eisenhower expressed his concern to the national press that Indochina would be the first of the dominoes to fall in Southeast Asia. The famous domino theory stemmed from the growing Communist threat in Indochina and Southeast Asia, which existed as a part of a much larger global conspiracy. In April 1954, the British cabinet unequivocally refused the American request to participate in United Action, preferring negotiations at Geneva scheduled to begin on April 26, 1954. Churchill and Eden placed little value on French Indochina, a French colony, and their subsequent lack of enthusiasm for United Action curbed any possibility for American military action in the region.[39]

Eisenhower agonized over the balance of power in the world, particularly in Asia, where he thought it hung by a thread like the sword of Damocles. The British assumed a war in French Indochina could not be won by the Western powers. They favored a negotiated settlement in Geneva. A major difference between the British and Americans concerned their views on the likelihood of military victory in Indochina. The British remained extremely skeptical about the likelihood of success in fighting a jungle war in Indochina. By contrast, Dulles believed a war could be won with the support of the indigenous people of the area.[40]

Disagreeing fundamentally with Eisenhower on the nature of the Communist threat in Asia, Churchill repudiated the domino theory and the value Eisenhower attached to Southeast Asia. He firmly refused to help Eisenhower bail out French colonialism. The real Cold War lay in Europe and not in Asia. This key distinction proved critical in the subsequent breakdown in Anglo-American relations. Asia should be simply downgraded as a theater of conflict in the Cold War. Churchill preferred diplomatic to military moves in the Far East and supported British national interests rather than guerrilla wars for strictly anti-Communist purposes. Dulles, on the other hand, became more and more infuriated with the British, in particular with his British counterpart, Eden. Historian Jeffrey A. Engel wrote: "Dulles privately told C. D. Jackson, one of Eisenhower's advisers, in the spring of 1954, 'At every turn we are blocked by the fact that our principal allies are not willing to take any risks.' He wanted allies who would risk their fortunes and even their peace to defeat global communism." The British thought fighting in French Indochina would lead to a military disaster.[41]

In order to save Dien Bien Phu, the American secretary of state, undoubtedly with the approval of Eisenhower, offered two atomic bombs to President Georges Bidault of France. Bidault wrote: "But it was I who answered without having to do much thinking on the subject, 'If those bombs are dropped near Dien Bien Phu, our side will suffer as much as the enemy. If we drop them on the supply line from China, we will be risking a world war. In either case, far from being helped, the Dien Bien Phu garrison would be worse off than before." The French refusal to use atomic bombs in their own defense led Dulles to demand a firm British commitment to a new regional military alliance in the Far East called the Southeast Asia Treaty Organization (SEATO).[42]

Expressing his intense annoyance at Dulles's remarkable single-mindedness and his bullying about the proposed SEATO, in a message to Makins on April 17, 1954, Eden wrote: "This is another of these exasperating examples of the American government rushing ahead without proper consultation. We have not yet decided upon the membership of this organization.

This matter was expressly reserved in London and I'm not prepared to decide it now." Eden continued to express his displeasure about Dulles, complaining in a later message to Makins: "Americans may think the time has passed when they need consider the feelings or difficulties of their allies. It is the conviction that this tendency becomes more pronounced in every week that is creating mounting difficulties for anyone in this country who wants to maintain close Anglo-American relations." Eden worried about the possible exclusion of some of Great Britain's Commonwealth partners from the new proposed treaty. He wanted to make sure that Makins pursued this point with the Americans, particularly with Dulles.[43]

On April 24, 1954, Dulles and Radford met with Eden in Paris to discuss United Action. In this key meeting, Dulles warned Eden that if Indochina fell, the United States was prepared to take military action against Communist China. These military actions included direct military attacks against China, a naval blockade of the Chinese coast, and the seizure of Hainan Island. The British considered Radford's planned war against China totally calamitous.[44]

Eisenhower sensed the British fears over a possible World War III. In his diary, he wrote: "I believe that the British government is showing a woeful unawareness of the risks that we run in that region." On the same day, Eisenhower wrote a letter to his old friend Swede Hazlet: "For more than three years I have been urging upon successive French governments the advisability of finding some way of 'internationalizing' the war; such action would be proof to all the world and particularly to the Vietnamese that France's purpose is not colonial in character but is to defeat communism in the region and to give the natives their freedom." Eisenhower sought to internationalize and expand the war in Indochina.[45]

Churchill may have been even more distressed had he known that Eisenhower behind the scenes had been preparing for nuclear air strikes against China. Historian Robert F. Burk contends: "In May 1954 Eisenhower upped the military stakes further by authorizing the preparation of nuclear strikes against China itself if it intervened directly in the Indochina war." Eisenhower's brinksmanship put heavy demands on the Soviets and the Chinese, who then apparently pressured Ho Chi Minh to accept the division of Vietnam along the 17th parallel.[46]

When Dien Bien Phu eventually fell on May 7, 1954, Eisenhower sent a message to French president René Coty stating: "I hope also that the gallant garrison at Dien Bien Phu may know that no sacrifice of theirs has been in vain; that the free world will remain faithful to the causes that they have so nobly fought." In his message, he clearly indicated that he had not given up the fight in Indochina over the loss of the men at Dien Bien Phu. In addition, Eisenhower and Dulles remained upset with Churchill and Eden for stalling on the development of SEATO until after the Geneva Conference.[47]

Genuinely fearing that direct American military intervention in Indochina would sabotage his negotiations with both the Chinese and the Soviets at the Geneva Conference, Eden wrote: "He [Molotov] added with a frosty smile that he had observed that Mr. Dulles had succeeded during his stay in Geneva in never once acknowledging a Mr. Zhou Enlai's existence." Dulles had deliberately snubbed Zhou Enlai by refusing to shake hands with him. Eden believed the Communists knew Eisenhower planned a military campaign in Indochina regardless of the result of the Geneva negotiations.[48]

The Chinese assumed the Americans planned on attacking them. Eden completely disagreed with Eisenhower's policy of brinksmanship, which threatened massive retaliation against the Chinese. He thought it diplomatically counterproductive to make such threats. It would not lead to better negotiations with the Soviets and the Chinese. Eden assumed Admiral Radford's policy of military action in Indochina had finally prevailed over Under-Secretary of State Walter Bedell Smith's preferred course of peaceful negotiations at Geneva. Smith, as the leader of the U.S. negotiation team, could not even directly contact the Chinese Communists or associate himself with any plan that might lead to the loss of any area of Indochina. Eden considered Dulles's talk of brinksmanship a catastrophic turn of events. Indeed, he wished to minimize the diplomatic damage caused by Dulles. Eden wrote: "I myself fear that this new talk of intervention will have weakened what chances remain of agreement at this conference. The Chinese, and to a lesser extent, the Russians, have all along suspected that the Americans intend to intervene in Indochina whatever arrangement we try to arrive at here." Eden completely rejected the efficacy of brinksmanship.[49]

Churchill backed the diplomatic efforts of his foreign secretary to the hilt in a parliamentary debate in the House of Commons by stating: "But our immediate task is to do everything we can reach an agreed settlement at Geneva for the restoration of peace in Indochina. Her Majesty's Government are resolved to do their utmost to achieve this aim and to exercise their influence to ensure that any acceptable settlement shall be backed by effective international guarantees." He sought peace in Indochina through diplomatic means in Geneva in order to avoid what he considered an unnecessary and unwanted war.[50]

Unlike the British, in a meeting with Dulles recorded by National Security Advisor Robert Cutler, Eisenhower proclaimed: "If he was to go to the Congress for authority he would not ask any half way measures. If the situation warranted it, there should be declared a state of war with China; and possibly there should be a strike at Russia." Cutler also noted that, "He would never have the United States going into Indochina alone," concluding that "if the U.S. took action against communist China, there should be no halfway measures or frittering around. The Navy and Air Force should go in with full power, using new weapons, and strike at air bases and ports in mainland China." Eisenhower proposed to use atomic bombs against air bases and naval ports in China. In an Eisenhower-led or -directed war there would be no dangerous stalemate. In a follow-up meeting with the Joint Chiefs of Staff on June 19, 1954, "he [Eisenhower] told the chiefs that an atomic assault against China would inevitably bring Russia into the war; therefore if the United States were to launch a preventive attack, it had to be against both Russia and China simultaneously." Eisenhower needed to take out both the Soviet Union and China with atomic weapons. While Eden feverishly worked on diplomatic initiatives at Geneva, Eisenhower confidently planned for global thermonuclear war.[51]

The U.S. military worried about the possible launch of a surprise Chinese air assault against the French in Vietnam, which could devastate French forces. On June 2, 1954, President Eisenhower, Secretary of State Dulles, Deputy Secretary of Defense Robert B. Anderson, Admiral Radford, Douglas MacArthur II, and Robert Cutler met at the White House. Cutler's notes of the meeting include the following:

> In the event of overt, unprovoked Chinese communist aggression in Southeast Asia which would be a direct threat to the security of the United States and to other nations having security interests in the re-

gion, Congress would be asked immediately to declare that a state of war existed with communist China, and the U.S. should then launch a large-scale air and naval attacks on ports, airfields, and other military targets in mainland China, using as militarily appropriate "new weapons," in the expectation that some of such other nations would join in opposing such aggression.[52]

In 1954, Eisenhower actually contemplated a first-strike attack against both the Soviet Union and China as a prelude to a thermonuclear global war against Communism.[53]

Meanwhile, Under Secretary of State Walter Bedell Smith and Anthony Eden worked amicably together at the Geneva Conference trying to resolve the Indochina situation peacefully. Eden wrote Churchill: "We judge that for most Americans here, except Bedell-Smith, any agreement with the communists is regarded as morally wrong and politically dangerous." Smith shared with Eden, possibly imprudently, the contents of two important telegrams he had just received, one from Saigon and the other from Eisenhower. The message from Saigon painted a depressing picture of the deteriorating French political and military position in Vietnam. The embassy's message indicated that the French planned to leave Vietnam. The only hope for the Vietnamese might be direct military intervention by the United States.[54]

In the second message, Eisenhower stated that the West needed to draw a line on Communism in Asia. Eden wrote to the British Foreign Office: "He [Eisenhower] was convinced that the communists would carry on until such a line had been drawn and the communists warned 'Thus far and no further.' In forging this chain the missing link was the United Kingdom since Her Majesty's Government could not be brought to a decision while the Geneva Conference continued, it was imperative to bring the conference to a close without delay." Eisenhower demanded an end to the Geneva Conference. He unmistakably preferred a policy of drawing a military line in Vietnam, with all of its dangerous military implications, to pursuing what he regarded as endless and fruitless negotiations with the Communists at Geneva.[55]

A Special National Intelligence Estimate maintained: "In this connection, U.S. use of nuclear weapons in Indochina would tend to hasten the ultimate Chinese Communist decision whether or not to intervene. It would probably convince the Chinese Communists of U.S. determination to obtain a decisive military victory in Indochina at whatever risk and by whatever means, and of the consequent danger of nuclear attack on Communist China." The United States' use of nuclear weapons in Indochina should act as a powerful deterrent to Chinese intervention. The United Kingdom, on the other hand, stubbornly held out for a negotiated peace agreement.[56]

Eisenhower might have been depressed had he known what Churchill really thought about Vietnam. In a message to Eden dated June 13, 1954, Churchill simply stated: "I heartily agree with you that Great Britain will in no circumstances intervene in Vietnam, on the other hand we have given our support in principle to SEATO which you and I both think has many advantages over ANZUS from which we were excluded." Churchill had been terribly offended by Great Britain's earlier exclusion, by the Truman administration, from ANZUS in 1951, a military alliance that included Australia, New Zealand, and the United States.[57]

Churchill feared a newly created SEATO might embroil him in an unwelcome war in Vietnam. Eden responded to Churchill on June 15, 1954, expressing his antipathy for the Americans' refusal to negotiate at Geneva: "The Americans appear to be building up a situation in which they will discuss nothing, Korea or other, with the Chinese. This can only lead to war. It is already resulting in intense American unpopularity here." He observed the Americans, under orders from Eisenhower, ending their negotiations in Geneva.[58]

Furthermore, Churchill identified Dulles as trying to undermine the British in the upcoming Washington summit planned for late June 1954. He wrote Eden: "Dulles evidently does not like our White House meeting. What he says counts for absolutely nothing here and the more he says it the more harmless does he become." Churchill planned the Washington summit with the intent of dealing directly with Eisenhower and avoiding Dulles. Churchill assumed, erroneously, that basic foreign policy differences existed between Eisenhower and Dulles.[59]

In another telegram to Eden on June 16, 1954, Churchill delivered what amounted to a vitriolic diatribe against the French: "A wise Frenchman would clear out of Indochina on the best terms possible and concentrate on saving North Africa which is in jeopardy. The French Chamber will go on playing its games and enjoying them without the slightest regard to the allies by whom they were rescued and on whom they have to live. It would be wrong, in my opinion, for this misbehavior to be further indulged." He doubted the French could save Indochina, just as the British could not save India. The best thing for Great Britain and France would be to concentrate on saving their colonies in North Africa and the Middle East. Churchill deeply resented how the problems of Indochina caused so many difficult problems for the Anglo-American relationship. He chose to project this loathing onto the French rather than the Americans.[60]

Conveying his concern to Eden about SEATO being an American contrivance to bring the British into an unwanted war in Vietnam, Churchill wrote: "As you invite my opinion I frankly give it. If disaster occurs, as the military think they may within the next month, you or we may be charged with having been sucked in by very obvious maneuvers." Churchill did not want to be viewed as naïve and subsequently trapped into an unwinnable war by the Americans. The British totally opposed any fighting in Vietnam, regardless of the commitments that might have been made to SEATO. Dulles believed the real issues in Vietnam concerned both French colonialism and the threat of Communism. In preparation for the Washington summit, "Dulles said he was sure that meant that the British were going to make a plea for a differentiation between French colonialism and British colonialism. The president interrupted to say, 'Sure the British always think their colonialism is different and better. Actually, what they want us to do is go along to help keep their empire.'" Eisenhower despised both French and British colonialism, knowing that they further complicated his arduous battle plan against global Communism.[61]

However, Eisenhower did recognize the importance of the Anglo-American relationship by comparing it to a bridge. In his comparison, he observed that people used bridges every day without noticing them at all. The trouble comes when a bridge becomes unusable and then everyone quickly notices. The bridge must be maintained and usable, and this provided the real purpose for the Washington summit. Any disruption in the Anglo-American relationship could only give aid and comfort to the enemies of freedom.[62]

Churchill's philosophy on Indochina can be found in a letter to President Eisenhower on June 21, 1954: "I have always thought that if the French meant to fight for their Empire in Indochina instead of clearing out as we did of our far greater inheritance in India, they should at least have introduced two years' service which would have made it possible for them to use the military power of their nation." He disagreed with the French using untrustworthy local troops and the French Foreign Legion, which seemed dominated by Germans. Churchill thought the French should get out of Indochina as quickly as possible, under the best possible circumstances.[63]

Churchill and Eisenhower desperately needed to coordinate their approach to the Chinese Communists. Eisenhower wanted Churchill's commitment to not allow the admission of China into the UN. On June 29, 1954, Press Secretary James C. Hagerty asked the president "if he had discussed the subject of Red China and its admission to the UN with Churchill, and he said that he had. 'I just had one conversation on the subject. I told him that it was politically immoral and impossible for the United States to favor the admission of Red China to the United Nations, and surprisingly enough Churchill agreed.'" Churchill unequivocally accepted the American position on excluding China from the United Nations, while Eden kept his opinions to himself. The British did get Eisenhower to agree to the division of Vietnam. At the end of the Washington Conference, Eisenhower and Churchill finally agreed to accept the partitioning of Vietnam, as long as South Vietnam, Cambodia, and Laos could establish independent non-Communist governments.[64]

After the Washington summit, in a follow-up letter to Churchill on July 8, 1954, Eisenhower reflected on his profound distrust of negotiations with the Soviets and the Chinese:

My appreciation of the acute need for peace and understanding in the world certainly far transcends any personal pride in my judgments or convictions. No one could be happier than I to find that I have been wrong in my conclusion that the men in the Kremlin are not to be trusted, no matter how great the apparent solemnity and sincerity with which they might enter into an agreement or engagement. . . . The bill of particulars against Red China includes, among many other things, its invasion of North Korea, where its armies still are stationed. Secondly, Red China, by its own admission, illegally holds a number of Americans as prisoners. This outrages our entire citizenry. Third, communist China has been the principal source of the military strength used in the illicit and unjust aggression in Indochina. Finally, Red China has been guilty of the most atrocious deportment in her dealings with the Western world. At Geneva it excoriated the United Nations and asked for the repudiation of decisions by that body. Red China has been worse than insulting in its communications to ourselves and others, while the public statements of its officials have been characterized by vilification and hatred.[65]

This letter profoundly disturbed the British. Roger Makins wrote to Eden on July 9, 1954: "Dulles told me that it was entirely his own work. I am afraid that the effects of this episode, the product of general frustration at the failure of American policy, or the lack of it, will linger on and drive American foreign policy still further into the impasse in which it now finds itself, e.g. the reluctance of Dulles and Bedell Smith to return to Geneva." The message came directly from Eisenhower without the assistance of the State Department.[66]

Rebuffing any talks with the Communists either at Geneva or anywhere else, Eisenhower continued to prefer a confrontational brinksmanship foreign policy over negotiations in Geneva. Initially, he wanted to pull all American diplomats out of Geneva, but worried about the negative reaction such a move might entail. Reluctantly, he decided to continue the American presence at Geneva, maintaining: "If we are not on record to oppose the settlement when it happens, it will plague us through the fall and give the Democrats a chance to say that we sat idly by and let Indochina be sold down the river to the communists without raising finger or turning a hair." He sent Bedell Smith back to Geneva to strictly observe the negotiations. Eisenhower's cynical analysis exposed his extreme skepticism of negotiations with the Communists and his underlying pessimism about domestic politics.[67]

The British disregarded American brinksmanship in favor of peaceful negotiations with the Communists at Geneva. Churchill passionately attacked Eisenhower's cynicism on a negotiated peace settlement and on July 20, 1954, sent a powerful message to Eden: "The supreme Geneva objective is cease-fire in stopping the war in Indochina, and no procedural differences with the United States should be allowed to prevent this."

The British cabinet stood completely united behind Churchill and Eden in overriding any possible disputes with the United States in achieving a cease-fire in Indochina.[68]

Foreign Secretary Eden's reputation as a great diplomat skyrocketed with the successful and popular peace agreement at the Geneva Conference in 1954, which may very well have been the high point of British diplomacy in the 1950s. Eden had overcome the objections of the Americans, the Soviets, the Chinese, and the Vietnamese in fashioning a settlement. Vietnam had been divided in two, with a Communist government in the north and a free government in the south. The plan called for free and open elections in the future in order to reunite the country. The planned elections would never be held, and the war would continue. Nevertheless, Churchill avowed, "I send you my sincere congratulations and those of your colleagues on the success which has at length rewarded your patient persevering skill at Geneva." Even Queen Elizabeth II joined in: "I am so delighted with your success and send you my warm personal congratulations." The Geneva Conference in 1954 was a tremendous diplomatic accomplishment for Anthony Eden.[69]

Unfortunately for Eden, this renown and unqualified success meant that he had to deal with a very somber and sullen John Foster Dulles, who emphatically refused to sign the peace agreement because it might be considered appeasement to the Communists even though, in theory, he accepted its usefulness in establishing a free and capitalist South Vietnam. Eden's enormous success led Eisenhower and Dulles to take a harder line on British and French colonialism in the Middle East. Eisenhower's predictably vindictive reaction to the Geneva Agreements reflected his extreme disappointment over the loss of North Vietnam. Dulles, at least, acknowledged that the Geneva Agreements might be the best that could be achieved under very difficult circumstances.[70]

Protecting Eisenhower and himself from attacks by Old Guard Republicans and Senator Joseph R. McCarthy by refusing to sign the Geneva Agreements, Dulles promised only "not to disturb them." Admiral Radford scornfully proclaimed: "Her Majesty's Government were being played upon by Nehru to back his neutralist proposal for what amounted to a sellout to the communists at Geneva; the British public was terrified at the thought of the hydrogen bomb; and there was a widespread feeling in Britain that, somehow or other, the Geneva Conference was going to settle all the problems of Asia." He accused the British of simply appeasing the Communists at Geneva in order to save London from the unlikely threat of a hydrogen bomb attack.[71]

Meanwhile, the British claimed:"The Americans tended toward impatience and naïveté, in diplomacy which often led to misguided bluster. Dulles' anti-communist zealotry compounded this American tendency and blinded him to realistic appraisal of the world stage." The Americans argued that the British based their foreign policy in Asia not on anti-Communism, but on a zealous defense of British colonialism. Eisenhower patronizingly wrote Churchill: "Colonialism is on the way out as a relationship among peoples. The sole question is one of time and method. I think we should handle it so as to win adherents to Western aims." British interests in Asia included Hong Kong, Malaya, and Singapore. Each country, the United States and Great Britain, fully understood the other's great weaknesses and prejudices. The Anglo-American relationship in the Far East remained strained. The British argued against a war in Indochina, which would shift much-needed resources from central Europe. These huge differences between the United States and Great Britain became further magnified with the momentous crisis over Quemoy and Matsu in 1955.[72]

Many historians have suggested that Eisenhower deliberately set up political and military impediments to his brinksmanship policy in Indochina. This analysis lacks both logical coherency and historical evidence because Eisenhower had deliberately sent Secretary of State Dulles and the chairman of the Joint Chiefs, Admiral Radford, to London to make their case for United Action. Too many historians pay no attention to the simple fact that Eisenhower favored sabotaging the negotiations going on in Geneva. He favored a military solution to what he perceived as a military problem in French Indochina. The lack of military cooperation from the British infuriated Eisenhower and Dulles. Numerous American historians overlook basic facts and have consistently misread Eisenhower's actions and statements. The serious falling out between Eisenhower and Churchill on Quemoy and Matsu proves, beyond the shadow of doubt, the vast ideological differences between the Americans and the British.

In 1954, the United States and Great Britain created the Southeast Asia Treaty Organization (SEATO) to halt further Communist subversion in Asia. This new international organization substantiated the many claims that collective security or United Action could not work in the fight against Communism in Southeast Asia. The British and the French continually evaded their responsibilities under the Manila Pact, leaving the United States virtually alone, without Western allies, in the political and military battle against Communism in Asia. For Eisenhower, the military situation in Asia went from bad to worse. The Americans had created SEATO to stop the Communists from taking over in Asia. Yet, European support of any military action proved problematic. Sherman Adams, Eisenhower's chief of staff, recorded: "Dulles said emphatically that the British and the French were giving us no military support in Asia and were opposed to our use of atomic weapons in a defense of Formosa. But we could not allow our policies in Asia to be dictated by our European allies." The United States, under Eisenhower's deliberate guidance, began shifting from a collective security approach in Asia to an entirely unilateral foreign policy, while the Soviet Union and China continued their unremitting demands for the removal of the Seventh Fleet and the elimination of American troops from Japan.[73]

Many Eisenhower revisionists have incorrectly praised the president for the way he avoided a war over Quemoy and Matsu, the Nationalist-controlled offshore islands of China. They have celebrated his "deliberate deception and ambiguity" with regard to a possible nuclear attack against mainland China. Robert Divine has written: "The beauty of Eisenhower's policy is to this day no one can be sure whether or not he would have responded militarily to an invasion of the offshore islands, and whether he would have used nuclear weapons." Of course, this only raises the perilous question of whether Eisenhower's "brinksmanship" was all bluff, a question frequently asked in 1956 by the Democratic presidential candidate, Adlai Stevenson.[74]

Historian Yi Sun insists that Eisenhower's hazardous stand on Quemoy and Matsu paid off. The Chinese had to take Eisenhower's threats of massive retaliation seriously. Eisenhower could wipe out the Chinese military and its military infrastructure through the use of atomic weapons. Sun reflects: "This strategy seemed effective. There is evidence to suggest that Mao at this time began to take the American nuclear threats more seriously. Although he continued to embrace the concept of 'people's war,' Mao came to realize nuclear weaponry, which he had discounted as a 'paper tiger,' could be a 'real tiger' capable of mass destruction." But beyond this latest assertion, historians have often disagreed on whether Eisenhower established himself as a wise statesman by threatening nuclear war over two tiny and relatively inconsequential Chinese islands.[75]

The initial shelling of Quemoy began in early September 1954 and immediately required the attention of Eisenhower with regard to the possible defense of the offshore islands. Having not gone to war over Korea and Indochina, would Eisenhower go to war with China over these small islands off the Chinese coast? The hazards in pursuing this calculatingly ambiguous or illusory brinksmanship policy was that Eisenhower confused not only the Chinese, but American and British policy makers as well. He became frustrated trying to explain his own unintelligible policies to Prime Minister Winston Churchill. In fact, Churchill and Eden fought against Eisenhower's policies on Quemoy and Matsu. They considered the threats of U.S. military actions as far too militant and unnecessarily threatening Europe with the possibility of a third world war. Churchill mistakenly blamed Dulles for these extreme foreign policy positions taken by the United States government. However, Eisenhower made clear in a letter to his old friend Swede Hazlett that he called the shots on American foreign policy: "So far as Dulles is concerned, he has never made a serious pronouncement, agreement or proposal without complete and exhaustive consultation with me in advance and, of course my approval." In addition, in his original draft letter to Hazlett with regard to Indochina, Eisenhower wrote: "What I really attempted to do was to get established in that region the conditions under which I felt the United States could and should intervene drastically." Eisenhower controlled this very radical and militant American foreign policy in the Far East.[76]

In an interview on NBC's *Meet the Press*, Anthony Nutting, British ambassador to the United Nations, made several imprudent remarks about Great Britain supporting the United States over Quemoy and Matsu. On December 13, 1954, he wrote Eden an apology:

I am more than sorry if my reply on Meet the Press caused embarrassment. Under considerable pressure I thought the safest let out was to refer to the United Nations. I carefully avoided speculating on what the United Nations would do and, in particular, refused to be drawn on what action, if any, we would take. I see the point about the international status of Formosa. But nevertheless I do not feel I could pretend that if Chiang Kai-shek were attacked by Communist China he would fail as a member of the United Nations to invoke United Nations assistance. Nothing I said went beyond or could be interpreted as exceeding the bounds of the charter of the United Nations.[77]

Eden responded coldly to Nutting on December 14, 1954:

Criticism of your interview is principally directed against implications that United Kingdom will necessarily be involved in hostilities if China attacks Formosa. It is by no means certain that an attack on Formosa "would no doubt call for collective action of the United Nations." Your references to the Korean parallel which is not a true one and that [to] China as the "potential enemy" are particularly criticized. They seem cumulatively to create the impression that it was your intention to declare that the United Kingdom would answer the war on the side of the United States if the Chinese launched an attack. "Times" Washington correspondent in his full account of your interview today states that you have in fact created the impression in America, and imply that we have undertaken something new. Consequently there is much concern here. I shall of course do all I can to meet criticism in the House. Meanwhile I rely on you to say as little as possible on this thorny subject and to limit your public interviews to the utmost.[78]

Eden carefully outlined an extremely legalistic and virtually anti-American position on the crisis in the Formosa Straits. The United States had a defense pact with Formosa, while Great Britain did not. The British might not even back UN actions or sanctions against China for attacking not only the offshore islands, but Formosa itself.

The Formosa Straits Crisis led to a dangerous split in the transatlantic alliance between the United States and Great Britain. The bombardment of Quemoy and Matsu started in September 1954. On January 1, 1955, the president of Formosa, Chiang Kai-shek, assumed that a war between China and Formosa would break out soon. Foreign Minister Zhou Enlai threatened a Chinese invasion of Formosa shortly. Once again, Eisenhower effectively threatened the Chinese Communists with nuclear weapons. He honestly expected to bomb China with atomic weapons in the defense of Formosa. Secretary of State Dulles mentioned "the use of atomic weapons in his conversations with Sir Anthony Eden related only to the most extreme hypothesis of the communists attacking Quemoy in so heavy a human wave as to make it impossible to stop them with ordinary firing power. He felt this was a remote possibility." Dulles suggested a limited use of nuclear weapons. Nevertheless, Churchill and Eden clearly understood the United States would be eventually forced to use nuclear weapons in order to protect the offshore islands.[79]

On January 25, 1955, Eisenhower wrote to Churchill describing the incredible differences between them on nuclear weapons. He thought the British failed to take into serious consideration the important power of surprise in military actions. Nuclear weapons provided an amazing ability to destroy targets with little or no warning. Eisenhower claimed that this gave the allies a tremendous advantage over the Chinese. He believed atomic bombs could be used against military targets.[80]

The president complained about the British having too negative an outlook on the usefulness of nuclear weapons and steadfastly claimed that with a dozen atomic bombs a nation could be completely paralyzed. China's infrastructure could be rapidly and completely destroyed by a skillfully launched nuclear attack. The British had not envisioned the use of atomic bombs in the same way. They felt nuclear weapons should be used as a deterrent to war, while Eisenhower regarded them, in the context of the Formosa Straits Crisis, as new and improved conventional weapons. In his disturbing letter to Churchill, he cautioned: "I think it possible that the very life of the nation, perhaps even Western civilization, could, for example, come to depend on instantaneous reaction to news of an approaching air fleet; victory or defeat could hang upon minutes and seconds used decisively at top speed or tragically wasted in indecision." Eisenhower depended on his vast military experience to give him the ultimate ability to make those kinds of decisions in seconds.[81]

Those kinds of letters from Eisenhower tended to appall Churchill, Eden, and the British Foreign Office into thinking that he might embroil the entire world in war. A nuclear attack against China could lead to the invocation of the Sino-Soviet Treaty and global thermonuclear war. Eisenhower daringly proposed the New Look defense built on logic and strategic studies, in order to know when, not if, to use nuclear weapons. Allies and adversaries faced the terrible dilemma of being pushed into war through miscalculation. Yet, Eisenhower took the utmost offense at British fears of the United States being drawn into a nuclear war with China. Eisenhower scathingly wrote Churchill: "I note that in the memorandum accompanying your letter, your government fears that during the next two or three years the United States may, through impulsiveness or lack of perspective, be drawn into a Chinese war. I trust that my message to the Congress reassured you as to our basic attitudes and sober approach to critical problems." He deeply resented being portrayed in British documents as either a warmonger or a fool. Finally, he said the United States could not abandon its friends, particularly Formosa, without the possibility of a major breakdown in the fight against Communism in Asia. The psychological impact of abandonment on the Asians could not be played down: "But I am positive that the free world is surely building trouble for itself unless it is united in basic purpose, is clear and empathetic in its declared determination to resist all forceful communist advances, and keeps itself ready to act on a moment's notice, if necessary." The sober tone of the letter indicates that Eisenhower lucidly recognized the Communists' preparations to take over Asia, unless met with military counterforce.[82]

Congressional resolutions on Formosa also confused the Chinese and Western allies. Zhou Enlai thought it a U.S. declaration of war. The Chinese, according to Zhou, were not afraid of war threats, and they continued to threaten Formosa with liberation. Churchill approved of the United States defending Formosa and the Pescadores Islands. These islands should be protected at "all cost and by all means." Eisenhower and Churchill basically agreed on the defense of Formosa and the Pescadores Islands.[83]

However, Churchill also supported the removal of the Nationalist Chinese from all coastal islands in the next three months:

If the Chinese Communists interfered with the Nationalists moving out all of their troops from the coastal islands then there should be a war between the United States and China. The United States should not have to worry about being attacked while removing 50,000 Nationalists on Quemoy. The removal of Chiang from the coastal islands meant that a clear demarcation could be made between Communist China and Formosa. This should be what the Americans really want. If this could be done as an ultimatum to the Chinese this would greatly reduce any kind of embarrassment the United States might feel in overseeing a Nationalist withdrawal. I do not know whether there is any chance of the Americans accepting this sensible withdrawal under cover of their formidable threats and military precautions and also the whole thing being on their initiative and decision. They would say in the fact: "as negotiations have become impossible nothing is left to us but to decide the matter for ourselves; this is what we are going to do. Beware!"[84]

Churchill promoted a hybrid policy incorporating American brinksmanship with British pragmatic substance.

On January 31, 1954, Eisenhower issued a statement to be delivered to Chiang Kai-shek to clarify America's position on the issue of Quemoy and Matsu: "It is the purpose of the President to assist in the defense of Quemoy and Matsu against armed attack if he judges such attack is of a character which shows that it is in fact in aid of and preparation for an armed attack on Formosa and the Pescadores and dangerous to their defense. An attack by the communists at this time on Quemoy or Matsu which seriously threatened their loss would be deemed by the president to be of this character." He ostensibly hoped to reassure Chiang Kai-shek and discourage Mao Zedong and Zhou Enlai.[85]

Disagreeing with Churchill and Eisenhower, Eden counseled for more patience in negotiating with the recalcitrant Chinese Communists: "Our object must surely be to bring the United States government along to a position which we will be able to support. Would it not be best to see whether the evacuation of the Tachens goes through without any communist interference?" Eden routinely recommended patience to the octogenarian prime minister, who preferred action to inaction. Eden optimistically suggested: "If it does we shall be in a stronger position to argue with the Americans over the other coastal islands. I would therefore urge that the message should be kept up our sleeves until (*a*) we know the result of the Tachen operation. (*b*) we have the promised Russian reply to us and the Indians." Eden's increasingly adversarial attitude toward Washington exemplified the breakdown of the transatlantic alliance. The new British role meant mediating between the East and West.[86]

On February 10, 1955, Eisenhower wrote a long letter to Churchill explaining his conviction that nothing could be worse than global war. He believed the Soviets did not want a global war at this time. Eisenhower disclosed to Churchill his confidence, in the event of a war with China, that the Soviets would prudently avoid any kind of direct military intervention. Eisenhower's National Security Council concluded: "So long as the Soviets are uncertain of their ability to neutralize the U.S. nuclear-air retaliatory power, there is little reason to expect them to initiate general war or actions which they believe would carry appreciable risk of general war, and thereby endanger the regime and the security of the USSR." Instead, the Soviets might be limited to supplying the Chinese with conventional weapons and using American intervention for propaganda purposes.[87]

The Soviets feared the possibility of an American nuclear bombing campaign against their homeland. Eisenhower certainly recognized the danger of U.S. intervention in China due to the Sino-Soviet Treaty, but for him this created even more of a dilemma for the Soviets, for they must decide whether they would plunge the world into a global war over China. He astutely wrote: "It would not be an easy decision for the men in the Kremlin, in my opinion. But all this is no excuse for fighting China. We believe our policy is the best that we can design for staying out of such a fight." Eisenhower refused to show any weakness to the enemy.[88]

The president wanted to draw a clear line on Communist expansion in Asia. If the Chinese crossed this line, he would eliminate China's capacity to wage war and conduct subversive activity throughout Asia even if that risked a global war with the Soviet Union. By raising the stakes in Asia so high, Eisenhower trusted Soviet leaders to choose their national interest over Marxist ideology. They would be forced to back down from the commitment required by the Sino-Soviet Treaty or face the horrible prospect of a thermonuclear attack by the United States.[89]

This signaled an American foreign policy of brinksmanship based on moral principles, inflexible and threatening, against both the Chinese and the Soviets. In a reply to Eisenhower on February 15, 1955, Churchill argued that the coastal islands legally belonged to China and therefore could not be a proper cause for war. Churchill, aided by Eden in the writing of this letter, made his case against Eisenhower based on his interpretation of international law and then added that a war to keep Quemoy and Matsu under Chiang Kai-shek could not be successfully supported in Great Britain's current political climate. The British prime minister argued strenuously against a war over Quemoy and Matsu, writing that "a war to keep the coastal islands for Chiang would not be defensible here." Churchill knew Formosa could easily be defended by U.S. naval and air forces. Furthermore, Chiang Kai-shek should be persuaded to remove his military forces from the indefensible coastal islands. Churchill wrote: "He deserves the protection of your shield but not the use of the sword." He made the diplomatic case for the evacuation of the offshore islands by the Nationalist Chinese.[90]

In his last months as prime minister, Churchill openly questioned the wisdom of Eisenhower's policy of defending the offshore islands of Quemoy and Matsu. He stressed the value of the Seventh Fleet in providing an absolute defense for the island of Formosa. Churchill unwaveringly doubted Eisenhower's basic premise on the need to keep Formosa, let alone Quemoy and Matsu. The Communists had successfully divided the West with its propaganda over Quemoy and Matsu.[91]

Expressing his extreme unhappiness with British policy in a protracted letter to Churchill on February 19, 1955, Eisenhower wrote: "It would surely not be popular in this country if we became involved in possible hostilities on account of Hong Kong or Malaya, which our people look upon as colonies, which to us is a naughty word. Nevertheless, I do not doubt that, if the issue were framed in this way, we would be at your side." Hong Kong and Malaya would be defended by the British and the Americans. Eisenhower openly attacked Churchill's hypocrisy and his failure to take Chinese threats seriously enough.[92]

In Eisenhower's mind, the Chinese really wanted to take over Formosa: "I am increasingly led to feel it would be dangerous to predicate our thinking and planning on the assumption that when the Chinese Communists talk about their resolve to take Formosa, this is just 'talk,' and that they really would be satisfied with the coastal islands. I suspect that it is the other way around. What they are really interested in is Formosa—and later on Japan—and the coastal islands are marginal." Eisenhower decided to draw the line between the free world and the Communist world somewhere between mainland China and the offshore islands of Quemoy and Matsu.[93]

Communicating his fears to his foreign secretary, who would soon be his successor, on February 19, 1955, Churchill wrote to Eden: "The Soviets, it seems to me, are playing a dangerous game if they are stimulating Communist China to talk big about Formosa. They are quite right in thinking that this provokes the Americans into an awkward and unhandy policy which loses them support in Britain and Europe. They are quite wrong if they think the consequences will divide the free world, or be very agreeable to China should they go too far." He thought the Chinese had gone too far in their insults of the Americans, possibly leading to a horrifying and unnecessary war.[94]

In a sense, Churchill, not Eisenhower, called for a "middle path" in diplomacy by pushing Chiang Kai-shek to give up the coastal islands in favor of a promise by the Communists not to take Formosa or the Pescadores Islands. However, Churchill and Eden, acting as mediators between the East and the West, continued to lose political influence with their powerful ally. Nearing the end of his second premiership, Churchill appeared completely powerless to influence American foreign policy. At age eighty, Churchill found himself battling against Eden, the Americans, the Soviets, and the Chinese.[95]

For his part, Dulles escalated the crisis with new warnings to the Chinese Communists. In defending Quemoy and Matsu, Dulles wrote Eisenhower on March 6, 1955: "I said that this would require the use of atomic missiles. The President said that he thoroughly agreed with this, and, indeed, he suggested my putting into my proposed speech a paragraph indicating that we would use atomic weapons as interchangeable with conventional weapons." While Eisenhower preferred to use conventional weapons, he actively prepared to use nuclear weapons if conventional weapons proved ineffective or nondecisive.[96]

In attacking China, Dulles had become convinced by the military that nuclear weapons would be needed. In the National Security Council Meeting on March 10, 1955, "Admiral Radford said that he merely wanted to say that the Joint Chiefs of Staff have consistently asserted that we should have to use atomic weapons. Indeed our whole military structure had been built around this assumption. He said that he was convinced that we could not handle the military situation in the Far East, particularly as regards aircraft, unless we could employ atomic weapons." The great question remained whether public opinion would allow Eisenhower and Dulles to use nuclear weapons in the defense of the offshore islands. They decided to prepare the public through their press conferences for the real possibility of nuclear weapons being used on military targets in China and along the Chinese coast.[97]

In a speech on March 12, 1955, Dulles explicitly stated that America had "new and powerful weapons of precision which can utterly destroy military targets without endangering unrelated civilian centers." He followed this up with more warnings to the Chinese Communists. In a news conference on March 16, 1955, Eisenhower stated: "Yes, of course they would be used . . . in any combat where these things can be used on strictly military targets and for strictly military purposes, I see no reason why they shouldn't be used just exactly as you would use a bullet or anything else." Eisenhower and Dulles deliberately blurred the distinctions between conventional and nuclear weapons. On March 17, 1955, Vice President Nixon also endorsed the use of nuclear weapons, asserting that "tactical atomic weapons are now conventional and will be used against the targets of any aggressive force." Everyone in the administration kept to their talking points.[98]

In a memorandum to the Joint Chiefs on March 22, 1955, Secretary Wilson ominously wrote: "Because of the Chinese Communist mentality and the announced U.S. policies regarding Formosa, the Pescadores and the offshore islands, there exists a real probability of war with Communist China." The Joint Chiefs had been put on notice to be prepared for war. To add even more fuel to the fire, Admiral Carney warned the press that the president was ready to destroy China and its ability to wage war. As Carney was a member of the Joint Chiefs, his message suggested that a nuclear war with China appeared imminent.[99]

H. W. Brands has written: "Preparing for the worst, Eisenhower directed the military to set war plans in motion. The Joint Chiefs responded by giving the commander of the U.S. Seventh Fleet authority to conduct reprisals against mainland installations in the event of attacks on American ships and by ordering the Strategic Air Command to begin, on an 'urgent basis' target selection for an 'enlarged atomic offensive' against the People's Republic of China." Obliterating China's capacity to wage modern war might make Eisenhower's troublesome problems in the Far East suddenly go away.[100]

On March 29, 1955, Eisenhower wrote his final letter to the departing Prime Minister Churchill about the Quemoy and Matsu crisis and the marked differences between the United States and Great Britain: "Although we seem always to see eye to eye when we contemplate any European problem, our respective attitudes towards similar problems in the Orient are frequently so dissimilar as to be almost mutually antagonistic." In this extended letter to Churchill, Eisenhower expanded on his view that the loss of Quemoy and Matsu could lead to the loss of Formosa, possibly the loss of the Philippines, and the rest of the Far East. He refused to put a lot of pressure on Chiang Kai-shek to remove his troops from Quemoy and Matsu. The United States and Great Britain continued to quarrel on this issue.[101]

The basic differences between Eisenhower and Churchill proved to be ideological. Churchill thought Eisenhower went much too far in his ideological opposition to Communism in the Far East. Yet, in a letter to Lewis William Douglas on March 29, 1955, at the height of the crisis over Quemoy and Matsu, Eisenhower explained: "The central fact of today's life is that we are in a life and death struggle of ideologies. It is freedom against dictatorship; communism against capitalism; concepts of human dignity against the materialistic dialectic. The communists and I mean Marx, Lenin, and Stalin and now their successors and offshoots—such as Mao and Zhou—have all announced their adherence to the theory of world revolution and overthrow of all other forms of government by force and violence." Under the real threat of nuclear war, Zhou Enlai reduced the tensions between the United States and China by making peaceful statements at the Bandung Conference. This effectively ended the crisis in the Formosa Straits. The shelling of Quemoy and Matsu finally stopped on May 1, 1955.[102]

Another significant difference between the United States and Great Britain in the Far East concerned the proper understanding of when and how SEATO should be implemented. Laotians had asked Secretary Dulles for reassurance about the Manila Pact. Would it go into effect if the Chinese Communists or Viet Minh entered their country? Dulles reassured them that the United States would pursue this under the Manila Pact. At the very same time, the British and the French assured the Laotians just the opposite. They would not intervene under SEATO provisions under any circumstances. The Americans felt double-crossed by the British failing to live up to their commitments with regard to SEATO. The French and the British could not be trusted. Eisenhower coldly reminded Churchill: "As a result, we have a situation in which the communists, in the affected areas of Laos, grow stronger and stronger, and we face a possibility of ultimately losing that entire territory to the communists, just as we lost North Vietnam." The Western allies had not lived up to their agreements and Communism could completely take over the Far East, particularly Indochina. Eisenhower continued: "We show ourselves fearful of the communistic brigands and create the impression that we are slinking along in the shadows, hoping that the beast will finally be satiated and cease his predatory tactics before he finally devours us." He harshly denounced what he considered British appeasement in the Far East. The United States would be forced into unilaterally supporting the Diem regime in South Vietnam.[103]

In conclusion, Eisenhower's ambiguous and deceptive diplomacy toward Quemoy and Matsu could have easily led to a nuclear war over two strategically insignificant Chinese coastal islands. The fact that no one knew whether he would use nuclear weapons led not only to a major crisis between the United States and China, but more importantly to a major division between the United States and Great Britain. Eisenhower's crisis management allowed him to keep his options open, but at the incredible cost of a possible third world war and the destruction of transatlantic relations. While military flexibility may have played an important role in his ending the Second World War, in the case of Quemoy and Matsu, it may very well have led to a major catastrophe. Through a bumbling misstatement, Eisenhower might have accidentally caused the Chinese to respond aggressively, thus setting off a chain of events that could have only ended in a tragic catastrophe.

Beyond any reasonable doubt, Eisenhower never bluffed about atomic warfare, but intended to use nuclear weapons if, in his mind, military necessity required it. He often rejected the advice of the Joint Chiefs of Staff, Congress, the British, and other U.S. allies. Eisenhower planned to use atomic bombs in North Korea and China if the Korean War remained a stalemate. With regard to Indochina, John Foster Dulles warned China of "massive retaliation." In March 1954, Dulles proposed United Action as a joint British-American military operation to save the French in Indochina. Admiral Radford recommended Operation Vulture, which involved dropping three atomic bombs to relieve the Vietminh siege of Dien Bien Phu. According to French president Georges Bidault, Dulles offered to give two atomic bombs to the French for use in rescuing the French forces at Dien Bien Phu.

With the fall of Dien Bien Phu, Eisenhower ordered preparations for nuclear strikes against China and the Soviet Union. Even more provocatively, he shut down American negotiations at the Geneva Conference. Eden deserved the full-credit for negotiating the peace accords at the Geneva Conference over the strenuous objections of Eisenhower and Dulles. With regard to Quemoy and Matsu, Eisenhower promoted the absolute necessity and the usefulness of nuclear weapons. In a press conference on March 16, 1955, he agreed with his secretary of state that tactical atomic weapons would be used against China in the event of a war. On March 25, 1955, Admiral Carney told the press about military plans to "take out" China.

The significant question is why Eisenhower did not follow through on his military threats to wage an all-out war on China and eliminate the Chinese menace to Asia and roll back Communism? Most historians believe the threat of war in Asia and the president's nuclear threats could never have been credible, and this eventually led to the demise of brinksmanship diplomacy. Others have shown Eisenhower, behind the scenes, as a master chess player and a model of balance and restraint. These depictions of Eisenhower are demonstrably false. The key to Eisenhower's actions or inactions can be seen in the context of his transatlantic relations with Churchill. With Churchill's agreement or at least acquiescence, Eisenhower felt free to threaten China with nuclear weapons and an expanded war in order to end the Korean War. He also sought and obtained Churchill's cooperation in the possible overthrow of President Syngman Rhee of South Korea in order to obtain a Korean armistice. At the same time, Churchill and Eisenhower agreed to Operation Ajax, the military overthrow in 1953 of Mossadegh in Iran. Having received a green light from Churchill, Eisenhower acted vigorously and ruthlessly in carrying out both overt and covert operations.

Still, they clashed on the internationalization of the Indochina War and the importance of the Geneva Conference. In effect, Churchill vetoed Eisenhower's military plans for Indochina, He allowed for American bellicosity on Formosa, but refused to wage a global thermonuclear war over Quemoy and Matsu. Only later, during his campaign for the presidency in 1956, did Eisenhower promote the astonishing myth of his waging peace, hiding the dark reality of his foreign policy from both journalists and historians.

CHAPTER 5

COVERT BRINKSMANSHIP

Iran and Guatemala

I n the Cold War, Eisenhower and Churchill often sat like Olympian gods, bypassing congressional and Parliamentary oversight while deciding the fate of nations. As the leaders of the transatlantic alliance, they decided to promote stable anti-Communist military dictators over reform-minded democrats in both Iran and Guatemala. Anti-Communism triumphed over the idea of promoting democracy, social justice, and the principles of international law. The legacy of this policy can be seen in the Bay of Pigs, Operation Mongoose, the Cuban Missile Crisis, Vietnam, and Iran-Contra Scandal. By engaging in secret wars hidden from the public, they set a dangerous precedent for the future of the Cold War and transatlantic diplomacy.

IRAN

After the Second World War, Iran remained an important battleground between East and West. The future of Iran in the early twentieth century depended on the fate of British colonialism and the influence of Communism in the country. Historian Barry Rubin has written: "In the early 1950s the British Embassy in Tehran was a gigantic compound, covering sixteen city blocks of lovingly landscaped ground. Nearby was the Russian Embassy, an only slightly less impressive expanse surrounded by a high brick wall. By contrast the American Embassy was tiny." Great Britain sustained a powerful sphere of influence throughout the Middle East. The Soviets sponsored Arab nationalism in order to weaken British influence in the region. The United States faced a growing Soviet expansionism in the Middle East and for this reason tolerated British colonialism. In 1951, in the Iranian Parliament, the Majlis elected a leading nationalist, Mohammad Mossadegh, as prime minister. In January 1952, *Time* named him "Man of the Year," explaining: "There were millions inside and outside of Iran whom Mossadegh symbolized and spoke for, and whose fanatical state of mind he had helped to create. They would rather see their own nations fall apart than continue their present relations with the West. . . . He is not in any sense pro-Russian, but he intends to stick to his policies even though he knows they might lead to control of Iran by the Kremlin." He championed Iranian nationalism and forced the British out of Iran.[1]

Ironically, Iran's Communist Tudeh Party did not back Mossadegh in his struggle to nationalize Iranian oil and eliminate British economic interests in the country. A nationalist, Mossadegh proved antagonistic to the Communists, who linked their own interests to the Soviet Union. Iraj Iskandari, a Tudeh Party leader, explained: "Mossadegh is fighting for the nationalization of Iranian oil, but the American imperialists are backing his movement, which means that they are guiding it. And so we drew the incorrect conclusion that the communists should not support the nationalist movement." The Tudeh Party should have stood for the nationalization of oil for strictly ideological reasons since the removal of British influence in Iran benefited the Soviet Union.[2]

The nationalization of Iranian oil in 1951 deeply traumatized the British government. This act had enormous political and economic repercussions. If the British government intended to pursue its interest in Iranian oil, it needed at least the moral assistance of the American government. The Truman administration refused to support British ambitions, including the overthrow of the Mossadegh government, based solely on their loss of oil revenues. By the fall of 1952, the new Churchill government took a far different approach than the previous Labour government by advising Truman and Acheson of the great danger of Iran falling to Communism and being dominated by the Soviet Union.

British intelligence officials alerted the United States to the important hazards of Communist influence in Iran in November 1952. Christopher Montague (C. M.) Woodhouse, a British intelligence officer who had previously worked in the British embassy in Tehran, said: "Not wishing to be accused of trying to use the Americans to pull British chestnuts out of the fire, I decided to emphasize the communist threat in Iran rather than the need to recover control of the oil industry. I argued that even if a settlement of the oil dispute could be negotiated with Mossadegh, which was doubtful, he was still incapable of resisting a coup by the Tudeh Party, if it were backed by Soviet support." The British Secret Intelligence Service (SIS) proposed to the CIA that Iran needed a much stronger anti-Communist leader than Mossadegh. This tactical shift by the British government in assailing the Iranian government as a threat in the Cold War, rather than merely trying to recover their oil revenues, proved to be completely successful.[3]

Asking for more economic assistance from the United States in early January 1953, Mossadegh wrote President-Elect Dwight D. Eisenhower to complain that the United States "has pursued what appears to the Iranian people to be a policy of supporting the British government and the former company [Anglo-Iranian Oil Company]. In this struggle it has taken the side of the British government against that of Iran in international assemblies." His letter posed a difficult dilemma for the new president: Eisenhower could support Mossadegh's nationalist agenda in Iran in the name of anticolonialism and anti-Communism, yet risk alienating America's closest and most important Western ally, Great Britain. The alternative, propping up British colonialism, might ruin American efforts to foster nationalist movements in the Middle East promoting anti-Communism.[4]

Numerous plots by the Iranian military and foreign countries sought to bring down the Mossadegh government. Ambassador Loy Henderson reported: "During my conversation with Mossadegh this evening he stated that British were intriguing in numerous ways to bring about overthrow of his government and at same time were pretending to United States government that they desired settlement of the oil problem." Historian Nikki R. Keddie discovered that "in late February 1953, General Fazlollah Zahedi, a former collaborator with Nazi Germany, was arrested for plotting with foreigners to overthrow the government. In March there were serious conflicts between Mossadegh and the Shah in which Mossadegh emerged victorious after large popular demonstrations in his favor." Zahedi would later be released by the Mossadegh government and become a key participant, along with the shah, in the Iranian revolution of August 1953.[5]

Secretary of State John Foster Dulles informed the National Security

Council (NSC) in March 1953 that Mossadegh totally dominated Iran. The grave danger to the United States would be the possible fall of the Iranian government. Such an event would be an open invitation for the Soviet Union to take over Iran and its oil assets. Dulles pointed out that the Soviets "would secure these assets and thus henceforth, be free of any anxiety about their petroleum situation. Worse still, if Iran succumbed to the communists there was little doubt that in short order the other areas of the Middle East, with some 60% of the world's oil reserves, would fall under communist control." The Soviets could take over Iranian oil and possibly all of the Middle East and drastically change the global balance of power.[6]

In this crucial NSC meeting on Iran, Vice President Richard M. Nixon predicted greater hostility from the Soviets even with the recent death of Stalin. He also suggested that the Soviets might indeed take over Iran in a coup d'état. Nixon thought the situation in Iran could lead to a world war. He emphasized Iran's dangerous state of affairs and condemned the British for being oblivious to the danger. Nixon insisted that the United States, rather than the Soviet Union, influence the government in Iran. Eisenhower seemed deeply troubled about the possibility of the Soviet Union moving against Iran, an action that could lead to total war. He stubbornly stipulated that in this case, if the U.S. government failed to move against the Soviets, it would be regarded as a "second rate power." Eisenhower wanted to maintain the independence of Iran: "If, said the President, I had $500 million of money to spend in secret, I would give $100 million of it to Iran right now." He wanted to discuss Iran with both Dulles and Eden in order to discern from the British what should be done. Nonetheless, he believed unilateral action by the United States might be required in order to save Iran from the Communists.[7]

In a message to Churchill on March 5, 1953, Eden related a detailed conversation he had just had with President Eisenhower and Secretary of State Dulles. Eden wrote that Eisenhower stated that "the American people would never be brought to understand the need to make sacrifices in the Middle East and that the consequences of an extension of Russian control of Iran, which he regarded as a distinct possibility, would involve the loss of the Middle East oil supplies or the threat of another world war." Unlike Eden, Eisenhower feared that Iran would become Communist and subsequently fall under the control of the Soviet Union. By contrast, Eden expected Mossadegh to continue to play the great powers against each other in order to maintain his power in Iran. They did have one major point of agreement: the constant bribing of Mossadegh through promises of economic aid had grown tiresome. The British and the Americans really preferred a new leader in Iran.[8]

After his meeting with Eisenhower, Eden telegraphed Churchill: "The difficulty of the situation remains that the Americans are perpetually eager to do something. The President repeated this several times. . . . For my part I had many times felt in the last two years that if we could just stay put for a while the chances of settlement would be improved." He told Churchill: "The President kept repeating that we could not do nothing. I said that I thought it unlikely that Mossadegh would link himself up with the West, but he was equally reluctant to join the East. He wanted to stay in the middle. This had been Persian policy for two thousand years and I saw no reason to suppose that it would change now." He had once again counseled patience to both Churchill and Eisenhower. They completely ignored his advice in favor of a policy of covert action, while Eden, seriously ill, took a long leave of absence from the Foreign Office through the fall of 1953.[9]

By authorizing the planning for Operation Ajax, the overthrow of Mossadegh, Eisenhower and Churchill began an infamous era of covert subversion of democratically elected governments. Historian H. W. Brands noted: "Historians of U.S. covert operations have placed the anti-Mossadegh coup near the beginning of a long and checkered history of U.S. paramilitary warfare, assassination attempts, economic sabotage, and political subversion throughout the Third World." Both the United States and Great Britain employed their intelligence services to come up with a secret plan to overthrow the Iranian government. CIA plans called for a new Iranian government to arrange for a "fair" Anglo-Iranian oil agreement and sustained opposition to the Communist Tudeh Party, all under the shah of Iran, Mohammad Reza Pahlavi.[10]

On April 4, 1953, CIA director Allen Dulles approved a $1 million expenditure for the overthrow of Mossadegh. The CIA and the British SIS worked jointly in planning the covert overthrow of the Iranian government. The vital question for historians is: Why did the British now support this covert operation? "The answer," as historian William Roger Louis has written, "can be summed up in one word: Churchill." He suggested that "after Eden became ill, Churchill took on responsibility for foreign affairs and changed the government's course." Churchill, disdaining timidity, authorized Operation Boot, a covert military operation designed to end the prolonged diplomatic stalemate in Iran.[11]

Anthony Eden's serious illness prevented him from opposing this extremely risky plan. "Eden may have been outraged by the Iranian act of nationalization," historian James A. Bill has argued, "but he was clearly not willing to approve this kind of intelligence adventure. Ultimately, he did not have to. In April he underwent the first of three operations related to a serious gallbladder problem and did not return to the Foreign Office until October." In his absence, Churchill took control of the Foreign Office and enthusiastically endorsed plans for the Anglo-American intervention in Iran.[12]

Meanwhile, Anglo-Iranian negotiations on the oil dispute had officially ended. The British rejected further negotiations. Selwyn Lloyd, minister of state, wrote Churchill on May 5, 1953: "Mossadegh has time and again acquired a new lease on life on the ground that he has been in negotiations. The Department thought it unwise to give him yet another opportunity, particularly now that the Americans and we are agreed that Mossadegh is hopeless." Much more than their predecessors, Attlee and Truman, Churchill and Eisenhower decided to fight the Communist threat posed by the Tudeh Party and an expansionist Soviet Union. They both preferred a covert operation, which their predecessors had desperately tried to avoid. The two leaders grasped the absolute necessity of direct intervention in Iran, a policy completely contravening international law. By the end of April, the CIA and SIS had settled on a coordinated plan.[13]

While Churchill and Eisenhower arranged his overthrow, Mossadegh continued to plead for more economic assistance from the United States. On May 28, 1953, he wrote: "The Iranian nation hopes that with the help and assistance of the American Government the obstacles placed in the way of the sale of Iranian oil can be removed." Mossadegh's desperate plea for help proved futile as Kermit Roosevelt, CIA chief of the Near East and Africa Division, finished his covert plan to overthrow him.[14]

Before the State Department would give final approval to Roosevelt's plan, it required some assurances of sufficient funds for economic aid to sustain an Iranian government headed by the shah. The Department also insisted that the British government formally express "its intention to reach an early oil settlement with a successor Iranian government in the spirit of goodwill and equity." In other words, the British must promise to negotiate in good faith with the prospective Iranian government. John Foster Dulles and State Department officials subsequently consented to the CIA plan.[15]

Eisenhower finally responded to Mossadegh's one-month-old plea for economic aid; his reply to Mossadegh turned out to be totally disingenuous. While Eisenhower wrote that Iran's foreign and domestic policies must be left to the government of Iran, at the same time, he secretly authorized direct American interference in Iranian affairs. He used his well-known obfuscation to deceive Mossadegh about why the United States would not extend more economic aid to Iran. Eisenhower lied when he wrote that the U.S. government's policies with regard to technical assistance and military aid had not changed from the previous year. He had already decided to reduce both technical assistance and military aid. Finally, he expressed his false hope that the United States could help the government of Iran. In his letter, Eisenhower intentionally misled the Iranian leader with the obvious purpose of protecting and proceeding with his clandestine plan.[16]

The men instrumental in organizing Operation Ajax included Under Secretary of State Walter Bedell Smith, CIA Director Allen Dulles, Secretary of Defense Charles Wilson, Kermit Roosevelt, Frank Wisner, and Secretary of State John Foster Dulles. The CIA planned to use millions of dollars to bribe military personnel and incite riots in Tehran. Dulles uttered his enthusiasm for the plan by proclaiming, "So this is how we get rid of that madman Mossadegh!" In July 1953, the Department of State and the British Foreign Office formally authorized the project. President Eisenhower approved giving the field command in Tehran to Kermit Roosevelt. Roosevelt would direct both the initial unsuccessful coup and the successful countercoup.[17]

Eisenhower firmly believed that Iran would soon be dominated by the Tudeh Party and that the Soviet Union would seize Iranian resources. He explicitly stated that Mossadegh "was moving closer and closer to the communists." Eisenhower wrote disdainfully of Mossadegh in his memoirs, calling him, "a semi-invalid who, often clad in pajamas in public, carried on a fanatical campaign with tears and fainting fits and street mobs of followers, to throw the British out of Iran, come what might." The expulsion of the British from Iran greatly reduced Western influence. Eisenhower knew that Mossadegh "was looking forward to receiving $20 million from the Soviet Union, which would keep his treasury afloat for the next two or three months. By the end of July the Tudeh Party came out openly for Mossadegh, the Soviet Union sent a new and hopeful ambassador to Tehran, and the Shah, his life in danger, was forced to take refuge." In his memoirs, Eisenhower expressed great admiration for the Iranian military coup without ever acknowledging his own crucial role in originating and authorizing it.[18]

Whether the shah would actively participate in the coup against Mossadegh remained the most important and unknown factor of Operation Ajax. The plan required the shah to give orders for a new prime minister to replace Mossadegh, but in this he proved both cowardly and indecisive. In fact, the CIA used Ashraf Pahlavi, the shah's twin sister, to buck up the shah's nerves in ordering the dismissal of Mossadegh.[19]

The chronology of the Iranian Revolution of 1953 remains murky and a bit mysterious even today, but a top-secret unsigned British memorandum entitled "Political Review of the Recent Crisis in Persia," dated September 2, 1953, and published in *Foreign Relations of the United States,* provides a fascinating and detailed account. Having signed off on final authorization of Operation Ajax, Eisenhower and Dulles created a vast political distance between Washington and Tehran. When asked about the increasing power of the Tudeh Party, in a press conference on July 28, 1953, Dulles stated: "Recent developments in Iran, especially the growing activity of the illegal communist party, which appears to be tolerated by the Iranian government have caused us concern. These developments make it more difficult for the United States to give assistance to Iran so long as its government tolerates this sort of activity." In a follow-up speech to U.S. governors on August 4, 1953, Eisenhower stepped up the mounting political pressure on the Iranian government, suggesting that Mossadegh had "moved toward getting rid of his parliament and of course he was in that move supported by the communist party of Iran." Eisenhower continued to distance himself from the Iranian government.[20]

By August 1953, a military coup to overthrow Mossadegh seemed imminent. General Norman Schwarzkopf, former advisor to the Persian Gendarmerie, discussed the full details of the military coup d'état with the shah. This first plan for a military coup leaked to Communist sympathizers in the Iranian military and then to the Tudeh press on August 8, 1953. On August 11, 1953, the shah and queen took a vacation at Ramsar on the Caspian Sea. From there, on August 13, 1953, the shah finally issued a decree removing Mossadegh as prime minister and replacing him with General Fazlollah Zahedi. This order came from Ramsar to Tehran by way of Colonel Nematollah Nasiri of the Imperial Guards. The Tudeh press publicly announced further details about the upcoming military coup on August 14, allowing Mossadegh time to plan for counter military action. On August 15, 1953, Colonel Nasiri delivered the shah's message to Mossadegh replacing him as prime minister. Shortly after receiving the message, Mossadegh had Colonel Nasiri placed under house arrest. This first military coup failed due to numerous leaks in the Iranian army, most likely originating from Communist sympathizers. On August 16, 1953, as a result of the failed military coup, the shah fled to Baghdad. In Baghdad, Gordon Mattison, a counselor to the State Department, wrote that the shah had confessed that "he is utterly at loss to understand why the plan failed. Trusted Palace officials were completely sure of its succeeding." The failure of the coup against Mossadegh caused considerable consternation in Washington.[21]

Walter Bedell Smith reported directly to the president on August 18, 1953: "The old boy wouldn't accept this and arrested the messenger and everybody else involved that he could get his hands on. We now have to take a whole new look at the Iranian situation and probably have to snuggle up to Mossadegh if we're going to save anything there. I daresay this means a little added difficulty with the British." The initial military coup in Iran turned out to be a total failure.[22]

Numerous demonstrations against the shah took place in Tehran on August 17, 1953. The protestors insisted that by fleeing the country, the shah had abdicated the throne and therefore a new Iranian republic should be established. Mossadegh's opposition, in contrast, believed that the shah had legally replaced Mossadegh with General Zahedi as prime minister, and therefore that Zahedi legally represented the government. A second coup sought the ouster of Mossadegh and occurred shortly after the American ambassador Loy Henderson returned to Tehran. The next day, the

Tudeh Party tipped off Mossadegh about an imminent political coup and requested ten thousand rifles to defend his rule. The shah, in the meantime, fled Baghdad for the much safer and more luxurious exile of Rome. Two days later, a final political coup started at 8:00 a.m. with a crowd of three thousand men holding sticks and clubs. The hooligans appeared to have royalist sympathies, but most likely were paid by the CIA. As the demonstrators roamed menacingly through the streets, the police chief ordered the police not to arrest the protestors. The Iranian police force fully supported the political protests, while Mossadegh ordered the military to disperse the unruly crowds. Instead, diverse segments of Iranian society—businessmen, police, and the military—joined in the demonstrations against Mossadegh. By late afternoon, General Zahedi had officially proclaimed himself the new prime minister. This new political coup succeeded because it had been well planned, kept secret, and amply funded by the United States. The new Iranian government detained Mossadegh the next day, and on August 22, 1953, the shah of Iran returned in triumph to Tehran and received a hero's welcome.[23]

In a prescient memorandum dated September 2, 1953, an unknown British analyst warned about the success of Operation Boot and the shah's problems with the progressive elements in Iran: "It should not be forgotten that measures adopted by Dr. Mossadegh to restrict the Shah's interference in the army had the universal support of the people, and that any future infringement of the Constitution by the Shah would be met by the opposition of all progressive elements in the country." The British memorandum suggested important people in Iran favored Mossadegh's removal and the elimination of the threat of a Communist takeover. Any hidden fears about the shah as a possible tyrannical dictator would be left for the future. The mastermind of Operation Ajax, Kermit Roosevelt, met with Lord Salisbury, the acting British foreign secretary, and also with the ailing British prime minister, Winston Churchill, on August 26, 1953. Roosevelt remembered the shah speaking of reconciliation with Great Britain and the United States: "The past is past. I don't intend to fight over the old issues. I recognize that Great Britain is anti-communist, which is what I care most about, and also that she is strong in this part of the world. It is essential that Persia should have good relations with her." The shah backed a fair and equitable oil deal with the United States, Great Britain, and Iran.[24]

Later that afternoon, Roosevelt met with the ailing Churchill at 10 Downing Street. Recovering from a stroke of the previous June, Churchill appeared physically weak. Roosevelt remembered that "he had great difficulty in hearing; occasional difficulty in articulating; and apparent difficulty in saying to his left. In spite of this he could not have been more kind personally nor more enthusiastic about the operation." Churchill told Roosevelt that Operation Ajax was "the finest operation since the end of the war." He had gambled on a high-risk policy and won. Churchill supported financial aid to Iran and the immediate restoration of diplomatic relations. Roosevelt reported: "He commented that the Anglo-Iranian Oil Company (AIOC) had really 'fouled things up' in the past few years and that he was determined that they should not be allowed to foul things up any further." Churchill hoped the political situation in the Middle East had been massively improved. C. A. E. Shuckburgh, however, counseled in a memo: "It is clear that the Shah has an almost pathological distrust of the British, and it is necessary to deal most delicately with him." Nevertheless, Churchill and Eisenhower had once again effectively used covert measures to achieve their political objectives in the Cold War.[25]

GUATEMALA

Eisenhower's patronizing view of Central Americans in the 1950s could be seen in both his cynical attitude and his deeply flawed policies. Eisenhower once told Mexican ambassador Robert Hill: "You know, they're rascals at heart. You can't trust them and so forth, but they're lovable types, and you know, I sure would like to get away on holiday and go back to relive that youth of mine in the military, those happy days in Mexico." This condescending attitude especially colored U.S. foreign policy with regard to Guatemala.[26]

The British openly worried about the Guatemalan government being Communist and hostile to British interests by early 1953. Selwyn Lloyd, minister of state for foreign affairs, cautioned Churchill on May 9, 1953: "Guatemala is in effect now a communist country, and her attitude towards us is unfriendly. We are maintaining troops in British Honduras specifically as a deterrent to armed action on the part of Guatemala." The British deemed a Communist Guatemala to be a possible threat to neighboring British Honduras. The American government agreed with the British assessment of Guatemala.[27]

Secretary of State Dulles also believed the United States should maintain a strong anti-Communist stance in Latin America. The fundamental issue in U.S. diplomacy toward Latin America involved the question of whether or not the United States should risk promoting democracy and possibly political instability over anti-Communist but stable military dictators. The hazard of promoting democracy in Latin America meant the real possibility of political, economic, and cultural turmoil. This led to a philosophical dilemma for John Foster Dulles: Should he support the American ideals of democracy and freedom or play it safe with corrupt anti-Communist dictators who happened to be pro-American? Eisenhower and Dulles backed stable military dictators over unstable democracies in the region. Anti-Communist policies supporting military dictators allowed little room for concern about political and civil liberties. A well-educated lawyer trained to follow the law, Dulles saw no problem in directly violating treaties or organizational commitments in order to keep Communism out of the Western Hemisphere. Eisenhower's foreign policy in Latin America required the overthrow of the democratically elected President Jacobo Arbenz of Guatemala in 1954.[28]

President Eisenhower initiated the overthrow of Arbenz only months after the successful removal of Mossadegh from Iran. Eisenhower, John Foster Dulles, Allen Dulles, and a few others kept the operation top secret. Historian Richard Immerman has written: "Any operative brought in on the project was sworn to secrecy. In all likelihood, a good deal of the discussion took place in Eisenhower's study late in the afternoon, when the president would meet with the secretary over cocktails, or at the Sunday lunch that Eleanor Dulles hosted for her two brothers each week." The secrecy of the planning furnished Eisenhower the option of plausible deniability, absolutely necessary if the operation failed and became public.[29]

Operation PBSUCCESS, formally approved on August 12, 1953, by the National Security Council, began after the success of Operation Ajax in Iran. Piero Gleijeses notes: "The decision was taken with little internal debate and a heartening unanimity among the few policymakers involved. Eisenhower reserved the right to grant or deny the final approval before H-hour, but this was standard procedure for operations of this nature."

Subversion and the undermining of democratically elected governments became a standard feature of U.S. foreign policy. The amazing paradox at the center of this planned operation involved the United States needing to deny its participation in the overthrow of Arbenz, while at the same time understanding that the operation really depended on Arbenz believing the United States fully backed the operation to overthrow him. Eisenhower engaged in psychological warfare against Arbenz. Strong condemnations of the Guatemalan government by State Department officials might reveal American intentions, but the State Department saying nothing about Communism in Guatemala could also be noticed as unusual behavior. Eisenhower and Dulles walked a very fine line in their public pronouncements on Guatemala.[30]

The new U.S. ambassador to Guatemala, John E. Peurifoy, arrived in November 1953 to "manage" the Guatemalan government. He had been briefed by the CIA about Guatemala continuing to move toward a Communist state. The CIA had been authorized by the president to take "strong action" against Arbenz in order to move toward a more democratic Guatemala. In his first meeting with Arbenz, Peurifoy bluntly indicated the importance of having the Communist elements in the Guatemalan government purged. In a letter to Assistant Secretary of State John Cabot, Peurifoy wrote: "As a result of my conversation with President Arbenz and general evaluation of the situation since my arrival here two months ago I am fully convinced that continuance of his administration until its term expires in 1957 will result in a further and dangerous advance of communism in this country, with all the attendant peril to our security and economic interests in this area." In January 1954, Peurifoy publicly communicated his views on Guatemala in an interview for *Time* magazine: "We cannot permit a Soviet republic to be established between Texas and the Panama Canal." He alerted the American public to the serious dangers of Communism in Guatemala.[31]

In a cabinet meeting in February 1954, Dulles claimed: "The major interest of the Latin American countries at this [Caracas] conference would concern economics whereas the chief United States interest is to secure a strong anti-communist resolution which would recognize communism as an international conspiracy instead of regarding it merely as an indigenous movement." Anti-Communism in Latin America remained the highest priority of the U.S. government.[32]

Human rights and economic development were only secondary issues, while Eisenhower refused to lose any sleep over the possible nationalization of United Fruit Company. He did not care about United Fruit, although John Foster Dulles and Allen Dulles had financial interests in the company. Eisenhower's concern was that Communism would gain a major foothold in Guatemala, then in all of Central America: "'My God,' Eisenhower told his Cabinet, 'just think what it would mean to us if Mexico went communist!' He shook his head at the thought of that long, unguarded border, and all those Mexican Communists to the south of it. To prevent the dominoes from falling, he was prepared to, and did, take great risks over tiny Guatemala." Eisenhower identified Guatemala as the first of the dominoes that might fall in Latin America.[33]

At a meeting of the Organization of American States (OAS) in March 1954, Dulles secured a resolution forcefully condemning Communism in the Western Hemisphere. The Declaration of Caracas, entitled "Declaration of Solidarity for the Preservation of the Political Integrity of the American States against Communist Intervention," denounced Communism as "alien intrigue and treachery" and concluded by proposing that Communist domination or control of any country would justify "appropriate action in accordance with existing treaties." Guatemala dissented on the vote for the declaration at the OAS meeting. Ambassador Peurifoy decided in late April that his diplomacy no longer sufficed and Arbenz needed to be overthrown. As a result, "in May, the State Department recommended specific OAS action against Guatemala, noting: 'The contest is of crucial importance in the global struggle between free nations and the communist forces. . . . [W]hat has happened in Guatemala is a part of Moscow's global strategy." The State Department demonized Guatemala as already under the control of the Kremlin.[34]

Any direct link between Guatemala and the Kremlin, nonetheless, remained unsubstantiated. Historian Richard Immerman argued: "Yet even President Eisenhower conceded that the expropriations were not conclusive proof. He wrote of Guatemala in his memoirs, 'Expropriation in itself does not, of course prove communism; expropriation of oil and agricultural properties years before in Mexico had not been fostered by communists.'" Nevertheless, this reality did not deter Eisenhower from employing covert military actions against Guatemala.[35]

The Eisenhower administration considered Guatemala a Communist refuge in Central America directed by the Kremlin to undermine U.S. political and economic interests in Latin America. The British Foreign Office disapproved of the Americans' unsophisticated and frightening analysis of Central America. British historian John Young determined: "Officials at the Foreign Office, already annoyed at Washington's simplistic view of events and its tendency to threaten Guatemala, were inclined to treat Guatemalan anti-Americanism as originating in more than mere communism. In particular, they held the United Fruit Company responsible for widespread discontent." Although the British recognized the Communist elements in the Guatemalan government, they preferred a much more nuanced view of the situation rather than the stark black-and-white picture drawn by Washington.[36]

The differences between the United States and Great Britain over Guatemala focused on two important policies, a strict naval blockade of Guatemala and the ouster of the Arbenz government. Guatemala's purchase of military arms from Czechoslovakia triggered a strong reaction from Washington. The British Foreign Office, interested in maintaining good transatlantic relations, normally deferred to Washington on issues involving Central America. The British looked unfavorably on the American plan to search ships going to Guatemala, especially during peacetime. Indeed, the British Foreign Office considered the stopping of ships on the high seas as illegal, even possibly an act of war. If the U.S. Navy stopped a British ship, the British public and the Labour Party would certainly react negatively against such a rash action.[37]

Responding to U.S. policy, Eden and the British Foreign Office looked for a compromise with Dulles on the naval blockade of Guatemala. By May 31, 1954, a British cabinet paper proposed: "If Washington were willing to guarantee compensation, the British would put pressure on merchants to halt shipments and would try to persuade suspected vessels on the high seas to sail to a British-controlled port to be searched; ultimately they would even let the U.S. Navy search suspected British ships, on condition that Whitehall be notified in good time and permission be obtained in each case." The British tried to pursue a reasonable compromise with Dulles.[38]

On June 2, 1954, British ambassador Roger Makins informed Dulles of this latest British proposal, forcing Dulles to confess that the United States might have to search a British ship without warning. Dulles's interpretation of the Monroe Doctrine did not allow for any interference by any European countries, including Great Britain. The United States reserved the right to act as the sole policeman in the Western Hemisphere. This diplomatic snub and Dulles's bullying tactics shocked the British. To the British Foreign Office, the boarding of neutral ships amounted to a serious breach of international law. Permanent Under-Secretary at the Foreign Office Sir Ivone Kirkpatrick stated: "I have written a private letter to Sir R Makins asking him whether Mr. Dulles is going fascist. I can think of no other explanation." Anglo-American relations continued to deteriorate over the American naval blockade of Guatemala.[39]

Selwyn Lloyd, minister of state, wrote a diplomatic note intended for British ambassador Makins, but he first sought Eden's approval for his note on June 9, 1954, about the naval blockade of Guatemala: "Mr. Dulles still does not seem to understand that we have to keep within the law and expect the Americans to do the same. You should let him know that the Secretary of State is personally deeply concerned at this unwillingness to give an assurance that no British ship will be diverted without our consent. He wishes you to make clear to Mr. Dulles beyond doubt that if the Americans do this they really will raise a row." On June 10, 1954, Eden, recognizing the reality of the situation, vetoed Lloyd's intended note to Makins.[40]

British newspapers published stories on June 19, 1954, about the ongoing nautical dispute between the United States and Great Britain. On June 21, 1954, Eden forcefully defended Great Britain's naval policy on the high seas: "that she condemned the sale of arms to Guatemala; that the Royal Navy in the West Indies would do all possible to prevent this; and that Great Britain would not allow her ships to be searched by the United States." Eden reasserted Great Britain's rights on the high seas and unequivocally disputed U.S. policy.[41]

Meanwhile, Colonel Castillo Armas, the leader of Guatemala's insurgents, code-named RUFUS by the CIA, invaded Guatemala from Honduras on June 18, 1954, in an effort to overthrow Arbenz. The success of the

CIA's efforts in Guatemala depended on U.S. air support. Even the ever-secretive Eisenhower referred in his memoirs to the significance of planes in the removal of Arbenz. He gave Armas the planes necessary to success-fully complete Operation PBSUCCESS. Allen Dulles told the president that the operation had no chance of success without the planes, but with the planes the operation might have a 20 percent chance. Eisenhower did not hesitate and immediately authorized the planes for the operation. A 20 percent chance of success was far better than no chance of success. Eisenhower gambled and won in Guatemala.[42]

This contrasts rather dramatically with President Kennedy's decision making at the Bay of Pigs. When Kennedy faced a similar situation, hav-ing to decide whether to provide U.S. air support to the Cubans at the Bay of Pigs, he failed to provide the requested air support and a fiasco ensued. Eisenhower later expressed contempt for President Kennedy's decision-making process during the Bay of Pigs. Kennedy, fearing the real possi-bility of international condemnation for an illegal military intervention, stepped on the brakes, consequently suffering a grievous political and mili-tary defeat. Eisenhower, knowingly breaking international law, stepped on the gas and persevered on to victory. If an American president commits himself to a military action, Eisenhower firmly believed, the U.S. govern-ment must be willing to provide the necessary military support to see it through successfully.[43]

The British and the Americans continued to disagree over the thorny issue of whether the United Nations or the Organization of American States should investigate the violence in Guatemala. The United States maintained that Guatemala was merely in the throes of a civil war, an issue outside the jurisdiction of the United Nations. The Organization of Ameri-can States should investigate Guatemala. Eisenhower planned on manipu-lating and managing the investigation by the Organization of American States. Nevertheless, the British announced that a UN team should in-vestigate the Guatemalan situation. On June 24, 1954, the British delega-tion at the United Nations backed a UN peace commission. Dulles asked Eisenhower how he wanted to handle the British proposal in the United Nations. Historian John W. Young has asserted: "He [Eisenhower] was pre-pared to overrun any opposition, if necessary to invoke the United States' UN veto, hitherto not used weapon, but one capable of grave harm to the

UN organization. The US was 'being too damned nice to the British on this,' said Eisenhower. 'The British expect us to give them a free ride . . . on Cyprus and yet they won't even support us in Guatemala. Let's give them a lesson.'" Eisenhower's intense anger with the British on the Guatemalan investigation would later develop into full-blown rage over Suez.[44]

Eisenhower gave Dulles his marching orders: Dulles was to tell the ambassador to the United Nations, Henry Cabot Lodge Jr., to block the British move in the United Nations. Dulles then called Ambassador Lodge at 9:55 a.m. on June 24, 1954:

DULLES: the president said he thinks you should let the British and French know that if they take independent line backing Guatemalan move in this matter, it would mean we would feel entirely free without regard to their position in relation to any other such matters as any of their colonial problems in Egypt, Cyprus, etc. If they feel they can take independent line, the counterpart will be that they must consider that we will be free equally to be independent when any of the matters such as North Africa, Middle East, etc., comes up before the UN.

LODGE: I will do that.

DULLES: He (the President) wanted to avoid making it in the form of a threat but make it a clear understanding that if they don't take into account our needs and consideration in this matter, it will be a two-way street and they must accept it.

LODGE: Yes, I see. It's a terrible thing. I will get this to them. Will determine just when and how to do it.

DULLES: Use your own judgment as to the time.

LODGE: If there is an open split between British and French, Russians will be very much pleased. But we cannot put off a meeting much longer.

DULLES: Guatemala itself, as I understand it, is violating the terms of the Charter article 53 (2), I think. The whole status of regional organizations is at stake in this particular matter. That was the thing we fought for (Vandenberg and I) at San Francisco. The whole concept is being destroyed.

LODGE: No question about it. At the same time, I will have to have a meeting, probably tomorrow. If the British and the French pursue this, we will have an open split. I will try to keep agenda from being adopted. I put it to the Frenchman this morning, and he didn't like it at all. Thank you very much. I will be guided accordingly.[45]

Lodge did meet with Pierson Dixon, permanent representative of the United Kingdom to the United Nations, and Henri Hoppenot, permanent representative of France to the United Nations, "and told them bluntly that if Great Britain and France took an independent line on Guatemala, they need no longer count on US support in Egypt or Cyprus, Tunisia or Morocco; this was not a threat, he insisted, merely a statement of position." British UN ambassador Dixon claimed that the British did not oppose an OAS oversight role, but if it failed he saw no problem with a UN investigation: "Lodge however 'listened without much interest' and professed not to understand the British arguments; if London wanted to oppose US policy they knew what the price would be." Lodge acted cunningly in stonewalling any UN investigation of Guatemala.[46]

In the meantime, Winston Churchill and Anthony Eden had just arrived in Washington on June 25, 1954, to discuss international affairs with Eisenhower and Dulles. While this Washington conference dealt with a number of challenging issues, including relations with the Soviet Union, Indochina, Egypt, and the European Defense Community, the real sticking point turned out to be Guatemala. Dulles, who told Makins that "Guatemala 'might well be the touchstone of the Anglo-American alliance,' was now, even before reaching the White House, pressing Eden for full support." Unquestionably, Dulles was ordered to do so by Eisenhower.[47]

Once again, Churchill came to the rescue of the Americans and completely disavowed the official British policy on Guatemala established by Eden, Dixon, and the British Foreign Office. Eden considered the Americans hypocritical on Greece and Turkey, particularly after they overthrew

Guatemala. Churchill, however, really did not care about Eden's views on Guatemala. He worried more about Britain's failing relationship with the United States than over such minor matters as Guatemala, and he believed that Guatemala should not be allowed to disrupt transatlantic relations: "I'd never heard of this bloody place Guatemala until I was in my seventy-ninth year. We ought not to allow (it) to jeopardize our relations with the United States, for on them the safety of the world might depend." He preferred playing the role of world statesman rather than acting like a country lawyer prosecuting a minor case.[48]

Eventually, Lodge and Churchill had a conversation at the White House on June 26, 1954. As Lodge remembered: "He said that he was not at all sympathetic with the communist government in Guatemala and, as a matter of fact, that he does believe that it would have been much better to have organized world peace on the basis of a few strong regional organizations, which might then choose representatives to a central world organization." Churchill cheerfully backed the American plan for an investigation of Guatemala by the Organization of American States. Minutes later, Lodge engaged in a similar conversation with Eden. He thanked Eden for abstaining in the Security Council vote. Lodge recorded Eden's reply: "'it will mean a lot of trouble for me explaining that in the House of Commons.' I said that it should not make too much trouble for him in as much as two minutes earlier I had been told by the Prime Minister himself that he longed favored [sic] strong regional organizations." The United States successfully overthrew the Guatemalan government and covered it up by suppressing an investigation by the United Nations. Eisenhower had masterfully controlled events without getting caught. Churchill and Eisenhower carefully defused the explosive issue of Guatemala, while the ongoing feud between Dulles and Eden persisted.[49]

Unlike Truman, Acheson, and Kennan, Eisenhower made the important case for rolling back Communism, irrespective of international law, particularly in the Western Hemisphere. Dulles happily proclaimed Guatemala "the biggest success in the last five years against communism." President Eisenhower personally invited the CIA agents involved in the overthrow of Arbenz to the White House: "He joshed with them, wondering why they had let Arbenz escape. And he shook everyone's hand, ending with Allen Dulles, and said: 'Thanks Allen, and thanks to all of you. You've averted a Soviet beachhead in our hemisphere." Eisenhower had fulfilled his presidential duties by strictly enforcing the Monroe Doctrine.[50]

In using the CIA, Eisenhower employed various covert operations to overthrow a variety of Communist-oriented regimes, but he cannot be held fully responsible for what happened to later presidents in Iran and South Vietnam. He certainly cannot be blamed for the mistakes those less experienced presidents made years later. Eisenhower's complicated and nuanced diplomacy, although at times confusing and even perilous, today seems far more attractive to many historians than the catastrophic policies that led later presidents into long and drawn-out wars in Vietnam, Kuwait, Iraq, and Afghanistan.[51]

Yet new documentation recently released by the CIA shockingly reveals the CIA planning political assassinations in Guatemala. Even today the names of the people targeted for assassination remain classified. How far would Eisenhower go in fighting the Communists? Could the United States legitimately destroy other nations or the freedom of other people in protecting itself? Once committed to military force, Eisenhower refused to allow covert actions to fail. Failure was not an option. This president dangerously escalated events, allowing for a second coup in Iran and pushing for planes to support Colonel Armas in Guatemala. Could he have walked away from these actions had they failed? Eisenhower believed, like Karl von Clausewitz, that battles are won before they are fought.[52]

In conclusion, U.S. policy on Iran and Guatemala set a terrifying trend for the rest of the 1950s and beyond. The United States and Great Britain initiated a new era in which the transatlantic partnership ruthlessly engaged in political subversion, insurrections, rebellions, military coups, economic sabotage, economic disruptions, guerrilla wars, and assassinations. These secret wars gave presidents of the United States and British prime ministers unprecedented and almost unlimited power. An American president could order the CIA to overthrow a democratically elected government. A British prime minister could order MI6, the British secret service, to assassinate a troublesome Middle East leader without telling his cabinet or the British Foreign Office. Anything could be justified in the Cold War, as long as the world could be kept in the dark.

CHAPTER 6

DIPLOMATIC BRINKSMANSHIP

The Suez Crisis

Throughout 1956, Prime Minister Eden and President Eisenhower became increasingly concerned with Soviet influence in the Middle East. Eden regarded Egyptian president Gamal Abdel Nasser as a tool of the Soviet Union who wanted to undermine British political hegemony in the region. In his 1954 book *The Philosophy of the Revolution,* Nasser called for Egypt to take the lead in creating an Arab Islamic empire that would stretch from North Africa through the rest of the Middle East. He also advocated the complete destruction of the State of Israel. While Eden deemed Nasser a new Hitler or Mussolini, Eisenhower saw Nasser as a nationalist Arab leader fighting against British colonialism. This difference in outlook partly explains the incredible differences in strategy and tactics employed by the British and the Americans in dealing with the Suez Crisis.[1]

Throughout the Suez Crisis, Eden charged Eisenhower and Dulles with undermining British national interests. He authorized MI6, on a number of occasions, to assassinate Nasser. President Eisenhower, having been made aware of British assassination plans, consistently opposed the killing of Nasser. The British and Americans did manage to cooperate on Operation Omega, a covert plan to overthrow the Nasser regime. They also agreed on Operation Straggle, a planned overthrow of the pro-Soviet Syrian government. But with the Egyptian seizure of the Suez Canal, the British cabinet unilaterally authorized Operation Musketeer, direct military intervention into Egypt for the purpose of taking back the Suez Canal and removing Nasser from power. Eisenhower vigorously resisted this direct British military intervention. He publicly favored negotiations with Egypt on the canal while at the same time secretly supporting Operation Omega.[2]

In their memoirs on the Suez Crisis, Eden and Selwyn Lloyd dishonestly blamed Eisenhower and Dulles for the failure of their diplomacy during the Suez Crisis. If the British had wanted a negotiated deal with Nasser on the Suez Canal, they could have had one. The British, however, imagined Nasser as a new Hitler. They insisted on direct military intervention and wrongly assumed the United States would follow their lead. The British military attack on Suez took place at a most inopportune time for Eisenhower—days before the vote that would secure his reelection. In response, Eisenhower turned on the British with a fury still incomprehensible to this day.

President Eisenhower's rage led him to declare economic war against Great Britain. He organized the actions of the Federal Reserve and Wall Street as they dumped sterling holdings at an excessive discount, lowering the value of sterling and the pound. This sank the British economy. Eisenhower also made a secret deal with King Saud of Saudi Arabia to cut off all oil from the Middle East going to Great Britain and France. Moreover, he halted all official U.S. communications with the British government, most notably with Eden and the British Foreign Office. Finally, through the ambassador to Great Britain, Winthrop Aldrich, Eisenhower actively conspired with Macmillan, Butler, and Salisbury to remove Anthony Eden from the premiership in order to end the Suez Crisis.

Having received reports from MI6 in the fall of 1955 about Soviet activity in Egypt and Syria, Prime Minister Anthony Eden became increasingly alarmed about the dangers of Communism in the Middle East. He informed Eisenhower: "It becomes increasingly clear that the Saudis, the Russians, the Egyptians and the Syrians are working together. If we don't want to see the whole of the Middle East fall into communist hands, we must first back the friends of the West in Jordan and in Iraq." Eden anticipated a variety of Soviet moves in the Middle East.[3]

In trying to counteract Soviet expansionism, Eden initiated the Baghdad Pact of 1955, in which Iran, Iraq, Turkey, and Pakistan pledged to act as an anti-Communist barrier to Soviet penetration of the northern area of the Middle East. Furthermore, the British retained protectorates over Bahrain, Kuwait, Qatar, and Oman in the Persian Gulf. They also maintained military bases in Libya, Cyprus, Malta, and Iraq. Jordan, protected by the Arab Legion, had an army subsidized by the British government and controlled by British officers. Eden wanted to strengthen the British military presence throughout the Middle East in order to promote British political hegemony throughout the region.[4]

MI6 began making secret plans to assassinate President Nasser of Egypt as early as February 1956. George Young, SIS officer, spoke to James Eichelberger, a CIA officer in London: "He talked openly of assassinating Nasser, instead of using a polite euphemism like liquidating. He said his people had been in contact with suitable elements in Egypt and the rest of the Arab world, and . . . with the French, who were thinking along the same lines." Another CIA officer in London, Chester Cooper, also knew that Young wanted Nasser either removed or assassinated. Although Eden spurned the use of nuclear weapons, he readily approved the use of assassination in the Middle East. Eisenhower, the old soldier who had proposed the use of nuclear weapons in the Far East, unwaveringly opposed political assassinations. Intriguingly, Eichelberger leaked British assassination plans to Nasser in order to thwart the assassination. Eden and Eisenhower, who had disagreed on both strategy and tactics in the Far East, quarreled violently about strategy and tactics in the Middle East. The British wanted to maintain their political, economic, colonial, and military hegemony over the region. The Americans favored an evolutionary change, which included the development of independent and modern Arab nations. Nasser correctly perceived how far the interests of Great Britain and the United States diverged in both North Africa and the Middle East.[5]

Churchill thought Eden was unprepared to be prime minister, which had prolonged Churchill's wish to stay in power. "I don't believe Anthony can do it," he concluded. In addition, Winston Churchill's center-right political beliefs differed radically from Eden's center-left views, and this may have considerably lengthened Churchill's second premiership. Lord Moran, Churchill's physician, testified: "The P.M. always claims that Anthony and he agree on most things in the field of foreign affairs, though it is not often very noticeable; they don't seem, for instance, to have much in common about Suez, or China, or in their approach to the Americans." Churchill and Eden fought bitterly over Anglo-American relations.[6]

One of the more profound differences between Churchill and Eden involved their ability to recognize changing political circumstances. Eden had modeled himself as a politician, not after Winston Churchill, but after Stanley Baldwin, the British prime minister he most admired. A left-of-center Conservative, Eden believed in manipulating the votes of the Labour Party while hoping to hold the support of staunch Conservatives. His political principles and personality made him a far different political leader than Churchill. Churchill recognized the shrinking British role in world affairs, while Eden tried to maintain the fiction of Great Britain's tremendous influence in the world. Churchill knew when to stand up to the Americans, and, more importantly, he knew when to back down. Eden did not know when to back down. Nevertheless, Eden had assumed the prime ministership and no longer deferred to Eisenhower in the Middle East, particularly after the Baghdad Pact. Eisenhower acidly wrote: "Jordan has not only withdrawn from the Pact, but did so under a compulsion of riots, etc., that incidentally, was directed against this nation as well as against Great Britain. The Arabs apparently take the assumption that Britain does nothing in the area without our approval. Nothing could be further from the truth." Much more than Churchill, Eden tended to act independently of the United States. He refused to recognize the changing nature of the Anglo-American relationship and Britain's declining power on the world scene.[7]

Eden wanted to preserve the British Empire throughout the Middle East by a military presence despite the drain on Great Britain's economy and vital financial resources. By killing Nasser, Eden would eliminate the leader of insurrectionary forces in the Middle East. By contrast, Eisenhower preferred an evolutionary change, covertly supporting anti-Nasser elements in Egypt. The British and the Americans agreed only on these anti-Nasser covert activities. When on March 1, 1956, King Hussein of Jordan summarily dismissed Lt. General John Bagot Glubb, the British commander of the Arab Legion, he distanced Jordan from the British Empire. This infuriated Prime Minister Eden. He personally blamed Nasser and his agents for this dismissal and for the loss of British influence in Jordan. He soon began referring to Nasser as a Hitler or a Mussolini.[8]

Eden's assessment of Nasser could not have been more brutal than his description of him in his memoirs: "Some say that Nasser is no Hitler or

Mussolini. Allowing for a difference in scale, I am not so sure. He has followed Hitler's pattern, even to concentration camps and the propagation of Mein Kampf among his officers. He has understood and used the Goebbels pattern of propaganda in all its lying ruthlessness." He considered Nasser a dictator who tried to hide the right-wing nature of his regime through a socialist label, just as Hitler had done.[9]

On March 12, 1956, Eden told Evelyn Shuckburgh, assistant undersecretary at the Foreign Office in charge of the Middle East, "It is either him or us and don't forget that." He viewed Nasser as the self-proclaimed leader of Pan-Arabism, an ideology favoring Arab nationalism under one leader for all of the Arab people. This new Arab leader, presumably Nasser, would then rule an Islamic empire from North Africa to Asia. Eden became more and more irrational with regard to Nasser's growing threat to the British Empire. Surgery on Eden's bile duct failed in 1953, which led to a slow poisoning of his entire system. While Benzedrine kept the manifestation of the poison under some control, one of the well-known side effects of Benzedrine, an amphetamine, is severe paranoia. Another example of Eden's increasing mental instability occurred in a meeting with the famous British historian Liddell Hart: "In the ensuing silence, Eden's face reddened, then he threw an old fashioned inkwell at the historian. Liddell Hart watched for a moment as the blue stains spread through his light summer suit, then he stood up, grasped a wastebasket, jammed it over the head of the prime minister and walked out." Illness and drugs had clearly affected Eden's mind.[10]

Eden's natural aptitudes had made him a formidable foreign secretary, but his training for the top job remained in many ways critically deficient. As Anthony Nutting has argued: "Eden was not tough; he had not been hardened by criticism. For too long he had been the 'Golden Boy' of the Conservative Party, the man who resigned over Neville Chamberlain's appeasement policy and was proved right within less than two years, the 'Crown Prince' who basked in the sunshine of Churchill's admiration." Churchill had shielded Eden from his political enemies for almost twenty years. This protective sheltering did not serve Eden well when he became prime minister in 1955.[11]

In a memorandum to the prime minister, Anthony Nutting, minister of state for foreign affairs, proposed having the United Nations intervene in the Middle East. He thought Nasser should be politically isolated rather than assassinated. That evening, during a dinner party, Nutting received a phone call from the prime minister. Eden shouted, "What's all this poppy-cock you've sent me? . . . What's all this nonsense about isolating Nasser or neutralizing him, as you call it? I want him destroyed, can't you understand? I want him murdered, and if you and the Foreign Office don't agree, then you better come to the Cabinet and explain why." Eden had a similarly astonishing conversation with Sir Ivone Kirkpatrick, permanent under-secretary at the Foreign Office: "'I don't think we have a department for that sort of thing, Prime Minister,' Kirkpatrick replied, 'But if we do, it certainly is not under my control.'" Without bothering to inform the British Foreign Office, Eden had ordered MI6 to come up with plans to assassinate Nasser.[12]

Working directly with MI6 on a number of plans to assassinate Nasser, Eden apparently kept the British Foreign Office completely in the dark including, presumably, his foreign secretary, Selwyn Lloyd. Eden directed these activities through Patrick Dean, chairman of the Joint Intelligence Committee (JIC): "It would appear that Eden and Dean, in turn, did not seek the approval of the Chief of MI6, 'Sinbad' Sinclair, who was seen as a weak figure by senior officers. Instead, decisions on priorities in the Middle East, and on Egypt in particular, and those concerning any assassination attempts, were left to George Young, a man on a high after the success of the 1953 coup against Mossadegh in Iran." He used George Kennedy Young and MI6 for his top-secret assassination plans against Nasser.[13]

On March 9, 1956, Eisenhower wrote Eden agreeing with his view that Nasser was helping the Soviets in the Near East. Still, he was not ready to completely give up on Nasser: "I do not think we should close the door yet on the possibility of working with him. For one thing, such a decision would cancel out any prospects of obtaining now an Arab-Israeli settlement." In a reply letter on March 15, 1956, Eden warned Eisenhower about Nasser intending to remove the pro-Western leaders of Iraq, Jordan, and Libya. Nasser's ultimate goal was to lead these new Arab republics. On March 21, 1956, Selwyn Lloyd argued before the British cabinet that British foreign policy must fundamentally change in the Middle East with the goal of undermining the anti-Western governments of Egypt and Syria.

The United Kingdom and the United States needed to isolate Egypt from the rest of region.[14]

Eisenhower authorized a secret Anglo-American political initiative to undermine Nasser in Egypt called Operation Omega. British historian Christopher M. Andrew argued: "Ike approved Operation Omega, designed to avoid 'any open break which would throw Nasser irrevocably into a Soviet satellite status,' but to use both diplomacy and covert action to thwart his ambitions in the Arab world." Eisenhower and Eden agreed to Operation Omega and covert measures to destabilize Nasser's leadership. A political or military coup within Egypt probably would not inflame public opinion in the surrounding Arab countries or in the Soviet Union.[15]

The British and Americans continued to discuss the possible assassination of President Nasser. While the CIA actively discouraged the British from assassinating Nasser, SIS, with the full approval of the British cabinet, proposed overthrowing the Soviet-backed Syrian government. The CIA then agreed to join SIS in planning and executing the overthrow of the Syrian government. In July 1956, Eisenhower officially approved Operation Straggle.[16]

Nasser continued to infuriate Eisenhower and Dulles when, in May 1956, he officially recognized Communist China. He also persisted in his political intrigues concerning the funding of the Aswan Dam by pitting the United States against the Soviet Union. The Soviets had earlier provided Egypt with military support through a Czech arms deal in 1955. In June 1956, the Soviets offered to fund the Aswan Dam through a $1.2 billion loan at 2 percent interest. Nasser successfully played the East off against the West.[17]

British foreign secretary Selwyn Lloyd correctly reasoned in his memoirs that Nasser's actual goals had been plainly stated in his book *The Philosophy of the Revolution*: "Therefore, Egypt must be the head of the Arab states, the Arab circle, with oil as its motive power. Second, the white man must be eliminated from the Middle East and Asia. Third, a universal Islamic Empire must be created, with limitless power." Nasser explicitly promoted the complete destruction of the State of Israel. Like Hitler's *Mein Kampf,* Lloyd felt that Nasser's *Philosophy of Revolution* could be a blueprint for his future actions. The real trigger for the Suez Crisis occurred when

Secretary Dulles formally withdrew U.S. aid for the Aswan Dam on July 19, 1956. The results of this decision should have been carefully weighed by President Eisenhower. Selwyn Lloyd wrote: "The president had only been consulted that morning. Makins, British Ambassador, was informed one hour before the meeting. I had no idea that there was going to be this abrupt withdrawal. We had discussed it in Cabinet on July 17 without any sense of urgency, and I had promised to circulate a memorandum on how the withdrawal of our offers should be put to the Egyptians." Obviously upset with Dulles's precipitous action, Eden had been once again "informed but not consulted." The denial of the funds for the Aswan Dam led directly to Nasser's nationalization of the Suez Canal. Apparently, Nasser understood that if he were to nationalize the canal, the Soviets would provide the funds necessary to build the Aswan Dam.[18]

From the very beginning, Eisenhower and Eden exhibited basic differences about how to resolve the Suez Crisis. Eisenhower's goals included stopping Soviet expansionism in the Middle East and North Africa while protecting American access to Arab oil. While the United States, in theory, supported the Baghdad Pact, Eisenhower and Dulles had consistently refused to formally join the alliance with Turkey, Iran, Iraq, and Pakistan out of the fear of alienating Jewish voters in the United States during the election of 1956. Selwyn Lloyd asserted that many of the American diplomats in the Middle East were plainly anti-British: "At best, they were indifferent; at worst, the McGhees in Iran, the Sweeneys in the Sudan, the Cafferys in Cairo, Aramco in Saudi Arabia, had shown themselves openly anti-British. Herbert Hoover Jr., Under-Secretary of State, was thoroughly anti-British, judging at least by what he said and did. It was a mixture of anti-colonialism and hardheaded oil tycoonery." Lloyd's analysis proved essentially correct.[19]

Meanwhile in Algeria, the French were engaged in a war against Islamic rebels who had the financial backing of Nasser. Nasser's dream of an Islamic empire stretching across North Africa clashed with French colonialism as well as British colonialism. The French, like the British, coveted Nasser's destruction. Nonetheless, French and British colonialism came into direct conflict with both Eisenhower's reelection plans and his genuine anticolonialism. Eisenhower, assuming that the peace of the world depended on his reelection, thought Nasser posed only a minor threat to world peace. Eden, on the other hand, expected Nasser to be a major troublemaker in the Middle East and a grave danger to Western civilization. This crucial divergence on the nature of the threat posed by Nasser would lead to disastrous results.[20]

Nasser created a terrible political dilemma for Eden: How could Eden negotiate in good faith with someone he regarded as a Hitler or a Mussolini since dictators could never be trusted? Consequently, Eden approved assassination attempts, covert operations, Operation Omega, military plans, Operation Musketeer, all of which had been designed to obliterate Nasser. A successful diplomatic negotiation with Nasser might have led to the unintended consequence of actually strengthening him. Throughout his memoirs, Eden blames Eisenhower and Dulles for deliberately damaging his diplomacy with Nasser, which led to the Suez debacle. The truth is that Eden never negotiated in good faith with Nasser. The negotiations at the London Conference and at the United Nations proved to be nothing more than a British charade designed to cover a well-planned military operation.

In his memoirs, Lloyd echoed Eden on the nature of the threat posed by Nasser: "Here we were confronted with what we regarded as another megalomaniac dictator, leader of a less powerful nation but with much easier targets to attack, who if unchecked would do infinite damage to Western interests, as Eisenhower admitted when he wrote his book nine years later." Lloyd dutifully defended the untruth about the Americans weakening their diplomatic negotiations while he and Eden had sought a peaceful resolution to the conflict. But why would one negotiate with a megalomaniac? Why would Eden or Lloyd risk enhancing Nasser's political standing in the Middle East?[21]

Eisenhower took a much more measured view and ridiculed the British view of Nasser as a Hitler or Mussolini. Nasser had operated within his legal rights in nationalizing the Suez Canal. Rather than a Hitler or Mussolini, Nasser had acted in the tradition of George Washington fighting against British imperialism. Nonetheless, Nasser's nationalization of the Suez Canal genuinely upset British prime minister Eden: "An angry Eden told conservative MP Robert Boothby that 'we must crush this man at all costs.' Shortly after, Boothby bumped into Kirkpatrick at the Foreign Office and told him: 'I believe our Prime Minister is mad.' Kirkpatrick replied, 'I could've told you that weeks ago.'" Eden looked to intervene militarily in Egypt.[22]

The British cabinet set up a special Egypt Committee consisting of Eden, Lloyd, Macmillan, Salisbury, Alec-Douglas Home (secretary of state for Commonwealth relations), and Walter Monckton (minister of defense). British historian Howard Dooley maintained: "The Egypt Committee acknowledged, somewhat cryptically, that toppling Nasser 'might perhaps be achieved by less elaborate operations than those required to secure physical possession of the canal itself, but as Great Britain's case before world opinion was based on the need to secure international control over the canal,' a diplomatic charade would be necessary." Meanwhile, MI6 produced several more assassination plans looking for a far more permanent solution to the problem of Nasser in Egypt.[23]

Many of the MI6 assassination plots against Nasser involved the use of poison. In one attempt, James Mossman, a BBC correspondent in Cairo and former MI6 official, would drop off a package meant for Nasser's doctor: "The package had contained 20,000 pounds in English banknotes which was intended as a bribe to Nasser's doctor to poison Nasser." Another plan included injecting poison into boxes of chocolates, but some members of MI6 became concerned about the morality of passing on poisoned chocolates. Major Frank Quinn worried that an innocent might be handed one of these chocolates. For the most part, though, moral considerations played no real role in designing MI6 assassination plans.[24]

Another MI6 assassination plan included the use of nerve gas. MI6 officials John Henry and Peter Dixon thought nerve gas would be the best way to kill Nasser. The plan required gassing Nasser's headquarters in Cairo, which would have led to the deaths of a large number of innocent people. Eden morally opposed this plan because he "personally disliked the idea of poison gas. During the Second World War, he had been against what he termed 'the war crimes business,' but by 1956 he seems to have had no qualms about other bizarre methods of assassination which MI6 dreamed up." Other proposed methods of assassination included the use of poison darts.[25]

Available evidence indicates that Eisenhower opposed Nasser's assassination. He worried about the reaction of the Arab world to such a transparent abuse of power. He also feared that such an action would catapult the Arab world into the Soviet camp. Facing reelection, Eisenhower required the illusion of his waging peace during his first term. A military intervention or a political assassination by the British in Egypt needed to be avoided at all costs. A covert operation *after* the November election would be his preferred course of action against Nasser. For the moment, Dulles's numerous calls for diplomatic negotiations forced the British to seek peaceful means to resolve the crisis.[26]

Eden set a confrontational tone in his speech to the House of Commons on the morning of July 27, 1956: "The unilateral decision of the Egyptian government to expropriate the Suez Canal Company, without notice and in breach of the Concession agreements, affects the rights and interests of many nations." Eden's legalistic attack on Egypt based on a treaty negotiated in 1888 appeared problematic to State Department lawyers. Nasser took a much different approach in explaining Egypt's expropriation of the Suez Canal. He put it in terms of Egyptian nationalism resisting British imperialism: "It is a battle against imperialism and the methods and tactics of imperialism, and a battle against Israel, the vanguard of imperialism. . . . As I told you; Arab nationalism has been set on fire from the Atlantic Ocean to the Persian Gulf." Eden's internationalist outlook collided with Nasser's Egyptian nationalism.[27]

Eden warned the world of the dangers of Middle East oil being cut off from most of western Europe. He reasoned against any legalistic interpretation supporting the right of the Egyptian government to nationalize the canal, which had been the position of the State Department's lawyers. Eden took a much broader view of Nasser's nationalization of the canal. World opinion and economic pressure would not be enough to force Nasser to relinquish the Suez Canal. The British prime minister sent a telegram to Eisenhower on July 27, 1956: "My colleagues and I are convinced that we must be ready, in the last resort, to use force to bring Nasser to his senses. For our part we are prepared to do so. I have this morning instructed our Chief of Staff to prepare a military plan accordingly." Eden's telegram landed in Eisenhower's White House like a bombshell.[28]

The president quickly decided to send U.S. Ambassador-at-Large Robert Murphy to London to find out exactly what the British planned to do and to discourage them from any hasty actions. Eden and Macmillan told Murphy confidentially that the British government had made a definite decision to get rid of Nasser. They wanted Eisenhower and Dulles to support them on their policy on Nasser. Instead, Murphy convinced Eden to agree to an international conference to determine the fate of the Suez Canal. On July 31, 1956, Eisenhower met with Allen Dulles, John Foster Dulles, Admiral Arleigh Burke, Herbert Hoover Jr., Secretary of the Treasury George Humphrey, and Colonel Andrew Goodpaster. According to Goodpaster's notes: "In essence it stated that the British had taken a firm, considered decision to 'break Nasser' and to initiate hostilities at an early date for this purpose (estimating six weeks to be required for setting up the operation). Eisenhower opened the discussion by saying 'he considered this to be a very unwise decision on (Eden's) part.'" British negotiations merely provided a cover for planned military action.[29]

The United States required congressional approval for any type of military action, and this approval seemed highly unlikely in the case of Eden's military plans to take back the canal. Believing Eden had overreacted to the crisis, Eisenhower decided to send Dulles to London to make the case for negotiations rather than military intervention. Eisenhower worried about the impact of a military intervention on the Third World. He sternly warned: "To join with the British against Nasser might well array the world from Dakar to the Philippine Islands against us." Dulles wanted Nasser to give up the Suez Canal, but worried that "the British went into World War I and World War II without the United States, on the calculation that we would be bound to come in." Eisenhower sent Eden a firm letter on July 31, 1956, discouraging any type of plans for using military force to resolve the Suez Crisis.[30]

The president dispatched Dulles to London on August 1 in order to slow down plans for British military intervention in Suez. Dulles concurred with the British that "a way had to be found to make Nasser disgorge what he was attempting to swallow. . . . [W]e must make a genuine effort to bring world opinion to favor the international operation now. . . . [I]t should be possible to create a world opinion so adverse to Nasser that he would be isolated." Eden later wrote in his memoirs: "These were forthright words. They rang in my ears for months." Eden understood Dulles's words as wholly justifying Operation Musketeer, the British military plan to take back the Suez Canal. Operation Musketeer had just been approved by the Egypt Committee on August 2, 1956.[31]

The next day, after ruminating on the problems of British colonialism, Eisenhower wrote to his old friend Swede Hazlett: "We unavoidably give to the little nations opportunities to embarrass us greatly. The great Western nations had no choice but to swallow their pride, accept insults, and attempt to work to bolster the underlying concepts of freedom, even though this was frequently costly. Yet there can be no doubt that in the long run such faithfulness will produce real rewards." Returning from London, Secretary Dulles supported a peaceful solution to the nationalization of the Suez Canal, declaring, "We do not, however, want to meet violence with violence." Unlike the Far East, in the Middle East, Dulles really anticipated a peaceful solution.[32]

The London Conference proceeded from August 16 to August 23, 1956, with eighteen of twenty-two countries coming to an agreement on the need for international control of the Suez Canal. The Suez Canal should be run by an international board rather than by the Egyptians. Dulles reported: "The British were determined to move militarily unless there was a clear acceptance of the 18-Power plan by Nasser by around the 10th of September. I said that Eden had indicated that their military planning would have to take a definite and irrevocable status by about that time and could not be left up appreciably longer in a state of indecision." The British had planned to retake the canal regardless of the outcome of the negotiations. On August 29, 1956, the British authorized French troops to be stationed in Cyprus and asked British subjects to leave the area of the Middle East.[33]

Dulles wisely remarked: "I had come to the conclusion that, regrettable as it might be to see Nasser's prestige enhanced even temporarily, I did not believe the situation was one which should be resolved by force. . . . They would make bitter enemies of the entire population of the Middle East and most of Africa lost for a generation, if not a century." The British government would permanently alienate the entire Arab world. This opened up the Middle East for the alarming possibility of additional Soviet expansionism. American and British interests had totally diverged in the region.[34]

In an important letter to Eden on September 2, 1956, Eisenhower pointed out the grave dangers of any British military intervention in Egypt:

I am afraid, Anthony, that from this point onward our views upon this situation diverge. As to the use of force or the threat of force at this juncture, I continue to feel as I expressed myself in the letter Foster carried to you some weeks ago. Even now military preparations and civilian evacuation exposed to public view seemed to be solidifying support for Nasser which has been shaky in many important quarters. I regard it as indispensable that if we are to proceed solidly together to the solution of this problem, public opinion in our several countries must be overwhelmingly in support. I must tell you frankly that American public opinion flatly rejects the thought of using force, particularly when it does not seem that every possible peaceful means of protecting our vital interests has been exhausted without result. Moreover, I greatly doubt we could here secure congressional authority even for the lesser support measures for which you might have to look to us.[35]

Using the same reasoning that Eden had used against him concerning military intervention in Indochina in 1954, Eisenhower favored peace negotiations. Eden claimed the Americans had tried to sabotage the Geneva Convention in order to intervene militarily in Indochina. Eisenhower charged the British with deciding on military intervention and not pursuing every means possible for a peaceful resolution of the Suez Crisis. Eisenhower used Eden's own arguments against him: "I really do not see how a successful result could be achieved by forcible means. The use of force would, it seems to me, vastly increase the area of jeopardy. I do not see how the economy of Western Europe can long survive the burden of prolonged military operations, as well as the denial of Near East oil." He thought a war between Great Britain and Egypt might not only bring down the economies of western Europe, but also alienate almost every Arab, African, and Asian. The Third World would be lost not for just a generation, but for a century or more. Moreover, Britain's war on Egypt could open the door to massive Soviet expansionism in the Middle East.[36]

In a letter dated September 6, 1956, Eden charged Eisenhower with sounding like those who had championed appeasement in the 1930s: "It was argued either that Hitler had committed no act of aggression against anyone or that he was entitled to do what he liked in his own territory or that it was impossible to prove that he had any ulterior designs or that the covenant of the League of Nations did not entitle us to use force and that it would be wiser to wait until he did commit an act of aggression." He emphasized that the nationalization of the Suez Canal amounted to an act of aggression against the international community.[37] On the same day, Dulles cautioned Eisenhower: "They could pass the blame to us and the subsequent losses they might incur in the Middle East and Africa as a result of Nasser's 'getting away with it.' I said if this happened, it could have a serious effect for some time upon good relations between our countries and certainly the existing British and French governments would have a tendency to try to find an alibi for themselves in our action." Dulles rightfully worried that a bad outcome in the Suez Crisis would be attributed to the United States.[38]

Responding to Eden on September 8, 1956, Eisenhower reiterated his position opposing the British government's use of force. Such an action would lead many Arabs to support Nasser. Eisenhower frankly warned: "It might cause a serious misunderstanding between our two countries because I must say frankly that there is as yet no public opinion in this country which is prepared to support such a move, and the most significant public opinion that there is seems to think that the United Nations was formed to prevent this very thing." Using the same arguments the British had used against his own position on Indochina in 1954, he advised Eden: "Nasser thrives on drama. If we let some of the drama go out of the situation and concentrate upon the task of deflating him through slower but sure processes such as I described, I believe the desired results can more probably be obtained." In short, Eden and Eisenhower had reversed roles in 1956. Eisenhower, the five-star general, became a dove, while Eden, the master diplomat, became a hawk.[39]

Predictably, Nasser officially rejected the Menzies mission on September 9, 1956. The Menzies mission, a delegation headed by Prime Minister Robert Menzies of Australia, attempted to sell the London Conference plan to Nasser. In their memoirs, Eden and Lloyd put the blame for failure squarely on Eisenhower for undermining their negotiating position with Nasser. In a press conference, Eisenhower indicated his preference for a peaceful solution to the Suez Crisis. The British persisted in threatening the Egyptians with the possible use of force. This bolstered their negotiating position with Nasser, the exact same argument made by Dulles in threatening military intervention in Indochina during the Geneva Conference of 1954. Eden, Lloyd, and Menzies decided that Eisenhower's comments had badly damaged their position in the subsequent negotiations. Nasser rejected the London Conference's proposals, which Lloyd regarded as a great tragedy. By publicly opposing military intervention, Eisenhower had done to the British what the British had done to the Americans at the Geneva Conference in 1954. Eden and Lloyd failed to appreciate the irony of the situation.[40]

Sir Ivone Kirkpatrick, permanent under-secretary of state at the Foreign Office, analyzed the situation this way: "Dulles, having rejected the idea of going to the Security Council, having refused to stop paying dues to the Egyptian Authority, having decided that other economic pressure was not possible, having thought up SCUA, . . . would very soon find out that SCUA did not work. The choice would then be force or surrender to Nasser." Kirkpatrick continued in a similar vein: "The Americans never believed that the Chinese would wreck them. . . . But for the reasons I have outlined very sketchily above, we, rightly or wrongly, believe that if we are denied the resources of Africa and the Middle East, we can be wrecked within a year or two." Kirkpatrick's evaluation of the crisis suggested diplomacy may have merely delayed the inevitable military confrontation between Great Britain and Egypt.[41]

The British began to think that Dulles was acting less like a diplomat and more like a campaign manager for Eisenhower's reelection campaign. In his press conference on September 11, 1956, Eisenhower stated: "I don't know exactly what you mean by backing them. As you know, this country will not go to war ever while I am occupying my present post unless the Congress is called into session and Congress declares such a war." In a press conference the following day, Dulles made the situation even worse by declaring: "We do not intend to shoot our way through. It may be we have the right to do it but we don't intend to do it as far as the United States is concerned." Eisenhower and Dulles had abandoned the gunboat diplomacy favored by Eden, Lloyd, and the British Foreign Office. Eden and Lloyd, once again, reprimanded Eisenhower and Dulles for undercutting their negotiations on the Suez Canal Users Association (SCUA).[42]

Meanwhile, British pilots left their jobs running the Suez Canal on September 14, 1956. New Egyptian pilots came in the following day, and the canal ran smoothly. Once Nasser rejected the SCUA proposals, the British and French in late September finally brought their case before the

United Nations Security Council. Whether the British or French genuinely desired peace at the UN or only needed to cover their moves toward a war on Egypt still remains unclear. In retrospect, Eden and Lloyd really needed a cover for a path to war. The proposal in September for SCUA again delayed British military intervention. SCUA had only the half-hearted backing of the British, but this time Dulles undermined his own project. The success of the Egyptian government in running the canal with Egyptians rather than the British proved to ultimately doom any chance of success for Dulles's proposal. Selwyn Lloyd believed Dulles's undermining of SCUA stood as the second tragic mistake made by the Americans.[43]

Dulles vigorously opposed any British military action in Egypt, at least until Eisenhower had been safely reelected. Eden mentioned this in a letter to Churchill: "Foster assured us that U.S. is as determined to deal with Nasser as we are—but I fear he has an incidental caveat about November 6. We cannot accept that." He then wrote a top-secret memorandum on September 23 telling Harold Macmillan, his chancellor of the Exchequer: "The Americans' main contention is that we bring Nasser down by degrees rather than on the Mossadegh lines. Of course if this is possible we should warmly welcome it and I am all for making every effort provided the results show themselves without delay." Eden looked for action sooner rather than later, while Eisenhower demanded he wait until after the presidential election.[44]

The next day, Macmillan met with Eisenhower in the White House. He recounted: "On Suez, he [Ike] was sure that we must get Nasser down. The only thing was how to do it. I made it quite clear that we could not play it long, without aid on a very large scale—that is, if playing it long involved buying dollar oil." The key differences related to tactics. The Eisenhower administration preferred a slow, covert war against Nasser, while the British supported a swift military intervention to take back the canal and destroy Nasser in the process. Macmillan had inadvertently revealed Britain's Achilles' heel to Eisenhower: its serious economic weakness in the event of a prolonged war.[45]

With the British government having recently announced the Anglo-French proposal to place the Suez Crisis on the agenda of the UN Security Council, Macmillan visited Dulles at the State Department. Having not been consulted in advance but merely informed of this British decision, Dulles looked surprised and angry. Macmillan wrote: "He was, there-fore, deeply hurt to find that we had taken this decision without further consultation. We should get nothing but trouble in New York; we were courting disaster. (From the way Dulles spoke you would have thought he was warning us against entering a bawdy house.)" Dulles regarded the United Nations as a hopeless diplomatic quagmire. While Dulles viewed the United Nations as a dangerous obstacle, the leader of the Labour Party; Hugh Gaitskill, viewed it as the only hope for the world. Macmillan walked a fine line at the UN and resented the attitude of the Labour Party and its leader Gaitskill, comparing it to the Catholic belief in papal infallibility: "The new doctrine about the infallibility of the United Nations, whether in the Security Council or in the Assembly, was declared by Gaitskell and his colleagues with all the infatuation of ultramontanism. Gaitskell in this respect resembled in 1956 Cardinal Manning in 1870." Macmillan did not embrace the high hopes of the Labour Party for a peace-ful solution to the crisis in the United Nations. Dulles believed that Nasser needed to be brought down by political and economic means rather than by military force.[46]

In a letter to Eisenhower on October 1, 1956, Eden tied Nasser to So-viet expansionism in the Middle East: "There is no doubt in our minds that Nasser, whether he likes it or not, is now effectively in Russian hands, just as Mussolini was in Hitler's. It would be ineffective to show weakness to Nasser now in order to placate him as it was to show weakness to Mus-solini. The only result was and would be to bring the two together." Eden linked Nasser to various Communist movements throughout the Arab world seeking the downfall of the West.[47]

The following day, Secretary of State Dulles made clear in a press con-ference the tangible differences between the British and the Americans: "The shift from colonialism to independence will be going on for another 50 years, and I believe that the task of the United Nations is to try to see that this process moves forward in a constructive, evolutionary way, and does not come to a halt or go forward through violent, revolutionary pro-cesses which would be destructive of much good." The Americans favored evolutionary change, while the British sought revolutionary change. The British responded to Dulles by charging the secretary of state with under-mining their negotiating position at the United Nations. In his memoirs,

Eden wrote: "It would be foolish to pretend that Mr. Dulles's remarks on colonialism did not represent his feelings and those of many of his countrymen. These sentiments certainly played their part in the reaction of some Americans to the Anglo-French intervention at Suez." Yet, Dulles could not have been more clear in advocating the American idea of evolutionary change in the Middle East rather than upholding British colonialism or endorsing radical and violent Arab or Islamic revolutions. Eden and Eisenhower quarreled over fundamental questions of strategy and tactics in the Middle East and North Africa.[48]

To help resolve these policy differences, Patrick Dean, British Joint Intelligence Committee chairman, came to Washington to review Operation Omega with U.S. officials in early October 1956. Dulles wrote: "I referred to the various projects of the British seemingly in different directions— one favoring a settlement by negotiation, another favoring overthrow by economic pressures; another favoring overthrow by a covert operation and another favoring open use of military force. The president felt that we should have nothing to do with any project for a covert operation against Nasser personally." The British had too many contradictory policies on Egypt. How could they support all of their policies at once? The British needed to decide which of these contradictory policies they would implement. Unlike Eden, Eisenhower categorically rejected British plans, specifically MI6 plans, to assassinate President Gamal Abdel Nasser of Egypt.[49]

In making a special point of rebuffing British plans for assassination, Eisenhower specifically rejected any American assassination plans against Nasser: "On October 8, 1956, Herbert Hoover, Jr., the Under-Secretary of State, told Eisenhower that 'one of our agencies' had devised a plan that was quicker and more direct 'on how to topple Nasser.' Whether or not that was a euphemism for assassination, Eisenhower rejected the basic premise. Goodpaster noted, 'the President said that an action of this kind could not be taken when there is as much active hostility as at present." Despite Eisenhower's unwavering opposition, the British continued their plans to assassinate Nasser.[50]

While visiting his wife in the hospital on October 5, 1956, Eden found himself struck by a life-threatening fever. Kennett Love wrote: "Eden was felled that day, a Friday, by a chill, ague, and raging fever during a visit to his wife in the University College Hospital, where, it was authoritatively said, she was recuperating from a miscarriage. Eden lost consciousness in an elevator in a fit so severe that his aides thought he was going to die. His fever mounted to 106 degrees." Eden remained in the hospital for the weekend and then miraculously returned to work the following Monday. The physical strain and the psychological pressure from the Suez Crisis had completely overwhelmed the British prime minister.[51]

In a press conference on October 12, Eisenhower cheerfully announced the end of the Suez Crisis: "I have got the best announcement that I could possibly make to America tonight. The progress made in the settlement of the Suez dispute this afternoon at the United Nations is most gratifying. Egypt, Britain and France have met through their foreign ministers and agreed on a set of principles on which to negotiate, and it looks like here is a very great crisis that is behind us." In fact, he was totally wrong. The Soviet Union vetoed the United Nations resolution and the Suez Crisis began to grow, not diminish.[52]

In mid-October 1956, Eisenhower learned through intelligence gathered by U-2 flights over Israel, that the Israelis had purchased sixty new French Mystere jets. The purchase of these jets violated the Tripartite Agreement of 1950, an agreement between the United States, Great Britain, and France to maintain the military status quo in the Middle East by restricting arms sales in the region. The United States had approved the sale of twenty-four French Mystere jets to Israel, but not sixty. Paradoxically, the brand-new U-2 planes had not been used to spy on the Soviet Union, but to observe America's allies, the British, the French, and the Israelis.[53]

The British deliberately concealed their diplomatic and military actions from Eisenhower. Selwyn Lloyd wrote: "Eisenhower's mind was concentrated on the election campaign, appearing as the candidate who could preserve the peace of the world. The fact was that he had twice let us down and relieved the pressure on Nasser at critical moments." He and Eden unfairly blamed Eisenhower and Dulles for the breakdown in the peace negotiations. However, if the British had truly coveted a peaceful resolution of the conflict, they could have easily attained one.[54]

In his book *The Art of the Possible*, R. A. Butler described what happened on October 18, 1956: "If war broke out in the Middle East between Israel and Egypt, Britain and France would jointly intervene in the canal area to stop hostilities. Selwyn Lloyd seemed anxious about my own reaction. At that moment I was summoned into the Cabinet Room." The British cabinet began planning for a war to take back the Suez Canal and oust Nasser from power. Shockingly, Lloyd had just admitted to the Israelis the day before that Great Britain and Egypt were within seven days of reaching a peace agreement on the Suez Canal. Moshe Dayan, chief of staff of the Israeli Defense Forces, recorded in his memoirs: "If all was so well and good, why, then, was he here? Because, he [Lloyd] explained, such an agreement would not only fail to weaken Nasser, it would actually strengthen him, and since her Majesty's Government considered that Nasser had to go, it was prepared to undertake military action in accordance with the latest version of the Anglo-French plan." This shocking admission by Lloyd manifestly contradicted his thesis about Eisenhower sabotaging the peace negotiations.[55]

The new Anglo-French military plan called for the Israelis to reach Suez within forty-eight hours. The Anglo-French ultimatum would then be issued for the Israelis and the Egyptians to withdraw. If, as planned, Egypt rejected the ultimatum, the British and French would seize the Suez Canal and overthrow Nasser. Negotiated between October 22 and 24, 1956, between Great Britain, France, and Israel, the Protocol of Sevres formally sealed the compact. Deeply worried about the existence of a written document of the war plans, Eden sent Patrick Dean back to Paris requesting that all the other copies of the document be destroyed. The French refused, while the Israelis had already returned to Israel with their copy.[56]

On October 23, 1956, Selwyn Lloyd deliberately misled U.S. Ambassador to Great Britain Winthrop Aldrich about Israeli intentions in the Middle East. He told Aldrich: "A major Israeli attack either on Jordan or Egypt at this time would put Britain in (an) impossible situation. . . . He (was) unwilling (to) believe the Israelis would launch a full scale attack upon Egypt despite the temptation to do so, in present circumstances. . . . Lloyd's major concern is (the) threat (of) further large-scale attacks on Jordan." Aldrich was deceived into thinking that the Israelis planned to attack Jordan. Aldrich's inability to grasp the collusion of the British, French, and Israelis stemmed from a crafty British diplomat engaging in prevarication.[57]

On October 29, 1956, the Israelis launched a military attack, not against Jordan, but against Egypt. At a meeting in the White House, Eisenhower quickly recognized the British deception: "We should let them know at once . . . that we recognize that much is on their side in the dispute with the Egyptians, but that nothing justifies double crossing us." After this meeting, Eisenhower called in the British diplomat J. E. Coulson and asked him about French collusion with Israel, pointing to the sixty French Mystere jets that had been sold to Israel. He did not charge the British with collusion but wanted only to "redeem (their) word about supporting any victim of aggression." Eisenhower referred to the Tripartite Agreement of 1950. The treaty called for the United States, Great Britain, and France to defend any Middle Eastern nation against an aggressor. In this case, the treaty required the United States, Great Britain, and France to defend Egypt against Israel.[58]

Eisenhower wanted to know what the British and the French planned to do. British historian Christopher Andrew has written: "Ike was so much in the dark that he speculated that 'the hand of Churchill,' rather than of Eden, might be behind the British Suez adventure, since it was 'in the mid-Victorian style.'" Eisenhower received reports that British and French military forces had attacked Egypt. He questioned the apparent repudiation of the Tripartite Agreement by Piers Dixon, the British ambassador to the UN. Eisenhower later wrote: "We were astonished to find that he was completely unsympathetic, stating frankly that his government would not agree to any action whatsoever to be taken against Israel. He further argued that the tri-partite statement of May, 1950, was ancient history and without current validity." Eisenhower had not been notified of the change in the British government's position in advance. The American position on the Tripartite Agreement had not changed.[59]

In the final message on October 30, 1956, the salutation from Eisenhower had changed from "Dear Anthony" to "Dear Prime Minister":

I have just learned from press of the 12-hour ultimatum which you and the French Government have delivered to the Government of Egypt requiring, under threat of forceful intervention, the temporary occupation by Anglo-French forces of key positions at Port Said, Ismailia and Suez in the Suez Canal Zone. I feel I must urgently express to you my deep concern at the prospect of this drastic action even at the very time when the matter is under consideration as it is today by the United Nations Security Council. It is my sincere belief that peaceful processes can and should prevail to secure a solution which will restore the armistice condition as between Israel and Egypt and also justly settle the controversy with Egypt about the Suez Canal.[60]

He transmitted this message recognizing Eden's ultimatum as a pretext for the very military intervention he had long opposed: "When news of the ultimatum reached Eisenhower, it is reported that 'the White House crackled with barrack-room language the kind of which had not been heard since the days of General Grant.' The president rang Eden but was connected to his Press Secretary, William Clark, by mistake. 'Anthony,' Ike told Clark, believing him to be the prime minister, 'you must have gone out of your mind.'" Eisenhower felt double-crossed by his good friend and ally Anthony Eden.[61]

Other foreign events muddled the Suez Crisis. The new Hungarian prime minister, Imre Nagy, announced a new coalition government including non-Communist members on October 31, 1956. The Soviets promised to quickly evacuate the Red Army from Hungary. The Dulles brothers wrongly assumed the new coalition government signaled "the beginning of the collapse of the Soviet Empire." Meanwhile, the British and the French had begun hostilities by bombing Egyptian airfields. Eisenhower's immediate reaction: "How could we possibly support Britain and France if in doing so we lose the whole Arab world?" After serious reflection, Eisenhower coldly chose the Arab world over his Western allies.[62]

Eden had lost the support of the U.S. government. British historian Howard J. Dooley noted: "Eisenhower administered a lesson about superpower authority and British dependency. In the Mediterranean, the United States used its powerful Sixth Fleet as a weapon of intimidation, harassing the Anglo-French invasion fleet, submerging submarines in its path, buzzing the ships with aircraft, rattling its commanders, and perhaps delaying its arrival off Port Said by twenty-four hours." Eisenhower rattled his saber and demonstrated his rage with Great Britain and France through military harassment. He was playing a very dangerous game, particularly if the U.S. military had made a serious mistake through some type of military miscalculation.[63]

In his memoirs, Eden tried to explain the differences between the United States' and Great Britain's view of the Suez Canal Crisis: "It is obvious truth that safety of transit through the canal, though clearly a concern to the United States, is for them not a matter of survival as it is to us and, indeed, to all Europe and many other lands. Indeed, Mr. Dulles himself made this clear on August 28 when he said the United States' economy is not dependent on the canal." For Eden, the Suez Crisis meant life or death.[64]

The National Security Council met at the White House on November 1, 1956, to discuss the two ongoing crises, the Hungarian Revolution and the Suez Crisis. Allen Dulles reported on Hungary. Dulles erroneously believed the Soviet Empire was coming apart and that Hungary would soon be free. In the same meeting, his brother John Foster Dulles spoke out on Suez: "For many years now the United States has been walking a tight rope between the effort to maintain our old and valued relations with our British and French allies on the one hand, and on the other trying to assure ourselves of the friendship and understanding of the newly independent countries who have escaped colonialism." The United States chose ideology over friendship and endorsed Arab nationalism over British and French colonialism.[65]

The president restated his belief that in a choice between Great Britain and France or the Arab world, he must choose the Arab world. His main concern in the Middle East was not defending Anglo-French colonialism, but rather defeating Soviet Communism. Eisenhower even worried about the Soviets giving the Egyptians atomic weapons. In the United Nations, Secretary of State Dulles sponsored a resolution calling for a cease-fire. On November 2, this UN resolution passed by a 64–5 vote with six abstentions. The five votes against the resolution included Britain, France, Israel, Australia, and New Zealand.[66]

Prime Minister Eden later bitterly wrote: "It was not Soviet Russia, or any Arab state, but the government of the United States which took the lead in Assembly against Israel, France and Britain. Their Secretary of State said he moved the resolution with a heavy heart." A cease-fire would not resolve the existing problems, but would instead exacerbate the existing problems in the Middle East. Eden complained about the United Nations not creating an effective international force to maintain the Suez Canal. The U.S.-sponsored move for a cease-fire would merely restore the unacceptable status quo. Selwyn Lloyd worried that that the United States, in conjunction with the Arab states, might impose an oil embargo on Great Britain.[67]

On the same day as the UN vote, Vice President Richard Nixon delivered a campaign speech celebrating America's declaration of independence from British and French colonialism: "That Declaration of Independence has had an electrifying effect throughout the world." The British scorned the vice president's statement as sheer political electioneering. A short time later, Eisenhower told General Alfred Gruenther, supreme commander of NATO: "If one has to fight then that is that. But I don't see the point in getting into a fight to which there can be no satisfactory end and in which the whole world believes you are playing the part of the bully and you do not even have the firm backing of your entire people." The British, French, and Israelis assumed that Eisenhower, distracted by a presidential election, would be forced to go along with them. They badly misjudged him.[68]

In the meantime, Secretary of State Dulles underwent emergency cancer surgery at Walter Reed Hospital on November 3, 1956, allowing the Anglophobe Herbert Hoover Jr. to take over in the State Department. Prime Minister Eden rejected the cease-fire as called for by the United Nations. The Soviet Union then vetoed the American resolution demanding the withdrawal of the Red Army from Hungary. Eisenhower, who had originally inspired Hungarian freedom fighters with his broadcasts from Radio Free Europe, refused to help the Hungarians against the Soviets. He rejected the CIA's request to assist Hungarian freedom fighters, and he prohibited the use of American troops because he considered Hungary "as inaccessible to us as Tibet." Sadly for the Hungarians, Eisenhower's commitment to rolling back Communism in Eastern Europe turned out to be nothing more than empty rhetoric. Eisenhower's rhetoric on "rolling back" Communism was incredibly inconsistent with his actual actions regarding the Hungarian Revolution.[69]

The Joint Chiefs of Staff provided another dire warning for the president about Communism in the Middle East: "By use of propaganda, agents and local communist parties the Soviets can cause extensive anti-Western rioting, sabotage and general disorder throughout the area, particularly at Western oil installations. To direct and assist in such operations the Soviets could introduce small numbers of professional agents and saboteurs." The Soviets could create political and economic chaos in the Middle East, which might spread quickly to Western Europe.[70]

Shockingly, Soviet troops totaling two hundred thousand redeployed on Budapest, crushing the Hungarian Revolution on November 4. Eisenhower's feeble response to the Soviets: "We could do nothing." Eisenhower's refusal to come to the aid of the Hungarian freedom fighters revealed his fear of using covert or overt military intervention to stop the Soviets in their recognized sphere of influence in Eastern Europe. This fear of the Soviets by an American president would be repeated in 1968 with the Soviet invasion of Czechoslovakia. Ronald Reagan, learning from the failures of his predecessors, finally stood up to the Soviets when they threatened Poland in the 1980s. The Soviets backed down after hearing Reagan's threat of military intervention. Years later in his memoirs, Eisenhower wrote: "I still wonder what would have been my recommendation to the Congress and the American people had Hungary been accessible by sea or through the territory of allies who might have agreed to react positively to the tragic fate of the Hungarian people." By November 7, 1956, the serious fighting in Hungary had ended in tragedy for the brave Hungarian freedom fighters.[71]

On November 5, 1956, British and French troops finally landed in Egypt near the Suez Canal. According to a memorandum by Andrew Goodpaster, Herbert Hoover Jr. weighed in: "The question may well be 'Eden or Nasser.' He added that Nasser's position is wobbly at the moment. The President said this is something quite new, said the British have always said their aim was to 'deflate' Nasser. Mr. Hoover suggested for consideration the possibility that Hammarskjold tell Nasser he must resign. The British may still have a coup in mind, as Nasser's position deteriorates." Indeed, the question did become, Eden or Nasser? Would the United States stand with their British friend Eden or with the Arab nationalist named Nasser?[72]

President Bulganin of the Soviet Union entered the picture by conveying letters to the leaders of Great Britain, France, and Israel denouncing their unwarranted aggression against Egypt and making a veiled threat to use nuclear weapons against London and Paris unless British, French, and Israeli forces withdrew from Egypt. He warned of a third world war and suggested a joint Soviet-American force to clear the region of British and French troops. Eisenhower dismissed the proposal of joint Soviet-American action against Britain, France, and Israel as a ridiculous idea.

Eisenhower compared the Soviets to Hitler: "Those boys are both furious and scared. Just as with Hitler, that makes for the most dangerous possible state of mind. And we better be damned sure that every intelligence point and every outpost of our armed forces is absolutely right on their toes." Eisenhower continued: "We have to be positive and clear in our every word, every step. And if those fellows start something, we may have to hit 'em—and, if necessary, with everything in the bucket." Howard Snyder, Eisenhower's doctor, heard him say, "if he were a dictator, he would tell Russia if they moved a finger, he would drop our entire stock of atomic weapons upon them." While refusing to help the Hungarian freedom fighters in Eastern Europe, Eisenhower began planning an all-out nuclear attack against the Soviet Union over the Middle East. He did not see any inconsistency in his foreign policy or even blink over the likelihood of a total global thermonuclear war.[73]

On Election Day, Eisenhower remained apprehensive over the possibility of Soviet unilateral military action against British, French, or Israeli forces: "If the Soviets attacked the British and the French we would be in war, and we would be justified in taking military action even if Congress were not in session." Colonel Goodpaster gloomily noted: "The President asked if our forces in the Mediterranean are equipped with atomic anti-submarine weapons." Eisenhower gravely pondered nuclear war in the Middle East without seeking the advice or consent of the U.S. Congress.[74]

At the same time, Eden and Lloyd wanted the British military intervention to continue until the Suez Canal had been taken. Due to an economic crisis in Great Britain, Eden agreed to a UN cease-fire by midnight on November 6, 1956. Eden had no real choice but to surrender to Eisenhower and agree to a cease-fire. Churchill later stated: "When things become known it will turn out, I think, that Anthony has been bitched, and that he wanted to go and complete the military operation. When the Cabinet wouldn't let him he tried to resign, but they told him that he would split the Conservative Party." Prime Minister Eden would ultimately bear the full responsibility for the political and military fiasco at Suez.[75]

CHAPTER 7

ECONOMIC BRINKSMANSHIP

The Fall of Anthony Eden

During the Suez Crisis, Eisenhower secretly declared an all-out economic war against Great Britain. He initiated a highly successful speculative financial attack on the value of sterling, which threatened to completely destabilize the British monetary system and economy. Herbert Hoover Jr., an expert at international finance, recommended the very arcane and elaborate strategy of the Federal Reserve quickly dumping their sterling holdings at basement prices, launching an attack on Britain's currency. Eisenhower played political and economic hardball to compel the British to withdraw from Suez.

Eden discussed Eisenhower's economic threats with French foreign minister Christian Pineau. "According to Pineau, the prime minister [Eden] said that he had received a call from Eisenhower, 'who told me if you don't get out of Port Said tomorrow, I'll cause a run on the pound and drive it to zero." Eisenhower's actions escalated the existing speculation on British sterling resulting from the Suez Crisis. Britain could not, under this type of economic attack, maintain the price of sterling or a fixed exchange rate for the pound. Cameron F. Cobbold, governor of the Bank of England, declared that this "would probably lead to the breakup of the sterling area (possibly even the dissolution of the Commonwealth), the collapse of (the European Payments Union), a reduction in the volume of trade and currency instability at home leading to severe inflation." In short, Great Britain faced an American-made economic catastrophe.[1]

Cobbold seriously understated the economic problems awaiting England, if one merges the sterling crisis with the resulting oil shortage from the Persian Gulf. Having blown up ships to block the Suez Canal, Nasser stopped the flow of virtually all Middle Eastern oil to western Europe. In addition, Eisenhower, through Deputy Secretary of Defense Robert Anderson, quietly negotiated with King Saud an order to stop the flow of virtually all Middle Eastern oil to Britain and France. Ambassador George Wadsworth wrote: "King then said: 'I have great confidence in USG and approve its plan for redistribution of oil, confident at the same time USG will minimize loss which Saudi Arabia will sustain as result [of] its implementation. We will welcome plan after withdrawal British-French forces in accordance UN resolutions, and thereafter it may be possible to restore relations with countries as before.'" Great Britain's sole supplier of oil, as a result of the Suez Crisis, would be the United States of America. American oil suppliers would reap hefty profits from Britain's economic crisis. Using the Federal Reserve and a secret deal with the Saudis, Eisenhower cunningly engineered a massive British economic crisis.[2]

The president's actions threatened the British with a near-term collapse of their economy. Economists Adam Klug and Gregor W. Smith confirmed this reality:

> We find that recent historians have been right to downplay the significance of the run on the pound in the first week of November 1956. Although this triggered a massive loss of reserves, the event did not significantly affect forward exchange rates. The historians have been wrong however to assert that there was no financial crisis. From the moment the Canal was nationalized the sterling exchange rate ceased to be credible and such credibility as had been regained was decisively reduced by the invasion. At the end of November these pressures came to a head, as reserve losses and falling exchange-rate credibility coincided and reserves fell below $2000 million. Moreover, the rate of reserve loss was greater than in other sterling crises.[3]

The day after his overwhelming reelection, President Eisenhower met with Secretary Dulles at Walter Reed Hospital to discuss the Suez Crisis: "The Secretary then said that the British and the French going into Egypt was 'a crazy act.' The President said yes, although it was somewhat understandable if in fact the Russians were going to act in any case. The President added, however, that even if this were true, the British and French action was still ill-advised." He then increased the political pressure on the British government by putting Prime Minister Anthony Eden into a permanent diplomatic deep-freeze. From November 7 until Eden's retirement in January 1957, Eisenhower communicated with Eden in the most minimal and perfunctory way. Eden had become persona non grata.[4]

British cabinet members, other than Eden and Lloyd, now needed to contact the U.S. government through Ambassador Winthrop Aldrich. Aldrich stated, "I was enormously helped at this time by the willingness of several important members of the British Cabinet to exchange views with me with great frankness and permit me to convey their view and ideas directly to Washington, without passing through the Foreign Office." Eisenhower had politically, economically, and diplomatically isolated the prime minister, the British Treasury Office, and the British Foreign Office from the U.S. government.[5]

The new British ambassador to the United States, Sir Harold Caccia, and Pierson Dixon at the UN had been frozen out as well. Aldrich recalled being "surprised at the vitriolic nature of Eisenhower's reaction to what happened. I think it was unstatesmanlike; indeed I think it was a dreadful thing the way the U.S. government permitted itself to act towards Eden because of pique or petulance. . . . [T]he President just went off the deep end. He wouldn't have anything to do with Eden at all. He wouldn't even communicate with him." This incredible state of affairs lasted until Macmillan succeeded Eden. Eisenhower flatly refused to deal with Prime Minister Eden or the British Foreign Office. This boycott of Britain's top leaders allowed Eisenhower, using Aldrich as a conduit, to conspire with British cabinet members such as Macmillan, Butler, and Salisbury to remove Eden from the premiership without leaving a paper trail.[6]

At a National Security Council meeting on November 8, 1956, Eisenhower still did not believe that the British had colluded with the French and the Israelis. Although he had originally thought the British misled him, he now believed that they would not have deliberately done so: "He said that the British were meticulous planners and he was sure that if they had been in on the scheme from the beginning that they would have seen to it that they were in a position to move into Egypt in a matter of hours after they declared their intention to do so." John Foster Dulles "thought that the British having gone in should not have stopped until they had toppled

Nasser. As it was they now had the worst of both possible worlds. They had received all the onus of making the move and at the same time had not accomplished their major purpose." The Suez Crisis was a total fiasco for Eden and Lloyd.[7]

R. A. Butler and Harold Macmillan could only communicate with Washington through Winthrop Aldrich, behind the back of their own prime minister. Aldrich wrote: "At evening reception Buckingham Palace November 8, Butler took me aside and said with great earnestness how deeply he deplored the existence of what he termed mutual misunderstandings of policy which had arisen between US and UK governments. He quite evidently was greatly disturbed by the course followed by a majority of the Cabinet although he did not specifically so state." All of the normal means of communication between Washington and London had completely broken down. Aldrich wrote that Butler said: "'I have been meaning to come and see you for a long time to tell you that in my opinion you are the only man who is in a position to explain to your government in detail the various attitudes of the members of our government. Never has an ambassador occupied a more important position that you do at the present moment.' He went on to urge me to see Macmillan at the earliest opportunity." The British cabinet had made preparations for a change in leadership.[8]

President Eisenhower only became fully cognizant of British collusion with the French on November 16, 1956. French foreign minister Christian Pineau admitted the collusion to CIA Director Allen Dulles. Selwyn Lloyd visited John Foster Dulles at Walter Reed Hospital on Saturday, November 17, 1956, with Dulles asking a quick question: "'Selwyn, why did you stop? Why didn't you go through with it and get Nasser down?' [Lloyd] replied, 'Well, Foster, if you had so much as winked at us we might have gone on.'" The differences between the United States and Great Britain concerned methods and tactics; Dulles had wanted Nasser overthrown as well.[9]

Dulles met with another important visitor, President Eisenhower, who refused to meet or confer with Lloyd. He talked gravely to Dulles about his negative opinion of Prime Minister Anthony Eden: "The President spoke of the reactions of British Generals, with whom he talked recently, concerning Prime Minister Eden. Both had expressed an increasing lack of confidence in the British Prime Minister." Dulles further noted, "He [Eisenhower] said that one of the most pleasant things in life was to find one's estimate of a man increased each time one had dealings with him. Conversely he thought one of the most disappointing things was to start with an exceedingly high opinion of a person and then have continually to downgrade this estimate on the basis of succeeding contacts with him. He indicated that Eden fell into the latter category." Eisenhower held Eden in complete contempt.[10]

Furthermore, Eisenhower, privately communicating with Macmillan and Butler through Aldrich, wanted the British to not only withdraw from Suez, but to seek the resignation of Anthony Eden. On November 19, 1956, a major cabinet shakeup seemed imminent, with the possible departure of Prime Minister Eden due to poor health. Aldrich reported: "Eden has had physical breakdown and will have to go on vacation immediately, first for one week and then for another, and this will lead to his retirement. Government will be run by triumvirate of Butler, Macmillan, and Salisbury." Macmillan could become the next prime minister. Thinking Eden's retirement would lead to the British withdrawing troops from Egypt, Aldrich continued: "Macmillan said, 'if you can give us a fig leaf to cover our nakedness' I believe we can get a majority of the Cabinet to vote for such withdrawal without requiring conditions in connection with location of United Nations forces and methods of re-opening and operating Canal, although younger members of the Cabinet will be strongly opposed." Macmillan's allusion to a "fig leaf to cover our nakedness" most likely represented a request for economic assistance.[11]

The next day, Ambassador Winthrop Aldrich called the president:

PRESIDENT: We have been getting your messages, and I want to make an inquiry. You are dealing with at least one person—maybe two or three—on a very personal basis. Is it possible for you, without embarrassment, to get together the two that you mentioned in one of your messages?

ALDRICH: Yes, one of them I have been playing bridge with. Perhaps I can stop him.

PRESIDENT: I'd rather you talk to both together. You know who I mean? One has the same name as my predecessor at Columbia University; the other was with me in the war. (Note: presumably, Butler and Macmillan)

ALDRICH: I know the one with you in the war. Oh yes, now I've got it.

PRESIDENT: Could you get them informally and say of course we are interested and sympathetic, and, as soon as things happen that we anticipate, we can furnish "a lot of fig leaves."

ALDRICH: I certainly can say that.

PRESIDENT: Will that be enough to get the boys moving?

ALDRICH: I think it will be.

PRESIDENT: Herb (Hoover) probably will send you a cable later tonight. You see, you don't want to be in a position of interfering between those two. But we want to have you personally tell them. They are both good friends.

ALDRICH: Yes, very much so. Have you seen all my messages? Regarding my conversations with them all?

PRESIDENT: Yes—with at least two.

ALDRICH: That is wonderful. I will do this—tomorrow?

PRESIDENT: Yes, first thing in the morning.

ALDRICH: I shall certainly do it. And will then communicate with you at once. Can do it without the slightest embarrassment.

PRESIDENT: Communicate through regular channels—through Herb.[12]

The president and the ambassador seemed to speak in code. One of the "fig leaves" may have been providing England with much-needed oil.

Goodpaster noted: "The President said that when the British and the French had withdrawn their troops, the United States 'would talk to the Arabs to obtain the removal of any objections they may have regarding the provision of oil to Western Europe.'" In the overall context of Aldrich and Macmillan's previous messages, Eisenhower may have agreed to give immense financial aid to Great Britain. The financial aid would be forthcoming as long as the British cabinet agreed to an immediate withdrawal of troops from Suez and Eden resigned. Unfortunately for Eisenhower, Macmillan's earlier prediction about Eden's poor health leading to his resignation proved to be wrong.[13]

Just before going on his long vacation to Ian Fleming's home, Goldeneye, in Jamaica, Prime Minister Eden renewed his orders for MI6 to kill Nasser on or about November 23, 1956. MI6, for whatever the reasons, failed in its mission to kill Nasser. Unfortunately for the prime minister, Eisenhower would not fail in his mission to destroy him. Eden ended up going into permanent political exile on a distant island, not unlike Napoleon. Eisenhower refused to work with him. Behind Eden's back and in concert with Eisenhower, a new pro-American, British political triumvirate had been set up, with R. A. Butler, Harold Macmillan, and Lord Salisbury. The new British leadership owed nothing to Eden. They simply informed Eden of their decisions, while conferring with Eisenhower.[14]

The harsh and punitive economic sanctions on Great Britain caused former prime minister Winston Churchill to directly intervene with his old friend in order to try to reduce the political and economic pressure on Great Britain. Churchill wrote Eisenhower on November 23, 1956: "Whatever the arguments adduced here and in the United States for or against Anthony's actions in Egypt, it will now be an act of folly, on which our whole of civilization may founder, to let events in the Middle East come between us." The United States and Great Britain must work together or face the real possibility of losing the Middle East and North Africa to the Soviet Union.[15]

Eisenhower replied: "Now I still believe that we must keep several facts clearly before us, the first one always being that the Soviets are the real enemy and all else must be viewed against the background of that truth. The second fact is that nothing would please this country more nor, in fact, could help us more, than to see British prestige and strength renewed and rejuvenated in the Mid-East." He wanted his appeal to appear reasonable and rational. Eisenhower continued: "We want those countries to trust and lean toward the Western World, not Russia. A third fact is that we want to help Britain right now, particularly in its difficult fuel and financial situation, daily growing more serious. All we have asked in order to come out openly has been a British statement that it would conform to the resolutions of the United Nations." This required a change in British leadership.[16]

Now, through economic blackmail, Eisenhower controlled the British government and the destiny of the British Empire. He demonstrated the wisdom of Sun Tzu: "An army is only the instrument which administers the coup de grace to an enemy already defeated by intelligence operations which separated the enemy from his allies, corrupted his officials, spread misleading information, and correctly assessed his strength and weaknesses—winning one hundred battles is not the acme of skill—to subdue the enemy without fighting is the acme of skill." Eisenhower, with the acme of skill, vanquished the wayward British.[17]

British historian Stephen Dorril has correctly deduced: "Harold Macmillan and Rab Butler had intrigued with US Ambassador, Winthrop Aldrich, 'to give assurances that Eden would not remain Prime Minister.' Indeed, the White House conspired to ensure that Macmillan was the next PM as part of a plan to prevent the emergence of a Labour government as a consequence of the crisis." Eisenhower's economic pressure on Great Britain had to be perfectly calibrated in order to be strong enough to remove Eden and overcome the anti-Americans in the British cabinet, but not so strong as to diminish Macmillan, Butler, and Salisbury, which would have created a Labour government.[18]

This political pressure took the form of economic blackmail. Secretary of the Treasury George Humphrey told British ambassador Harold Caccia: "You will not get a dime from the United States government if I can stop it, until you have gotten out of Suez! You are like burglars who have broken into somebody else's house. So get out! When you do, and not until then, you'll get help!" Humphrey dutifully described Great Britain's dire economic straits in a National Security Council meeting: "In point of fact the financial aspects of Britain's problems were even more serious than her physical situation. The British reserves were falling very rapidly. Even some slight indication of a run on currency could spell disaster for Great Britain." Nevertheless, Eisenhower prepared to bail out the British.[19]

On December 3, 1956, British ambassador Caccia successfully negotiated a financial deal with Treasury Secretary Humphrey and Robert Murphy of the State Department to rescue Britain. Initially, Caccia said he was unable to give a specific date for the British withdrawal from the Suez Canal area. Humphrey and Murphy thought this unacceptable. Caccia then promised a British withdrawal from Suez in fourteen days. For Eisenhower, this met his minimum requirements and British financial aid would soon become available. The British had been sufficiently humiliated.[20]

As promised, the United States ensured delivery of $1.3 billion in IMF funds to the British on December 10, 1956. Eleven days later, the British also received an additional $500 million loan from the Export-Import Bank. When Eden returned to England on December 14, he had lost virtually all of his political power. Eden no longer controlled the cabinet. On December 20, 1956, Eden addressed the House of Commons for the last time, where he falsely claimed "there was not foreknowledge that Israel would attack Egypt." This proved to be Eden's final and sad farewell to the House of Commons. He remained unrepentant to the end.[21]

Already campaigning for the premiership, Macmillan stated: "I like both Butler and Eden. They both have great charm. But it has been cruelly said that in politics there are no friends at the top. I fear it is so." Macmillan, the first man in and the first man out of the Suez Crisis, would soon become the queen's new first minister. Foreign Secretary Lloyd wrote in his memoirs: "My theme was that, after the serious difference of opinion with the United States, we must try to make Western Europe less dependent upon America. I did not get much sympathy from my colleagues. Most of them thought that the first priority must be the mending of our fences with the United States." His anti-American outlook failed to impress a reinvigorated British cabinet seeking reconciliation with Eisenhower.[22]

Remaining exceptionally loyal to Eden, Lloyd wrote: "Towards the end of the morning meeting Eden said that the discussion must continue in the afternoon without him. He had to go to Sandringham. There was some barrack-room language from one of my colleagues, who thought it was unreasonable and inconsiderate to break off the discussion in this way. Neither he nor I had any idea of the reasons for Eden's visit to see the

Queen." In his meeting with Queen Elizabeth II, Eden mentioned his debt to Mr. Butler and praised his service. Macmillan, however, was the queen's choice, and Eisenhower's longtime friend became prime minister. Macmillan led Great Britain into a junior partnership with the United States, a role that Churchill and Eden had long feared.[23]

The skilled deviousness and hypocrisy of Eisenhower knew no bounds when, on January 10, 1957, he wrote Eden: "I cannot tell you how deeply I regret that the strains and stresses of these times finally wore you down physically until you felt it necessary to retire. . . . The only reason for recalling those days is to assure you that my admiration and affection for you have never diminished; I am truly sorry that you had to quit the office of Her Majesty's First Minister." His disingenuous letter concealed his real feelings. Eden responded a week later: "Thank you so much for your letter and the kind thoughts in it. I confess that it is a wrench to go just now, but the doctors really gave me no choice. Clarissa joins me in every wish for happiness to you both." Ironically, Eden lived on with his bile duct problems for another twenty years.[24]

Eisenhower's support of Arab nationalism over British and French colonialism came from his extreme anti-Communist view of the region. British political hegemony in the region gave way to American backed anti-Communist Arab nationalism. While Nasser may have been an assassin and a thug, he was no Hitler or Mussolini. He had acted within his legal rights when he nationalized the Suez Canal. The British could not legally or morally justify direct military intervention in Egypt.

Having been warned numerous times by Eisenhower of the severe consequences of military intervention, Eden obviously did not fully understand the consequences of ignoring those warnings. Eden and Lloyd blamed Eisenhower for their own diplomatic defeats and then deceived him about direct British military intervention in Egypt. After he had been safely reelected, President Eisenhower's personal rage against Eden led to an American economic war against Great Britain. Eisenhower's extreme and drastic measures ended the Suez Crisis, forced the resignation of Eden, and vaulted the United States to the position of the West's unquestioned power broker in the Middle East.

CHAPTER 8

CONCLUSION

Many books have been written about the relationship between Dwight D. Eisenhower and Winston Churchill during the Second World War, but very few have been written about their relationship during the Cold War. Eisenhower and Churchill battled each other on how to end the war in Europe, specifically whether or not to let the Soviet army take Berlin. It is much less well-known how Eisenhower and Churchill fought each other during the Cold War. Churchill achieved fame for his absolute refusal to negotiate with Adolf Hitler and the Nazis, but by the 1950s, he favored negotiations with the Soviet Union and the Communists. Eisenhower's reputation during the Second World War was based on his ability to get along with difficult allies, including the Soviets, but by the 1950s, he openly rejected any type of negotiations with the Communists.

Eisenhower's conservatism exceeded the conservatism of the Old Right. His transatlantic foreign policy represented neither a continuation of Truman's containment policy nor a "middle path" between Democrats and far-right Republicans. If Eisenhower had been a mere continuation of Truman or a "middle path" Republican president, Winston Churchill and Anthony Eden would have easily adapted their pragmatic foreign policy to mesh with the foreign policy of the new president. Instead, Eisenhower intentionally adopted a distinctly far-right Republican foreign policy. Eisenhower's brinksmanship overwhelmed two Conservative British prime ministers and accelerated the decline of the British Empire.

This brinksmanship foreign policy represented a radical rejection of America's traditional European-based diplomacy and Great Britain's balance-of-power diplomacy. Rather than backing British colonial interests, the

United States moved to a conservative foreign policy, anticolonial and anti-Communist, that forced it to become the policeman of the world. The transatlantic alliance between the United States and Great Britain collapsed because the United States refused to be associated with British colonialism in the Far East and the Middle East. Instead, Eisenhower, who had promised collective security through NATO and SEATO, practiced personal diplomacy based on brinksmanship, unilateralism, and intense anti-Communism.

This unilateralism alienated the United States from its Western allies, forcing it in the future to go it alone in wars in the Far East, the Middle East, and the Western Hemisphere. Ironically, Eisenhower had created an environment for future U.S. presidents where the military-industrial complex could flourish, while completely undermining the American economy and what Eisenhower called "the American way of life."[1]

For his part, Winston Churchill advocated détente between the Soviet Union and the West. He believed in British colonialism as a force for good, elevating and civilizing Third World countries. Churchill understood the growing economic weakness of Great Britain and its waning influence in the world. He also knew the limits of British influence on American foreign policy.

Churchill championed a new concept of diplomacy, which later became known as détente. This British foreign policy became the model for Richard Nixon and Henry Kissinger in the 1970s. Yet Kissinger's balance-of-power diplomacy in the 1970s failed to stop a military buildup by the Soviet Union. Churchill's personal diplomacy really represented a prelude to the 1980s and Ronald Reagan's diplomacy. Churchill emphasized the importance of diplomatic negotiations, even during a disagreement with a demanding and difficult adversary. A constructive engagement with one's enemy proved to be the real legacy of Churchill's personal diplomacy.[2]

Churchill believed that the Soviet Union's national interest and a growing consumer demand for Western goods would ultimately force the Soviet government toward a détente with the West. In Great Britain's politics, he had suffered far too long from being called a warmonger; Churchill wanted to end his grand and glorious public career as a peacemaker. Unfortunately for him, Eisenhower, Dulles, and even his own foreign secretary, Anthony Eden, resisted his brilliant idea of a Big Three summit.

Conversely, Eisenhower's ideology led him to completely distrust the Communist leaders of the Soviet Union and China. Churchill, also distrustful of Soviet leadership, believed agreements of mutual interest were possible. Eisenhower's radical anti-Communist ideology completely thwarted the ambitions of British diplomacy. America's ideological war with the Soviet Union directly clashed with Britain's balance-of-power foreign policy. These ideological differences caused the break in the postwar Anglo-American relationship.[3]

In his campaign for the Republican presidential nomination against Senator Robert A. Taft in 1952, Eisenhower championed collective security agreements. He had directed a large military coalition in the Second World War and had been the leader of the North Atlantic Treaty Organization (NATO). Eisenhower advocated the development of the Southeast Asia Treaty Organization (SEATO) in the Far East in 1954. Paradoxically, by practicing "brinksmanship," Eisenhower moved toward a militant and unilateral foreign policy. In the Third World, he often rejected a collective approach to resolving problems or to peaceful negotiations.

Churchill and Eden learned the hard way that Eisenhower represented the return of the Old Right. Eisenhower adopted Douglas MacArthur's daring and dangerous strategy to end the Korean War with the threat to use atomic weapons. He also threatened President Syngman Rhee of South Korea with a proposed military coup, called Operation Everready, if Rhee did not cooperate with armistice talks in Panmunjom. Lord Salisbury, the acting British foreign secretary, appeared genuinely shocked by the possibility of a global thermonuclear war and a military coup against Rhee occurring at the same time.

For his part, Eisenhower always generously credited MacArthur for the strategy ending the Korean War, while dismissing British objections and concerns about the possible use of atomic weapons. This nuclear brinksmanship, which MacArthur advocated, illustrated a fundamental break with the Truman administration and two British governments of differing parties. They viewed MacArthur's plan for Korea as far too risky. Eisenhower accepted the risk of a possible war with the Soviet Union. Indeed, his success in ending the Korean War may have led to his overconfidence about the possible use of nuclear weapons in Asia. For this reason, MacArthur should be considered the true author of Eisenhower's "brinksman-

ship." Many historians often ignore or are unaware of Eisenhower's dangerous threats against South Korea's Syngman Rhee. The threat of a military
coup against Rhee did not end in May 1953, as H. W. Brands has written, but continued until Rhee finally agreed to an armistice in early July.[4]

While Eisenhower's actions did lead to an armistice in July 1953, they
did not lead to a peace agreement between the United States and North
Korea at the Geneva Conference of 1954. Technically speaking, a state of
war still exists between the two countries. North Korea has an army of 1
million on the border with South Korea, along with more than 8 million in
the active reserves. By contrast, South Korea has an army of 650,000, and
the United States has about 30,000 soldiers in South Korea and 47,000 in
Japan. A part of Eisenhower's legacy in the Far East was his failure to establish peace on the Korean peninsula. In addition, the danger of a possible
nuclear war in Korea has increased with the North Koreans' development
of nuclear weapons.[5]

Regarding Indochina, historians should admire the U.S. Congress,
Churchill, and Eden for urging restraint on Eisenhower. Instead, too
many historians mistakenly praise Eisenhower for restraining John Foster
Dulles. Churchill questioned Eisenhower's domino theory and doubted
the effectiveness of any Western military intervention in Southeast Asia.
Admiral Radford's Operation Vulture called for the use of three atomic
bombs to save Dien Bien Phu. Dulles offered the French president two
atomic bombs to save Dien Bien Phu. Eisenhower considered Indochina a
military problem requiring a military solution. Churchill, Eden, the British Foreign Office, and even the British military disputed the effectiveness
of any military solution in deciding the fate of Indochina. They preferred
peace negotiations in Geneva rather than a hopeless war in the jungles of
Vietnam.[6]

Nevertheless, Eisenhower continued to promote United Action, a proposed alliance for military intervention in Indochina. Churchill explicitly denounced this terrible idea to Eisenhower, Dulles, and Radford. The
British absolutely refused to fight in French Indochina. As a result, Eisenhower began making plans for a possible atomic attack on China as well
as the Soviet Union, while undermining British diplomatic efforts during the peace negotiations at Geneva. Churchill ordered Eden to override
all American diplomatic objections in order to obtain a peace agreement.

British foreign secretary Anthony Eden overcame American objections and successfully brokered a peace agreement in Geneva. Vietnam was divided into North Vietnam and South Vietnam.

The extreme ideological differences between the Americans and the British can be seen most easily in the Quemoy-Matsu Crisis of 1955. The British maintained that the coastal islands of Quemoy and Matsu belonged to the Chinese Communists. The Americans thought that the coastal islands belonged to the Chinese Nationalists on Formosa. Eisenhower threatened global nuclear war over two tiny islands located near China's mainland. For the British, the great question concerning Quemoy and Matsu was whether or not Eisenhower was bluffing in his plan for nuclear attacks on China.

In the crisis over Formosa, Eisenhower and Churchill engaged in a colossal battle over the importance of Quemoy and Matsu to world peace. Here again, Eisenhower publicly and dramatically threatened China with nuclear war. The British prudently counseled restraint and suggested that a negotiated deal could be made in which the islands would be given to the Communists in exchange for Communist promises not to invade Formosa. Eisenhower viewed this as appeasement. Churchill viewed Eisenhower's position as illegal and militarily untenable. Nevertheless, the Chinese Communists did buckle under American military pressure. Zhou Enlai, at the Bandung Conference, sought a peaceful resolution to the dispute.

Eisenhower did not limit his covert activities to Iran and Guatemala. He engaged in numerous covert activities throughout the 1950s. The perceived success of brinksmanship and Operation Everready, which threatened Syngman Rhee with a military coup in 1953, led to the CIA's Operation Ajax and the overthrow of Prime Minister Mohammad Mossadegh in Iran. Eisenhower and Churchill installed the shah of Iran as the new leader. In 1979, the shah was overthrown by the Ayatollah Khomeini in an Islamic revolution. The shah and SAVAK, Iran's secret police, have been tied to the American government since the Eisenhower administration. The takeover of the American embassy in Iran, with fifty-three Americans held hostage, can be seen as political blowback originating in the Eisenhower era.

Operation PBSUCCESS overthrew the democratically elected President Jacobo Arbenz of Guatemala and installed Colonel Castillo Armas as the leader of Guatemala in 1954. Eisenhower established a naval quarantine against Guatemala. This was an act of war against Guatemala. He then effectively forced the British to quash a UN investigation of the Guatemalan crisis in order to cover up his illegal activities. Eisenhower had acted both illegally and unilaterally in Guatemala while bristling over the superficial interference of the British at the United Nations. He took a completely unilateral approach to Guatemala by ignoring British interests in the Western Hemisphere. Eisenhower had antagonized the British Foreign Office with his naval blockade of Guatemala. Churchill acted alone, against the advice of Eden and the British Foreign Office, when he sided with Eisenhower and quashed a United Nations investigation of Guatemala.

Finally, the Suez Crisis in 1956 caused a complete breakdown in the transatlantic relationship between the United States and Great Britain. British prime minister Anthony Eden claimed that Nasser was a new Hitler and an agent of Soviet expansionism in the Middle East. Nasser represented an attack against not just Great Britain but the international community. Eisenhower, for his part, viewed Nasser as an Arab nationalist who strongly opposed British imperialism. Technically, Nasser had the legal right to nationalize the Suez Canal. Eisenhower chose to publicly support Arab nationalism over Anglo-French colonialism in North Africa and the Middle East. He supported slow evolutionary change in the region.

Nevertheless, Eisenhower approved and supported a covert joint MI6–CIA planned military coup in 1956 against the Syrian government called Operation Straggle. In addition, he secretly approved of Operation Omega, a British-American clandestine operation to undermine Nasser in Egypt in 1956. He wanted to eliminate these Soviet-backed governments surreptitiously. Yet, Eisenhower did not limit U.S. interventions to Soviet-backed governments. He directly intervened in western Europe as well.

In November 1956, using economic blackmail and political brinksmanship, Eisenhower forced the British cabinet to oust Prime Minister Anthony Eden. He manipulated Great Britain's currency by devaluing the sterling pound. Eisenhower made a secret deal with the Saudi king to eliminate Great Britain's oil supply from the Middle East. The British diplomatic corps and Anthony Eden became persona non grata. He then orchestrated Eden's removal by the British cabinet. American historians who claim that Eisenhower was the least interventionist of our modern presidents are dead wrong.

Several historians have claimed "the Eisenhower administration had grossly exaggerated the Soviet threat, misunderstood Arab nationalism, and stimulated Arab anti-Americanism." The historical evidence indicates a truth far more complicated. A Soviet threat did exist in places like Egypt and Syria. Moslem faith and culture, antidemocratic and authoritarian, had a far greater affinity with Communism than it did with Western values. Eisenhower ultimately decided that he needed to replace British colonial power with American influence to deal with the intractable political problems of the Middle East.[7]

On January 5, 1957, President Eisenhower delivered a historic address to a joint session of Congress on the importance of the Middle East to the United States. He unequivocally stated: "Our country supports without reservation the full sovereignty and independence of each and every nation of the Middle East." He put the United States on the side of those nations seeking independence from Anglo-French colonialism and those resisting Communist subversion. Eisenhower massively expanded the American commitment to the Middle East in order to counter the Soviet Union's attempt to cut off the region's oil supply to Europe, Africa, Asia, and the United States.[8]

As a result of the Suez Crisis, the United States took on the unprecedented responsibility of protecting virtually all of the sovereign nations of the Middle East. Previous American commitments in the Middle East included the Tripartite Agreement of May 25, 1950, and presidential assurances to Saudi Arabia on October 31, 1950. In his speech to the Congress, Eisenhower stated emphatically: "There is the presidential declaration of April 9, 1956, that the United States will within constitutional means oppose any aggression in the area. There is our declaration of November 29, 1956, that a threat to the territorial integrity of Iran, Iraq, Pakistan, or Turkey would be viewed by the United States with the utmost gravity." He had come to Congress to have them support and ratify his foreign policy strategy in the Middle East—the Eisenhower Doctrine. Eisenhower had massively expanded the role of the United States as the protector of the nations of the Middle East. He replaced British political influence with American political and military power.[9]

With the Eisenhower Doctrine for the Middle East in place, Eisenhower ordered U.S. Marines to invade Lebanon in 1958 in Operation Blue Bat. Twenty-five years later, in 1983, President Ronald Reagan sent the U.S. Marines into Lebanon only to have a suicide bomber kill 299 American and French servicemen in their barracks at the airport in Beirut. Reagan admitted that his decision to send the Marines into Lebanon was his biggest mistake as president. He completely withdrew them from that country in early 1984. Nevertheless, his military intervention stood as an unwelcome legacy from a previous Republican president.

In the last year of his presidency, Eisenhower authorized Operation Pluto, the CIA planning for the Bay of Pigs. Vice President Nixon "was a forceful advocate of bringing down Castro and urged the CIA to support 'goon squads and other direct action groups' operating inside and outside of Cuba." President Kennedy gave final authorization to Eisenhower's plan in April 1961, leading to the Bay of Pigs fiasco, which turned out to be the greatest foreign policy disaster of the Kennedy administration.[10]

Refusing to use the U.S. Air Force to back up the invasion of Cuba, Kennedy suffered the disgrace of the Bay of Pigs. As Nassir Ghaemi has written: "CIA and military leaders were appalled; they had expected him to take the next step when defeat was the only other option. Eisenhower would not have stopped, they told him. ('When you commit the flag, you commit to win,' Eisenhower had said during the 1954 overthrow of Guatemala's government.)" Kennedy decided to cut his losses at the Bay of Pigs. He also refused to send 150,000 U.S. combat troops to Laos in 1961 as Eisenhower had suggested.[11]

After the assassination of President Kennedy in 1963, Lyndon B. Johnson aggressively sought the advice of former president Eisenhower on the difficult question of whether or not he should increase the American troop presence in South Vietnam. Johnson fervently believed in Eisenhower's domino theory. Eisenhower enthusiastically and repeatedly endorsed Johnson's unilateral moves to escalate the number of U.S. troops during the Vietnam War. The governments of Britain and France, however, wisely followed the advice of Churchill and Eden and stayed out of the jungles of Vietnam.

On August 3, 1965, Eisenhower told General Andrew Goodpaster: "We should not base our actions on minimum needs, but should swamp the enemy with overwhelming force." In late 1967, Eisenhower spurned the "kooks and hippies and all the rest that are talking about surrender." By 1968, the United States had 550,000 men in Vietnam. President Richard M. Nixon, Eisenhower's former vice president, dragged out the Vietnam War for another four years, leaving a total of fifty-eight thousand American soldiers dead. In the end, the Communists won and seized Saigon, unifying the country under Communist rule.[12]

This study of Anglo-American relations and conservative ideology from 1953 to 1956 reveals and illuminates Eisenhower's foreign policy in the context of transatlantic relations with Winston Churchill and Anthony Eden. Eisenhower's prerogatives of zealous anti-Communism, dangerous brinksmanship, and colossal unilateralism outweighed his commitment to the Anglo-American alliance. While Eisenhower bragged about his risky brinksmanship, Churchill and Eden rightfully warned of the dangers and the possible consequences of unilateral policies and a Fortress America completely removed from its allies. In his Farewell Address, Eisenhower presciently warned his successors about the risk of the development of unwarranted power by the military-industrial complex. After all, he knew better than anyone the hazards and perils involved with covert military operations.

Ultimately, Eisenhower's foreign policy moved from one of accommodation and cooperation with the British to one intrinsically hostile to the British Empire. The Eisenhower administration's anti-Communist ideology set aside Truman's balance-of-power diplomacy in favor of a policy of rolling back Communism, while severely undermining British national security and economic interests in both the Middle East and the Far East. Eisenhower engaged in a new confrontational "brinksmanship" opposed to long-term British diplomacy and interests. Eisenhower's unilateral use of American power against perceived Communist threats and his new anti-colonial policies in the Third World had put him on an inevitable collision course with Churchill and Eden.

NOTES

CHAPTER ONE

1. John Lukacs, "Ike, Winston, and the Russians," *New York Times*, February 10, 1991, www.nytimes.com/1991/02/10/books/ike-winston-and-the-russians.html?pagewanted =all&src=pm.

2. George F. Kennan, *Realities of American Foreign Policy* (Princeton, N.J.: Princeton University Press, 1954), 76–90; John Lewis Gaddis, *Strategies of Containment: A Critical Appraisal of American National Security Policy during the Cold War* (New York: Oxford University Press, 2005), 142.

3. Dwight D. Eisenhower, *Mandate for Change, 1953–1956*, vol. 1 of *The White House Years* (Garden City, N.Y.: Doubleday, 1963); David G. McCullough, *Truman* (New York: Simon and Schuster, 1992); Fred I. Greenstein, "Eisenhower as an Activist President: A Look at New Evidence," *Political Science Quarterly* 94, no. 4 (Winter 1979–80): 94.

4. Edward Friedman, "Nuclear Blackmail and the End of the Korean War," *Modern China* 1, no. 1 (January 1975): 75–91.

5. Robert A. Taft, *A Foreign Policy for Americans* (Garden City, N.Y.: Doubleday, 1951), 78–81; H. W. Brands, "The Age of Vulnerability: Eisenhower and the National Insecurity State," *American Historical Review* 94, no. 4 (October 1989): 963–89. Brands argues, mistakenly, that Eisenhower created the very military-industrial complex that he deplored. The military-industrial complex really began with Kennedy's massive increase in nuclear weapons related to the missile gap. It continued with Lyndon Johnson's expansion of the Vietnam War.

6. Herbert Hoover, *Addresses upon the American Road, 1950–1955* (Stanford, Calif.: Stanford University Press, 1955).

7. John Foster Dulles, "A Policy of Boldness," *Life*, May 19, 1952; H. W. Brands Jr., "Testing Massive Retaliation: Credibility and Crisis Management in the Taiwan Strait," *International Security* 12 (Spring 1988): 124–51.

8. Robert A. Divine, *Eisenhower and the Cold War* (New York: Oxford University Press, 1981), 154.

9. H. W. Brands, "The Cairo-Tehran Connection in Anglo-American Rivalry in the Middle East, 1951–1953," *International History Review* 11, no. 3 (August, 1989): 434–56; Mary Ann

Heiss, "The United States, Great Britain, and the Creation of the Iranian Oil Consortium, 1953–1954," *International History Review* 16, no. 3 (August 1994): 511–35.

10. John Charmley, *Churchill's Grand Alliance: The Anglo-American Special Relationship, 1940–57* (New York: Harcourt Brace, 1995); Karl Larres, *Churchill's Cold War: The Politics of Personal Diplomacy* (New Haven, Conn.: Yale University Press, 2002).

11. Alan P. Dobson, *The Politics of the Anglo-American Economic Relationship, 1940–1987* (Brighton, Sussex, England: Wheatsheaf, 1988); Robin Edmonds, *Setting the Mould: The United States and Britain, 1945–1950* (New York: Norton, 1986).

12. Helen Leigh-Phippard, *Congress and US Military Aid to Britain: Interdependence and Dependence, 1949–56* (New York: St. Martin Press in association with the Mountbatten Centre for International Studies, University of Southampton, 1995); R. B. Manderson-Jones, *The Special Relationship: Anglo-American Relations and Western European Unity 1947–56* (London: London School of Economics and Political Science, 1972); Fraser J. Harbutt, *The Iron Curtain: Churchill, America, and the Origins of the Cold War* (New York: Oxford University Press, 1986); Timothy J. Botti, *The Long Wait: The Forging of the Anglo-American Nuclear Alliance, 1945–1958* (New York: Greenwood, 1987).

13. Chi-Kwan Mark, *Hong Kong and the Cold War: Anglo-American Relations 1949–1957* (Oxford: Clarendon, 2004), 22–23; Chi-Kwan Mark, "A Reward for Good Behaviour in the Cold War: Bargaining over the Defense of Hong Kong, 1949–1957," *International History Review* 22, no. 4 (December 2000): 837–61; Victor S. Kaufman, "'Chirep': The Anglo-American Dispute over Chinese Representation in the United Nations, 1950–71," *English Historical Review* 115, no. 461 (April 2000): 354–77; Kevin Ruane, "Refusing to Pay the Price: British Foreign Policy and the Pursuit of Victory in Vietnam, 1952–4," *English Historical Review* 110, no. 435 (February 1995): 70–92.

14. David Dutton, *Anthony Eden: A Life and Reputation* (New York: St. Martin's, 1997), 2.

15. Ibid., 334.

16. Ayesha Jalal, "Towards the Baghdad Pact: South Asia and Middle East Defence in the Cold War, 1947–1955," *International History Review* 11, no. 3 (August 1989): 409–33; David R. Devereux, "Britain, the Commonwealth and the Defence of the Middle East 1948–56," in "Studies on War," special issue, *Journal of Contemporary History* 24, no. 2 (April 1989): 327–45.

17. Dobson, *Politics of the Anglo-American Economic Relationship*, 118; Howard J. Dooley, "Great Britain's 'Last Battle' in the Middle East: Notes on Cabinet Planning during the Suez Crisis of 1956," *International History Review* 11, no. 3 (1989): 486–517.

18. Dianne B. Kunz, *The Economic Diplomacy of the Suez Crisis* (Chapel Hill: University of North Carolina, 1991); David A. Nichols, *Eisenhower 1956: The President's Year of Crisis: Suez and the Brink of War* (New York: Simon and Schuster, 2011); Christopher Grayling and Christopher Langdon, *Just Another Star? Anglo-American Relations since 1945* (London: Harrap, 1988), 11.

19. Robert J. McMahon, "The Illusion of Vulnerability: American Reassessments of the Soviet Threat, 1955–1956," *International History of Review* 18, no. 3 (August 1996), 591–619; U.S. Embassy Moscow to Secretary of State John Foster Dulles, telegram, November 18, 1956, Dulles, Foster, Nov. 56 (1), Box 8, Dulles-Herter Series, Ann Whitman File, Papers of Dwight D. Eisenhower, 1953–61, Dwight D. Eisenhower Presidential Library.

CHAPTER TWO

1. Ira Chernus, *Apocalypse Management: Eisenhower and the Discourse of National Insecurity* (Stanford, Calif.: Stanford University Press, 2008); Ira Chernus, *General Eisenhower: Ideology and Discourse* (East Lansing: Michigan State University Press, 2002); Ira Chernus, *Eisenhower's Atoms for Peace* (College Station: Texas A&M University Press, 2002); Martin J Medhurst, ed., *Eisenhower's War of Words: Rhetoric and Leadership* (East Lansing: Michigan State University Press, 1994); Chris Tudda, *The Truth Is Our Weapon: The Rhetorical Diplomacy of Dwight D. Eisenhower and John Foster Dulles* (Baton Rouge: Louisiana State University Press, 2006).

2. Stephen E. Ambrose, *The President, 1952–1969,* vol. 2 of *Eisenhower* (New York: Simon and Schuster, 1984), 160.

3. Dwight D. Eisenhower, Inaugural Address, January 20, 1953, *Public Papers of the Presidents of the United States: Dwight D. Eisenhower, 1953* (Washington, D.C.: U.S. Government. Printing Office, 1960), 1–8; Dwight D. Eisenhower, "World Freedom and Peace: The Responsibilities of Leadership," *Vital Speeches* 19, no. 8 (1 February 1953): 252–54.

4. John Foster Dulles, "Enlightened Self-Interest: Encirclement a Deadly Threat to United States," *Vital Speeches* 19, no. 9 (February 15, 1953): 265.

5. Dwight D. Eisenhower, *The Eisenhower Diaries,* ed. Robert H. Ferrell (New York: Norton, 1981), 232.

6. Meeting with President of the United States, March 6, 1953, Anthony Eden, Roger Makins, Dwight D. Eisenhower, John Foster Dulles, Bedell Smith, Winthrop Aldrich, FO 800/839, United States of America, March–April 1953, Private Papers of Sir Anthony Eden, Avon Papers, University of Birmingham Special Collections, Birmingham, England; Sir Douglas Veale, University Registry, Oxford, to Mr. Randolph S. Churchill, July 4, 1957, RDCH 3/2/1, Randolph S. Churchill Papers, Churchill Archives Centre, Churchill College, University of Cambridge: "Sir Anthony Eden took First Class Honours in the School of Oriental Studies, his two languages being Persian and Arabic. He took the Final Honour School in Trinity Term 1922."

7. Winston Churchill to Dwight D. Eisenhower, April 11, 1953, FO 800/839, United States of America, March–April 1953, Avon Papers.

8. Roscoe Drummond and Gaston Coblentz, *Duel at the Brink: John Foster Dulles' Command of American Power* (Garden City, N.Y.: Doubleday, 1960), 163.

9. Townsend Hoopes, *The Devil and John Foster Dulles* (Boston: Little, Brown, 1973).

10. Dwight D. Eisenhower, Address, "The Chance for Peace," Delivered before the American Society of Newspaper Editors, April 16, 1953, *Public Papers of the Presidents of the United States: Dwight D. Eisenhower, 1953,* 179–88; Dwight D. Eisenhower, Address, "Chance for Peace," April 16, 1953, Box 69, Duplicate Correspondence, John Foster Dulles Papers, Seeley G. Mudd Manuscript Library, Princeton University; Dwight D. Eisenhower, "Peace in the World: Acts, Not Rhetoric, Needed," *Vital Speeches* 19, no. 14 (May 1, 1953): 419; Bill Buzenberg, "A Half Century Later, Another Warning in Eisenhower's Address Rings True," Center for Public Integrity, January 17, 2011; Susan Eisenhower, "50 Years Later, We're Still Ignoring Ike's Warning, *Washington Post,* January 16, 2011, B3; Walter LaFeber, *America, Russia, and the Cold War, 1945–2000* (Boston: McGraw Hill, 2002), 194–97; and for a detailed history of

the origin of Eisenhower's speech, see Paper Prepared by Walt Whitman Rostow, Massachusetts Institute of Technology, Cambridge, May 11, 1953, *Foreign Relations of the United States* [hereafter cited as *FRUS*], *1952–1954,* vol. 8, *Eastern Europe, Soviet Union, Eastern Mediterranean,* 1173–83.

11. Eisenhower, "Peace in the World: Acts, Not Rhetoric, Needed," 419; Prime Minister Churchill to President Eisenhower, London, April 22, 1953, *FRUS, 1952–1954,* vol. 6, *Western Europe and Canada,* 975; President Eisenhower to Prime Minister Churchill, April 25, 1953, *FRUS, 1952–1954,* vol. 8, *Eastern Europe, Soviet Union, Eastern Mediterranean,* 1167: "Your comments about the reception of my speech were most welcome and I warmly appreciate the support contained in your statement in the House of Commons and Mr. Morrison's reply."

12. William Strang to Winston Churchill, April 25, 1953, FO 800/839, United States of America, March–April 1953, Avon Papers.

13. Larres, *Churchill's Cold War,* 213–14: "Churchill was not averse to considering a 'solitary pilgrimage' to Moscow to persuade Malenkov and Molotov of his peaceful intentions and the necessity of conversation at the highest levels." Martin, *Churchill: A Life* (New York: Holt, 1991), 915; Memorandum by the Acting Secretary of State for Foreign Affairs, Foreign Ministers' Meeting in Washington: Policy towards the Soviet Union and Germany, July 3, 1953, CAB/129/61, National Archives, Kew, London, United Kingdom; Colville, *The Fringes of Power,* 673.

14. John Foster Dulles, "Creating a Strong and Peaceful Europe: European Army Only 'Good Solution,'" *Vital Speeches* 19, no. 15 (May 15, 1953): 456; Gaddis, *Strategies of Containment;* Marc Trachtenberg, *A Constructed Peace: The Making of the European Settlement, 1945– 1963* (Princeton, N.J.: Princeton University Press, 1999).

15. Winston Churchill to Dwight D. Eisenhower, May 7, 1953, The President-Churchill, Jan. 20, 1953–May 28, 1953 (1), Box 18, International Series, Ann Whitman File, Papers of Dwight D. Eisenhower, 1953–61.

16. Statement by John Foster Dulles at Waldorf Astoria, May 7, 1953, Eisenhower, Dwight D. 1953, Box 69, Duplicate Correspondence, John Foster Dulles Papers, Seeley G. Mudd Library, Princeton University.

17. Richard Goold-Adams, *John Foster Dulles: A Reappraisal* (Westport, Conn.: Greenwood, 1962), 3.

18. Winston Churchill, *Hansard, House of Commons Debates,* vol. 515, May 11, 1953, 83–1004; Winston Churchill, "Survey of the World Scene: Change of Attitude and Mood in the Kremlin," *Vital Speeches* 19, no. 17 (June 15, 1953): 522–26.

19. Anthony Eden, *Full Circle: The Memoirs of Anthony Eden* (Boston: Houghton Mifflin, 1960), 55–56.

20. Robert A. Taft, "United States Foreign Policy: Forget United Nations in Korea and Far East," *Vital Speeches* 19, no. 17 (June 15, 1953): 530; Martin Gilbert, *Never Despair: Winston S. Churchill, 1945–1965* (Boston: Houghton Mifflin, 1988), 974.

21. Taft, "United States Foreign Policy," 531.

22. Churchill to Eisenhower, May 29, 1953, in *The Churchill-Eisenhower Correspondence, 1953–55,* ed. Peter Boyle (Chapel Hill: University of North Carolina Press, 1990), 64; Dwight D.

Eisenhower, The President's News Conference of May 28, 1953, *Public Papers of the Presidents of the United States: Dwight D. Eisenhower, 1953*, 328–29.

23. Memorandum to the President, June 5, 1953, John Foster Dulles to Dwight D. Eisenhower, Dulles, John F., June 1953, Box 1, Dulles-Herter Series, Ann Whitman File, Papers of Dwight D. Eisenhower, 1953–61.

24. Memorandum to the President, June 5, 1953, John Foster Dulles to Dwight D. Eisenhower, Dulles, John F., June 1953, Box 1, Dulles-Herter Series, Ann Whitman File, Papers of Dwight D. Eisenhower, 1953–61.

25. Winston Churchill to Dwight D. Eisenhower, June 19, 1953, FO 800/840, United States of America, May–December 1953, Avon Papers.

26. Tore T. Petersen, *The Middle East between the Great Powers: Anglo-American Conflict and Cooperation, 1952–7* (New York: St. Martin's, 2000), 3; Tore T. Petersen, "Anglo-American Rivalry in the Middle East: The Struggle for the Buraimi Oasis," *International History Review* 14, no. 1 (February 1992): 71–91.

27. Memorandum to the President, July 23, 1953, John Foster Dulles to Dwight D. Eisenhower, Dulles, John F., July 1953, Box 1, Dulles-Herter Series, Ann Whitman File, Papers of Dwight D. Eisenhower, 1953–61.

28. Gilbert, *Churchill: A Life*, 915; William Manchester and Paul Reid, *The Last Lion: Winston Spencer Churchill; Defender of the Realm, 1940–1965* (New York: Little, Brown, 2012), 1024; President Eisenhower to Prime Minister Churchill, Washington, July 20, 1953, *FRUS, 1952–1954*, vol. 6, *Western Europe and Canada*, 996: "Your own country, and indeed the world, can hardly spare you even in semi-retirement. Therefore, I am delighted that you expect to emerge in full vigor by September."

29. Eisenhower-Churchill Meeting, Mid Ocean Club, Bermuda, December 4, 1953, Memorandum of Conversation by the Secretary of State, Bermuda, December 4, 1953, *FRUS, 1952–1954*, vol. 5, *Western European Security*, 1739–40; Memorandum of Conversation between President Eisenhower and Prime Minister Churchill on December 4, 1953, Bermuda, State Department Report–Top Secret (1), Box 1, International Meeting Series, Ann Whitman File, Papers of Dwight D. Eisenhower, 1953–61; Gilbert, *Never Despair*, 918; Diary, December 4, 1953, EM, AWF, DDE Diaries Series, *The Presidency: The Middle Way*, vol. 15 of *The Papers of Dwight David Eisenhower*, ed. Alfred D. Chandler, Louis Galambos, and Duan Van Ee (Baltimore: John Hopkins Press, 1970), 728: "I informed him of our intention to strike every military target in the region, but to avoid useless attacks upon civilian centers. I also informed him that we intended to use every weapon in the bag, including our atomic types."

30. Memorandum of Conversation between President Eisenhower, Prime Minister Churchill, Admiral Strauss, and Lord Cherwell on December 4, 1953, Bermuda, State Department Report–Top Secret (1), Box 1, International Meeting Series, Ann Whitman File, Papers of Dwight D. Eisenhower, 1953–61.

31. Gilbert, *Never Despair*, 923.

32. Ibid.; Heads of Government Meeting, Mid Ocean Club, December 4, 1953, Bermuda-Hagerty Notes (1), Box 1, International Meetings Series, Ann Whitman File, Papers of Dwight D. Eisenhower, 1953–61; First Plenary Tripartite Meeting of the Heads of Govern-

ment, Mid Ocean Club, Bermuda, December 4, 1954, *FRUS, 1952–1954*, vol. 5, *Western European Security*, 1754–61.

33. Eisenhower-Churchill Meeting, Eisenhower Quarters, Mid Ocean Club, Bermuda, December 5, 1953, Notes prepared by Admiral Strauss, Bermuda, December 5, 1953, *FRUS, 1952–1954*, vol. 5, *Western European Security*, 1767–69; Michael Gordon Jackson, "Beyond Brinkmanship: Eisenhower, Nuclear War Fighting, and Korea, 1953–1968," *Presidential Studies Quarterly* 35, no. 1 (March 2005): 52–75, doi:10.1111/j.1741–5705.2004.00235: "British Foreign Minister Anthony Eden, according to his secretary Evelyn Shuckburgh, describes one of his discussions with the president about their use in Korea: 'Ike said the American public no longer distinguished between atomic and other weapons. . . . [N]or is there logically any distinction, he (Eisenhower) says. Why should they confine themselves to high explosives requiring thousands of aircraft in attacking China's bases when they can do it more cheaply and easily with atoms? The development of smaller atomic weapons and the use of atomic artillery make the distinction impossible to sustain.'" Gilbert, *Never Despair*, 936; Diary, December 6, 1953, EM, AWF, DDE Diaries Series, *The Presidency: The Middle Way*, vol. 15 of *The Papers of Dwight David Eisenhower*, 733; Diary, December 10, 1953, ibid., 743–44.

34. Gilbert, *Never Despair*, 936.

35. Dwight D. Eisenhower, Address before the General Assembly of the United Nations on Peaceful Uses of Atomic Energy, New York City, December 8, 1953, *Public Papers of the Presidents of the United States: Dwight D. Eisenhower, 1953*, 813–22; Atomic Power for Peace, An Address by President Eisenhower, December 8, 1953, Box 69, Duplicate Correspondence, John Foster Dulles Papers, Seeley G. Mudd Manuscript Library, Princeton University; Dwight D. Eisenhower, "An Atomic Stockpile for Peace: Dedicated to Serve the Needs Rather Than the Fears of Mankind," *Vital Speeches* 20, no. 6 (January 1, 1954): 163–65. For a chronology of the events leading to the "Atoms for Peace" speech, see Chronology of the "Atoms for Peace" speech, *FRUS, 1952–1954*, vol. 2, *National Security Affairs*, pt. 2, 1526–27.

36. Statement by the Secretary of State to the North Atlantic Council, December 14, 1953, *FRUS, 1952–1954*, vol. 5, *Western European Security*, 461–68; John Foster Dulles, "Unity Must Be Achieved Soon: It May Never Be Possible for Integration to Occur in Freedom," *Vital Speeches* 20, no. 6 (January 1, 1954): 165–66; Brian R. Duchin, "The 'Agonizing Reappraisal': Eisenhower, Dulles, and the European Defense Community." *Diplomatic History* 16, no. 2 (April, 1992): 201–22.

37. Winston Churchill to Dwight D. Eisenhower, December 22, 1953, FO 800/840, United States of America, May–December 1953, Avon Papers.

38. "Nixon's Secret Report Warns: Don't Recognize Red Chinese," *Newsweek*, January 4, 1954, 17.

39. Dwight D. Eisenhower, Annual Message to the Congress on the State of the Union, January 7, 1954, *Public Papers of the Presidents of the United States: Dwight D. Eisenhower, 1954* (Washington, D.C.: U.S. Government Printing Office, 1960), 6–23; Dwight D. Eisenhower, "The State of the Union: Building a Stronger America," *Vital Speeches* 20, no. 8 (February 1, 1954): 226.

40. The Secretary of State to the Department of State, Berlin, February 18, 1954, *FRUS, 1952–1954*, vol. 13, *Indochina*, 1057: "I have emphasized to Bidault that prospect of conference

on Indochina will increase Communist effort for knock out this season and must be met with corresponding determination to win good negotiating position."

41. John Foster Dulles, "The Ultimate Weapon Is Moral Principle: Conference Gave Post-Stalin Knowledge of Soviet Intentions," *Vital Speeches* 20, no. 11 (March 15, 1954): 325.

42. Roger Makins to John Colville, Private Secretary of Winston Churchill, March 13, 1954, FO 800/841, United States of America, January–May 1954, Avon Papers.

43. Dwight D. Eisenhower, Radio and Television Address to the American People on the Tax Program, March 15, 1954, *Public Papers of the Presidents of the United States: Dwight D. Eisenhower, 1954*, 313–18; Dwight D. Eisenhower, "The New Tax Program: Economic Conditions Do Not Warrant Additional Tax Reductions," *Vital Speeches* 20, no. 12 (April 1, 1954): 365.

44. Memorandum of Telephone Conversation between the Secretary of State and the Chairman of the Joint Chiefs of Staff (Radford), Washington, March 24, 1954, *FRUS, 1952–1954*, vol. 13, *Indochina*, 1151; The Secretary of State to the Embassy in the United Kingdom, April 1, 1954, ibid., 1203; Editorial Note, ibid., 1181; Nixon, *R. N.: The Memoirs of Richard Nixon* (New York: Grosset and Dunlap, 1978), 151; Statement from John Foster Dulles, Secretary of State, before the House Foreign Affairs Committee, April 5, 1954, Re: "Deterrent Strategy," Box 80, Duplicate Correspondence, John Foster Dulles Papers, Seeley G. Mudd Manuscript Library, Princeton University.

CHAPTER THREE

1. John F. Kennedy, "The War in Indochina: The Wholehearted Support of the Peoples of the Associated States Is Necessary for Victory," *Vital Speeches* 20, no. 14 (May 1, 1954): 418–19; David L. Anderson, *Trapped by Success: The Eisenhower Administration and Vietnam, 1953–1961* (New York: Columbia University Press, 1991); Editorial Note, *FRUS, 1952–1954*, vol. 13, *Indochina*, pt. 1, 1266: "On April 6, 1954, the question of Indochina was the subject of debate in the United States Senate. Senator John F. Kennedy delivered an address in which he stressed that a satisfactory outcome could not be achieved unless France accorded the Associated States true independence."

2. John Foster Dulles to Walter B. Smith and Dwight D. Eisenhower, telegram, April 13, 1954, Dulles–April 1954 (2), Box 2, Dulles-Herter Series, Ann Whitman File, Papers of Dwight D. Eisenhower, 1953–61.

3. Dwight D. Eisenhower to John Foster Dulles, April 23, 1954, Dulles–April 1954 (2), Box 2, Dulles-Herter Series, Ann Whitman File, Papers of Dwight D. Eisenhower, 1953–61; see Memorandum of Discussion at the 194th Meeting of the National Security Council, Thursday, April 29, 1954, *FRUS, 1952–1954*, vol. 13, *Indochina*, 1437: "Admiral Radford said he gathered the distinct impression that Sir Winston was presently unprepared to participate in collective action on any matter involving commitments of British resources or incurring any risks unless some British territory is under imminent threat."

4. John Foster Dulles to Walter B. Smith, telegram, April 26, 1954, Dulles–April 1954 (1), Box 2, Dulles-Herter Series, Ann Whitman File, Papers of Dwight D. Eisenhower, 1953–61.

5. Eisenhower, *Mandate for Change, 1953–1956*, 351–52; Radio and Television Address to the Nation by the Secretary of State Delivered in Washington, May 7, 1954, *FRUS, 1952–1954*, vol. 16, *The Geneva Conference*, 720–26; Editorial Note, ibid., 834–35. Churchill to the House of Commons on May 17, 1954: "But our immediate task is to do everything we can to reach an agreed settlement at Geneva for the restoration of peace in Indochina."

6. Ambrose, *The President, 1952–1969*, 205: "Bobby Cutler reported to the President that the NSC also believed that 'there was little use for discussing any defense of Southeast Asia; that U.S. power should be directed against the source of the peril, which was, at least in the first instance, China, and that in this connection atomic weapons should be used." Eden, *Full Circle*, 115.

7. Eden, *Full Circle*, 115.

8. Ibid., 117–19; Memorandum of Conversation by the Assistant Secretary of State for Far Eastern Affairs (Robertson) with the Rt. Hon. R.G. Casey, Australian Minister for External Affairs, John Foster Dulles, Secretary of State, and Walter S. Robertson, Assistant Secretary of State, Geneva, April 25, 1954, *FRUS, 1952–1954*, vol. 16, *The Geneva Conference*, 558: "The Secretary stated that President Eisenhower had asked Admiral Radford to ask the British why they were willing to wait until one of their greatest assets, some 300,000 Vietnamese troops, had been destroyed before deciding to take collective action. Casey replied that it was the British fear that British and American intervention in Indo-China at this time would bring in the Communist Chinese and get us all embroiled in a war with Red China."

9. Anthony Eden to Winston Churchill, April 28, 1954, FO 800/841, United States of America, January–May 1954, Avon Papers; Gilbert, *Never Despair*, 973–74: "I don't see why we should fight for France in Indochina when we have given away India."

10. Dwight D. Eisenhower to Winston Churchill, April 28, 1954, FO 800/841, United States of America, January–May 1954, Avon Papers.

11. John Foster Dulles, Memorandum of Conversation with Anthony Eden, April 30, 1954, Dulles–April 1954 (1), Box 2, Dulles-Herter Series, Ann Whitman File, Papers of Dwight D. Eisenhower, 1953–61; Memorandum of a Conference at the White House, Wednesday, May 5, 1954, *FRUS, 1952–1954*, vol. 13, *Indochina*, 1466–70.

12. Winston Churchill to Anthony Eden, May 5, 1954, FO 800/841, United States of America, January–May 1954, Avon Papers; President Eisenhower News Conference, May 12, 1954, *FRUS, 1952–1954*, vol. 13, *Indochina*, 1543: "I don't think the free world ought to write off Indochina."

13. D. R. Thorpe, *Eden: The Life and Times of Anthony Eden: First Earl of Avon 1897–1977* (London: Chatto and Windus, 2003), 393; Winston Churchill to Anthony Eden, May 18, 1954, FO 800/841, United States of America, January–May 1954, Avon Papers.

14. Roger Makins to Anthony Eden, May 29, 1954, FO 800/841, United States of America, January–May 1954, Avon Papers.

15. Anthony Eden to Winston Churchill, June 1, 1954, FO 800/842, United States of America, June 1954, Avon Papers. At 11:45 a.m., June 2, 1954, President Eisenhower met at the White House with the following individuals: John Foster Dulles, Robert B. Anderson, Admiral Arthur W. Radford, Douglas MacArthur II, and Robert Cutler. Cutler's summary of the meeting: "In the event of overt, unprovoked Chinese Communist aggression in Southeast

Asia which would be a direct threat to the security of the United States and to other nations having security interests in the region, Congress would be asked immediately to declare that a state of war existed with Communist China, and the U.S. should then launch large-scale air and naval attacks on ports, airfields, and other military targets in mainland China, using as appropriate 'new weapons,' in the expectation that some of such other nations would join in opposing such aggression" (*FRUS, 1952–1954*, vol. 13, *Indochina*, 1658).

16. Eisenhower, *Mandate for Change, 1953–1956*, 349; Eden, *Full Circle*, 127.

17. Eden, *Full Circle*, 142.

18. Ibid., 144.

19. Roger Makins to Anthony Eden, June 18, 1954, FO 800/842, United States of America, June 1954, Avon Papers.

20. Ibid.

21. Roger Makins to Anthony Eden, June 21, 1954, FO 800/842, United States of America, June 1954, Avon Papers.

22. Gilbert, *Never Despair*, 1016.

23. Memorandum of Breakfast Conversation with Former President Hoover, John Foster Dulles and Herbert Hoover, June 29, 1954, Dulles, John 1954 (1), Box 3, Dulles-Herter Series, Ann Whitman File, Papers of Dwight D. Eisenhower, 1953–61.

24. Dwight D. Eisenhower to Winston Spencer Churchill, July 7, 1954, EM, AWF, International Series: Churchill, *The Presidency: The Middle Way*, vol. 15 of *The Papers of Dwight David Eisenhower*, 1165.

25. Joseph W. Martin Jr., "Liberty, Intelligence, Our Nation's Safety: 'Coexistence' with Communism Impossible," *Vital Speeches* 20, no. 20 (August 1, 1954): 613–14; James J. Kenneally, *A Compassionate Conservative: A Political Biography of Joseph W. Martin Jr., Speaker of the U.S. House of Representatives* (Lanham, Md.: Lexington, 2003), 214.

26. Sir Winston Churchill, Anglo-American Talks, *Hansard, House of Commons Debate*, vol. 530, July 12, 1954, 34–49; Winston Churchill, "British Foreign Policy: Statement on Washington Talks," *Vital Speeches* 20, no. 20 (August 1, 1954): 613.

27. State Department Memorandum on John Foster Dulles News Conference on Geneva Negotiations, July 23, 1954, Eden, Anthony 1954, Box 80, Duplicate Correspondence, John Foster Dulles Papers, Seeley G. Mudd Manuscript Library, Princeton University.

28. Matthew B. Ridgway, "The Statesman and the Soldier: Foreign Policy Has a Military Aspect as Well as Peaceful Aspect," *Vital Speeches* 20, no. 22 (September 1, 1954): 674–75. See also Memorandum by the Chief of Staff, United States Army (Ridgway) to the Joint Chiefs of Staff, April 6, 1954, *FRUS 1952–1954*, vol. 13, *Indochina*, pt. 1, 1270: "Such use of United States armed forces, apart from any local successes that they might achieve, would constitute a dangerous strategic diversion of limited United States military capabilities, and would commit our armed forces in a non-decisive theatre to the attainment of non-decisive local ȯbjectives."

29. Jean Edward Smith, *Eisenhower: In War and Peace* (New York: Random House, 2012), 645; Robert T. Oliver, "American Foreign Policy in a World Adrift: We Must Assert Leadership Not Partnership," *Vital Speeches* 21, no. 1 (October 15, 1954): 778.

30. Anthony Eden, "Principles of British Foreign Policy: To Preserve Our Way of Life and to Live in Peace," *Vital Speeches* 21, no. 3 (November 15, 1954): 836.

31. Winston Churchill, "Peace through Strength: The London Agreement," *Vital Speeches* 21, no. 3 (November 15, 1954): 837; Prime Minister Churchill to President Eisenhower, London, December 7, 1954, *FRUS, 1952–1954,* vol. 6, *Western Europe and Canada,* 1056: "When I was young I used to hear much talk about 'the Yellow Peril.'. . . It is Soviet Russia that ought to dominate our minds."

32. Dwight D. Eisenhower, Annual Message to the Congress on the State of the Union, January 6, 1955, *Public Papers of the Presidents of the United States: Dwight D. Eisenhower, 1955* (Washington, D.C.: U.S. Government Printing Office, 1959), 7–30; Dwight D. Eisenhower, "The State of the Union: Three Main Purposes of Our Federal Government," *Vital Speeches* 21, no. 7 (January 15, 1955): 962.

33. John Foster Dulles, "The Peace We Seek: The Desperate Struggle against the War System," *Vital Speeches* 21, no. 8 (February 1, 1955): 1001; Memorandum of Conversation with John Foster Dulles, Roger Makins, Robert Scott, Mr. Robertson, and Mr. Merchant, January 20, 1955, *FRUS, 1955–1957,* vol. 2, *China,* 86–89.

34. Text of Douglas MacArthur's Address at a civic banquet sponsored by the Los Angeles County Council of the American Legion on the dedication of a monument to General MacArthur in MacArthur Park on January 26, 1955, *New York Times,* January 27, 1955, 8; Douglas MacArthur, "The Abolition of War: Triumph of Scientific Annihilation," *Vital Speeches* 21, no. 9 (February 15, 1955): 1043.

35. Address by the Honorable John Foster Dulles, Secretary of State, before the Foreign Policy Association, Waldorf-Astoria Hotel, New York City, Wednesday, February 16, 1955, Box 95, Duplicate Correspondence, John Foster Dulles Papers, Seeley G. Mudd Manuscript Library, Princeton University; John Foster Dulles, "Human Equality versus Class Rule: The Struggle for Power by Communist Party," *Vital Speeches* 21, no. 10 (March 1, 1955): 1063; see Memorandum from the Policy Planning Staff (Bowie) to the Secretary of State, Washington, February 7, 1955, *FRUS, 1955–1957,* vol. 2, *China,* 238: "A war arising over Quemoy would alienate our Allies in Europe and much of Asia. The lack of Allied support would handicap our conduct of even a limited war and might seriously impair our capabilities if hostilities spread."

36. Roger Makins, "The Balance of Power: Anglo-American Unity Vitally Necessary to World Peace," *Vital Speeches* 21, no. 12 (April 1, 1955): 1131.

37. Ibid., 1133–34; Secretary of State to the Department of State, Bangkok, telegram, February 25, 1955, *FRUS, 1955–1957,* vol. 2, *China,* 312.

38. Sir Winston Churchill, Defence, *Hansard, House of Commons Debate,* vol. 537, March 1, 1955, 1893–2012; Winston Churchill, "Defense through Deterrents: Free World Should Retain Superiority in Nuclear Weapons," *Vital Speeches* 21, no. 11 (March 15, 1955): 1090–94.

39. Address by the Honorable John Foster Dulles, Secretary of State, Report from Asia, March 8, 1955, Box 95, Duplicate Correspondence, John Foster Dulles Papers, Seeley G. Mudd Manuscript Library, Princeton University; John Foster Dulles, "Report from Asia: We Will Meet Force with Greater Force," *Vital Speeches* 21, no. 12 (April 1 1955): 1124.

40. Anthony Eden, Middle East, Southeast Asia and Formosa Straits, *Hansard, House of Commons Debate,* vol. 538, March 8, 1955, 157–66; Memorandum of Conversation with Sec-

retary of State, Ambassador Roger Makins, Mr. Robertson, and Mr. Merchant, March 9, 1955, *FRUS, 1955–1957,* vol. 2, *China,* 344; Eisenhower, *Mandate for Change, 1953–1956,* 475.

41. Address by the Honorable John Foster Dulles, Secretary of State, Report from Asia, March 8, 1955, Box 95, Duplicate Correspondence, John Foster Dulles Papers, Seeley G. Mudd Manuscript Library, Princeton University; J. Dulles, "Report from Asia," 1124; Memorandum of Discussion at the 240th Meeting of the National Security Council, Washington, March 10, 1955, *FRUS 1955–1957,* vol. 2, *China,* 345–50.

42. Press Conference of President Dwight D. Eisenhower, March 16, 1955, Box 91, Duplicate Correspondence, John Foster Dulles Papers, Seeley G. Mudd Manuscript Library, Princeton University; Eisenhower, *Mandate for Change, 1953–1956,* 479.

43. Adlai Stevenson, "China Policy: Condemns Force in Formosa Strait," *Vital Speeches* 21, no.14 (May 1, 1955): 1189.

44. Dwight D. Eisenhower, Address at the Annual Luncheon of the Associated Press, New York City, April 25, 1953, *Public Papers of the Presidents of the United States: Dwight D. Eisenhower, 1953,* 416–23; Dwight D. Eisenhower, "The Search for Peace: International Trade A Step on the Road to Universal Peace," *Vital Speeches* 21, no. 15 (May 15, 1955): 1219.

45. Dwight D. Eisenhower, Address at the Annual Luncheon of the Associated Press, New York City, April 25, 1953, *Public Papers of the Presidents of the United States: Dwight D. Eisenhower, 1953,* 416–23; Eisenhower, "The Search for Peace," 1219.

46. Nikolai A. Bulganin, "Relaxation of International Tension: Collective Security System for Europe," *Vital Speeches* 21, no. 20 (August 1, 1955): 1385.

47. John Foster Dulles, "The Power of the United Nations: An Era of Peaceful Change," *Vital Speeches* 22, no. 1 (October 15, 1955): 3.

48. Ibid., 4.

49. Harold Macmillan, "Diplomacy's Long Haul: The New Phase in East-West Relations," *Vital Speeches* 22, no. 1 (October 15, 1955): 12–13.

50. John Foster Dulles, "The Foundation for a Firm Peace," John Foster Dulles, Deterrent Strategy, 1955, file, Duplicate Correspondence Box 91, John Foster Dulles Papers, Seeley G. Mudd Library, Princeton University; John Foster Dulles, "The Struggle for Justice: The Spirit in Which Our Nation Was Conceived," *Vital Speeches* 22, no. 6 (January 1, 1956): 163.

CHAPTER FOUR

1. Evan Thomas, *Ike's Bluff: President Eisenhower's Secret Battle to Save the World* (New York: Little, Brown, 2012), 413.

2. Fred M. Leventhal and Roland Quinault, eds., *Anglo-American Attitudes: From Revolution to Partnership* (Burlington, Vt.: Ashgate, 1988), 279–80.

3. Sherman Adams, *First-Hand Report: The Inside Story of the Eisenhower Administration* (New York: Harper, 1961), 47; Dwight D. Eisenhower, "I Shall Go to Korea" speech, October 25, 1952, www.eisenhower.archives.gov/education/bsa/citizenship_merit_badge/speeches _national_historical_importance/I_shall_go_to_korea.pdf.

4. H. W. Brands Jr., "The Dwight D. Eisenhower Administration, Syngman Rhee, and the 'Other' Geneva," *Pacific Historical Review* 56, no. 1 (February 1987): 59; Conversation between Anthony Eden and General Eisenhower on Nov. 20, 1953, FO 800/782, Far East, July–December 1952, Avon Papers.

5. Memorandum on Ending the Korean War, Douglas MacArthur to Dwight D. Eisenhower, December 14, 1952, Douglas MacArthur file, Box 25, Administration Series, Ann Whitman File, Papers of Dwight D. Eisenhower, 1953–61; Korea file, Box 8, John Foster Dulles, Subject Series, ibid.; Eisenhower, *Mandate for Change, 1953–1956*, 179–80: "Finally, to keep the attack from becoming overly costly, it was clear that we would have to use atomic weapons. This necessity was suggested to me by General MacArthur while I, as President-elect, was still living in New York."

6. Winston Churchill to Anthony Eden and R. A. Butler, January 8, 1953, FO 800/783, Far East, January–April 1953, Avon Papers; Gilbert, *Never Despair*, 792: "Governor Thomas Dewey and John Foster Dulles had irritated him in an after-dinner conversation. Jock Colville wrote, 'W was really worked up and, as he went to bed said some very harsh things about the Republican Party in general and Dulles in particular, which Christopher and I thought both unjust and dangerous.'"

7. The President to the Congress, message, Washington, February 2, 1953, *FRUS, 1952–1954*, vol. 14, *China and Japan*, 140; Conclusions of the Meeting of the Cabinet on February 3, 1953, CAB/128/26, National Archives, Kew, London, United Kingdom; Eisenhower, *Mandate for Change, 1953–1956*, 123; Memorandum of Discussion at the 131st Meeting of the National Security Council, Wednesday, February 11, 1953, *FRUS, 1952–1954*, vol. 15, *Korea*, pt. 1, 770, 771: "Noted the President's desire that the Secretary of State undertake promptly to secure the agreement of our allies to termination of the existing arrangements in Korea connected with the armistice negotiations."

8. Meeting with French Ministers, Anthony Eden, and M. Bidault on February 13, 1953, FO 800/783, Far East, January–April 1953, Avon Papers.

9. Jeffrey A. Engel, *Cold War at 30,000 Feet: The Anglo-American Fight for Aviation Supremacy* (Cambridge: Harvard University Press, 2007), 167; Eisenhower, *Mandate for Change, 1953–1956*, 180.

10. Conversation between Anthony Eden and John Foster Dulles on March 9, 1953, FO 800/ 783, Far East, January–April 1953, Avon Papers; John Foster Dulles Statement on Korean War, undated 1952, Dwight D. Eisenhower File 1952, Box 60, Duplicate Correspondence, John Foster Dulles Papers, Seeley G. Mudd Manuscript Library, Princeton University.

11. Eden to Foreign Office on Naval Blockade of China on March 9, 1953, FO 800/783, Far East, January–April 1953, Avon Papers; John Norman's "MacArthur's Blockade Proposals against Red China," *Pacific Historical Review* 26, no. 2 (May 1957): 161–74; John Edward Wiltz, "The MacArthur Hearings of 1951: The Secret Testimony," *Military Affairs* 39, no. 4 (December 1975): 167–73.

12. Botti, *The Long Wait*, 112; *FRUS, 1952–1954*, vol. 15, *Korea*, pt. 2, 1961; Memorandum by the Administrative Assistant to the President for National Security Matters (Cutler) to the Secretary of Defense (Wilson), Washington, March 21, 1953, *FRUS, 1952–1954*, vol. 15, *Korea*, pt. 1, 815.

13. Friedman, "Nuclear Blackmail and the End of the Korean War," 79–80; Jackson, "Beyond Brinkmanship," 54–56.

14. Adams, *First-Hand Report*, 48–49; McGeorge Bundy, "Atomic Diplomacy Reconsidered," *Bulletin of the American Academy of Arts and Sciences* 38, no. 1 (October 1984): 29–30; Memorandum of Conversation with Prime Minister Nehru by Secretary of State, New Delhi, May 21, 1953, *FRUS, 1952–1954*, vol. 15, *Korea*, pt. 1, 1068n1: "There has been considerable speculation that at this meeting Dulles passed a warning to the Chinese through the Indian Government that unless an armistice was agreed upon, the United States would expand the war."

15. Memorandum of Discussion at the 143rd Meeting of the National Security Council, Wednesday, May 6, 1953, *FRUS, 1952–1954*, vol. 15, *Korea*, pt. 1, 977; *FRUS, 1952–1954*, vol. 15, *Korea*, pt. 2, 815–1571; Adams, *First-Hand Report*, 117.

16. Winston Churchill to Roger Makins, on possible bombings near Yalu River on May 8, 1953, FO 800/784, Far East, May to December 1953, Avon Papers.

17. Ibid.: "You need take no action." A. Timothy Warnock, "Air War Korea, 1950–1953," *Air Force-Magazine.com*, 83, no. 10 (October 2000).

18. Dutton, *Anthony Eden*, 13, Dutton quoting Moran.

19. Richard V. Damms, *The Eisenhower Presidency, 1953–1961* (London: Pearson Education, 2002), 33; E. Thomas, *Ike's Bluff*, 78.

20. Dwight D. Eisenhower to Winston Churchill, May 23, 1953, FO 800/784, Far East, May to December 1953, Avon Papers; Korean Warning Statement, undated 1953, FO 800/784, Far East, May to December 1953, Avon Papers: "We declare again our faith in the principles and purposes of the United Nations, our consciousness of our continuing responsibilities in Korea, and our determination in good faith to seek a settlement of the Korean problem. We affirm, in the interests of world peace, that if there is a renewal of any armed attack, challenging again the principles of the United Nations, we should again be united and prompt to resist. The consequences of such a breach of the armistice would be so grave that, in all probability, it would not be possible to confine hostilities within the frontiers of Korea."

21. Brands, "The Dwight D. Eisenhower Administration, Syngman Rhee, and the 'Other Geneva,'" 61–62: "Though this option had the support of the Joint Chiefs of Staff, it was opposed by Secretary of State John Foster Dulles, who considered the political risks of such a move to outweigh any military advantages. The United States, after all, had spent billions of dollars and tens of thousands of lives protecting Rhee's government; at this late date, the Eisenhower administration could hardly declare that he was not worth saving, or worse, that it would assist in his removal. Rejecting the coup plan, Dulles suggested soliciting Rhee's acquiescence in an armistice with the promise of a security pact. At a meeting on May 30, 1953, Eisenhower approved the recommendation."

22. Memorandum of Discussion at the 150th Meeting of the National Security Council, June 18, 1953, *FRUS, 1952–1954*, vol. 15, *Korea*, pt. 2, 1200–1205; Dwight D. Eisenhower to Syngman Rhee, June 18, 1953, EM, AWF, International Series: Korea, *The Presidency: The Middle Way*, vol. 14 of *The Papers of Dwight David Eisenhower*, 309; *New York Times*, June 19, 1953.

23. Dwight D. Eisenhower to Winston Spencer Churchill, June 19, 1953, EM, AWF, International Series: Churchill, *The Presidency: The Middle Way*, vol. 14 of *The Papers of Dwight David Eisenhower*, 315.

24. Roger Makins to Winston Churchill, top-secret letter on Syngman Rhee on June 21, 1953, FO 800/784, Far East, May to December 1953, Avon Papers.

25. Winston Churchill to Dwight D. Eisenhower, June 24, 1953, FO 800/784, Far East, May to December 1953, Avon Papers.

26. The Commander in Chief, United Nations Command (Clark) to the Department of State, Tokyo, June 25, 1953, *FRUS, 1952–1954*, vol. 15, *Korea*, pt. 2, 1271; The Joint Chief of Staff to the Commander in Chief, Far East (Clark), Washington, June 25, 1953, ibid., 1271, 1272n3.

27. Selwyn Lloyd to Winston Churchill, June 25, 1953, FO 800/784, Far East, May to December 1953, Avon Papers.

28. John Foster Dulles to Winston Churchill, June 26 1953, FO 800/784, Far East, May to December 1953, Avon Papers; Dwight D. Eisenhower to Winston Churchill, June 26, 1953, ibid.: "I am still chasing the word 'gainsaying' back and forth across the waves of the Atlantic. Certainly I have never been guilty of using such a ten shilling monstrosity." The guilty party was British ambassador Roger Makins.

29. Clay Blair, *The Forgotten War: America in Korea, 1950–1953* (New York: Times Books, 1987), 674.

30. Walter G. Hermes, *Truce Tent and Fighting Front* (Washington, D.C.: Center of Military History, United States Army, 2005), 479–97; The Deputy Secretary of Defense (Kyes) to the Commander in Chief, United Nations Command (Clark) Washington, June 29, 1953, *FRUS, 1952–1954*, vol. 15, *Korea*, pt. 2, 1287.

31. Lord Salisbury, Acting Secretary of State, to Winston Churchill, July 3, 1953, FO 800/784, Far East, May to December 1953, Avon Papers.

32. The Assistant Secretary of State for Far Eastern Affairs (Robertson) to the Department of State, Seoul, July 7, 1953, *FRUS, 1952–1954*, vol. 15, *Korea*, pt. 2, 1337.

33. Ambrose, *The President, 1952–1969*, 104.

34. Diary, July 24, 1953, EM, Diaries, *The Presidency: The Middle Way*, vol. 14 of *The Papers of Dwight David Eisenhower*, 420.

35. Eden, *Full Circle*, 96; "Strike in Indochina to Spark All-Out War, Dulles Warns Reds" *Milwaukee Sentinel,* September 3, 1953: "State Secretary Dulles warned the Chinese Communists Wednesday that they face the 'grave consequence' of an all-out war if they send an army into Indochina. . . . The blunt warnings were sounded in Dulles' major foreign policy speech to the American Legion convention." Frederick W. Marks III, "The Real Hawk at Dienbienphu: Dulles or Eisenhower?," *Pacific Historical Review* 59, no. 3 (August 1990): 297–99; Dobson, *Anglo-American Relations in the Twentieth Century*, 111–12.

36. Memorandum of Discussion at the 179th Meeting of the National Security Council, January 8, 1954, *FRUS, 1952–1954*, vol. 13, *Indochina*, pt. 1, 949; Memorandum, February 8, 1954, EM, AWF, DDE Diaries Series, in *The Presidency: The Middle Way*, vol. 15 of *The Papers of Dwight David Eisenhower*, 887n1.

37. Nixon, *RN: The Memoirs of Richard Nixon*, 150. Nixon's assertions are confirmed in a Memorandum from Douglas MacArthur II to the Secretary of State, April 7, 1954, *FRUS, 1952–1954*, vol. 13, *Indochina*, pt. 1, 1270–72: "The 'advance study group' in the Pentagon has

been making an estimate of whether atomic weapons could be used to clean up the Vietminh in the Dien Bien Phu area. It has reached the conclusion that three tactical A-weapons, properly employed, would be sufficient to smash the Vietminh effort there."

38. At 8:20 p.m., April 4, 1954, President Eisenhower held an off-the-record meeting on Indochina at the White House (*FRUS, 1952–1954*, vol. 13, *Indochina*, pt. 1, 1236).

39. The President's News Conference of April 7, 1954, *Public Papers of the Presidents of the United States: Dwight D. Eisenhower, 1954*, 381–90; *FRUS, 1952–1954*, vol. 13, *Indochina*, pt. 1, 1224–25, 1307–15, 1319–23, 1327–38; Jeremy Pressman, *Warring Friends: Alliance Restraint in International Politics* (Ithaca, N.Y.: Cornell University Press, 2008), 53.

40. Petersen, *The Middle East between the Great Powers*, 49: "Scholars have pointed out that Britain did not believe in the domino theory, and thought it was still possible for France to reach an acceptable negotiated settlement. Britain had, furthermore, little desire to be embroiled in what it regarded as a non-winnable war." Greenstein and Immerman, "What Did Eisenhower Tell Kennedy about Indochina?," *Journal of American History* 79, no. 2 (September 1992): 579: "At one point he (Eisenhower) went so far as to describe Indochina as 'the tale of the snake,' saying (evidently for rhetorical purposes) that before he struck it he would assemble his wisest advisers and ask them if the United States should attack the snake's head (presumably Moscow)."

41. Engel, *Cold War at 30,000 Feet*, 172.

42. Georges Bidault, *Resistance: The Political Autobiography of Georges Bidault*, trans. Marianne Sinclair (New York: Praeger, 1965), 196–97.

43. Anthony Eden to Roger Makins, telegram, April 17, 1954, FO 800/785, Far East, January to June 1954, Avon Papers; Anthony Eden to Roger Makins, April 19, 1954, ibid.

44. Memorandum of Conversation by the Assistant Secretary of State for European Affairs (Merchant), participants, The Secretary of State, Admiral Radford, Livingston Merchant, Mr. Eden, Sir Harold Caccia, C. A. E. Shuckburgh, April 26, 1954, *FRUS, 1952–1954*, vol. 13, *Indochina*, pt. 1, 1386–91; Memorandum by the Assistant Secretary of State for Public Affairs (McCardle) to the Secretary of State, Geneva, April 30, 1954, *FRUS, 1952–1954*, vol. 16, *The Geneva Conference*, 629.

45. Diary, April 27, 1954, EM, AWF, DDE Diaries Series, *The Presidency: The Middle Way*, vol. 15 of *The Papers of Dwight David Eisenhower*, 1041; Dwight D. Eisenhower to Edward Everett Hazlett, Jr., April 27, 1954, EM, AWF, Name Series, ibid., 1043.

46. Robert Fredrick Burk, *Dwight D. Eisenhower, Hero and Politician* (Boston: Twayne, 1986), 132; William J. Duiker, *Ho Chi Minh* (New York: Hyperion, 2000), 456–57.

47. Exchange of Messages between the President and the President of France on the Fall of Dien Bien Phu, May 7, 1954, *Public Papers of the Presidents of the United States: Dwight D. Eisenhower, 1954*, 463; Memorandum of Conversation with the President by the Secretary of State, Washington, May 19, 1954, *FRUS, 1952–1954*, vol. 13, *Indochina*, pt. 2, 1583–85.

48. Conclusions of a Meeting of the Cabinet, Indochina, May 3, 1954, CAB/128/27, National Archives, Kew, London, United Kingdom; Eden, *Full Circle*, 132.

49. Anthony Eden to Roger Makins and Paris Office, telegram, May 16, 1954, FO 800/785, Far East, January to June 1954, Avon Papers; The Secretary of State to the United

States Delegation, Washington, May 12, 1954, *FRUS, 1952–1954*, vol. 16, *The Geneva Conference*, 778–79; Eden-Smith Meeting, Geneva, May 15, The United States Delegation to the Department of State, ibid., 815.

50. Sir Winston Churchill, Southeast Asia (Defence), *Hansard, House of Commons Debate*, vol. 527, May 17, 1954, 1692–93; Conclusions of a Cabinet Meeting, Indochina, May 24, 1954, CAB/128/27, National Archives, Kew, London, United Kingdom.

51. Ambrose, *The President, 1952–1969*, 205–6; Conclusions of a Meeting of the Cabinet, Indochina, June 5, 1954, CAB/128/27, National Archives, Kew, London, United Kingdom.

52. Editorial Note, *FRUS,1952–1954*, vol. 13, *Indochina*, pt. 2, 1658.

53. Ambrose, *The President, 1952–1969*, 205–6; Editorial Note, *FRUS, 1952–1954*, vol. 13, *Indochina*, pt.2, 1657–58.

54. Anthony Eden to Winston Churchill, May 31, 1954, FO 800/761, Conferences and Meetings, January to June 1954, Avon Papers.

55. Anthony Eden to Foreign Office, June 12 1954, FO 800/785, Far East, January to June 1954, Avon Papers.

56. "Special National Intelligence Estimate," June 15, 1954, *FRUS, 1952–1954*, vol. 13, *Indochina*, pt. 2, 1704; Kevin Ruane, "Anthony Eden, British Diplomacy and the Origins of the Geneva Conference of 1954," *Historical Journal*, 37, no. 1 (March 1994): 153: "The British attitude to Geneva only became more positive in March–April 1954 when French fortunes reached their nadir and the alternative to a negotiated solution in Vietnam seemed to be American, or American-led, military intervention. Faced with this potentially catastrophic prospect, the previously 'unwanted' conference assumed a new relevance for Eden and British diplomacy."

57. Winston Churchill to Anthony Eden, telegram, June 13, 1954, FO 800/785, Far East, January to June 1954, Avon Papers.

58. Anthony Eden to Winston Churchill, telegram, June 15, 1954, FO 800/785, Far East, January to June 1954, Avon Papers.

59. Winston Churchill to Anthony Eden, telegram, June 16, 1954, FO 800/785, Far East, January to June 1954, Avon Papers.

60. Ibid.

61. Ibid.; Roger Dingman, "John Foster Dulles and the Creation of the South-East Asia Treaty Organization in 1954," *International History Review* 11, no. 3 (August 1989): 457–77; James C. Hagerty, *The Diary of James C. Hagerty: Eisenhower in Mid-Course, 1954–1955*, ed. Robert H. Ferrell (Bloomington: Indiana University Press, 1983), 74.

62. Hagerty, *The Diary of James C. Hagerty*, ed. Ferrell, 66.

63. Editorial Note, Prime Minister Winston Churchill to President Dwight D. Eisenhower, June 21, 1954, *FRUS, 1952–1954*, vol. 13, *Indochina*, pt. 2, 1728–29.

64. Hagerty, *The Diary of James C. Hagerty*, ed. Ferrell, 80; Agreed Minute on Southeast Asia, June 28, 1954, *FRUS, 1952–1954*, vol. 6, *Western Europe and Canada*, pt. 1, 1129.

65. Dwight D. Eisenhower to Winston Churchill, telegram, July 8, 1954, FO 800/786, Far East, July to December 1954, Avon Papers.

66. Roger Makins to Anthony Eden, telegram, July 9, 1954, FO 800/786, Far East, July to December 1954, Avon Papers; Conclusions of a Meeting of the Cabinet, Indochina, July 9, 1954, CAB/128/27, National Archives, Kew, London, United Kingdom.

67. Hagerty Diary, Friday July 9, 1954, *FRUS, 1952–1954*, vol. 13, *Indochina*, pt, 2, 1798; The French Prime Minister (Mendes-France) to the Secretary of State, Paris, July 14, 1954, *FRUS, 1952–1954*, vol. 16, *The Geneva Conference*, 1365–67; The Secretary of State to the French Prime Minister (Mendes-France), Paris, July 14, 1954, *FRUS, 1952–1954*, vol. 13, *Indochina*, 1834.

68. Winston Churchill to Anthony Eden, telegram, July 20, 1954, FO 800/786, Far East, July to December 1954, Avon Papers; Conclusions of a Meeting of the Cabinet, Indochina, July 20,1954, CAB/128/27, National Archives, Kew, London, United Kingdom.

69. Winston Churchill to Anthony Eden, July 21, 1954, FO 800/762, Conferences and Meetings, July to December 1954, Avon Papers; Queen Elizabeth II to Anthony Eden, July 21, 1954, FO 800/762, ibid.

70. *FRUS, 1952–1954*, vol. 16, *The Geneva Conference*, 1459–503.

71. Damms, *The Eisenhower Presidency*, 37; Arthur W. Radford, *From Pearl Harbor to Vietnam: The Memoirs of Admiral Arthur W. Radford*, ed. Stephen Jurika Jr. (Stanford, Calif.: Hoover Institution Press, 1980), 434.

72. James R. Arnold, *The First Domino: Eisenhower, the Military, and America's Intervention in Vietnam* (New York: Morrow, 1991), 179; Dwight D. Eisenhower to Winston Spencer Churchill, July 22, 1954, EM, AWF, International Series, *The Presidency: The Middle Way*, vol. 15 of *The Papers of Dwight David Eisenhower*, 1208; Jeremy Pressman, *Warring Friends: Alliance Restraint in International Politics* (Ithaca, N.Y.: Cornell University Press, 2008), 44.

73. D. Anderson, *Trapped by Success*; George M. T. Kahin, *Intervention: How America Became Involved in Vietnam* (New York: Knopf, 1986); Adams, *First-Hand Report*, 132; *FRUS, 1952–1954*, vol. 14, *China and Japan*, pt. 1, 745–46, 776–77.

74. Divine, *Eisenhower and the Cold War*, 65–66.

75. Yi Sun, "Militant Diplomacy: The Taiwan Strait Crises and Sino-American Relations, 1954–1958," in *The Eisenhower Administration, the Third World, and the Globalization of the Cold War*, ed. Kathryn C. Statler and Andrew L. Johns (New York: Rowman and Littlefield, 2006), 125; John Lewis Gaddis, *The Long Peace: Inquiries into the History of the Cold War* (New York: Oxford University Press, 1987); David A. Mayers, *Cracking the Monolith: U.S. Policy against the Sino-Soviet Alliance, 1949–1955* (Baton Rouge: Louisiana State University Press, 1986).

76. See Gordon H. Chang and He Di, "The Absence of War in the U.S.-China Confrontation over Quemoy and Matsu in 1954–1955: Contingency, Luck, Deterrence," *American Historical Review* 98, no. 5 (December 1993): 1500–1524; Leonard H. D. Gordon, "United States Opposition to Use of Force in the Taiwan Straits, 1954–1962," *Journal of American History* 72, no. 3 (December 1985): 637–60; Ambrose, *The President, 1952–1969*, 238–40; Dwight D. Eisenhower to Edward Everett Hazlett, Jr., October 23, 1954, EM, AWF, Name Series, *The Presidency: The Middle Way*, vol. 15 of *The Papers of Dwight David Eisenhower*, 1353n7, 1355.

77. Anthony Nutting to Anthony Eden, telegram, December 13, 1954, FO 800/786, Far East, July to December 1954, Avon Papers.

78. Anthony Eden to Anthony Nutting, telegram, December 14, 1954, FO 800/786, Far East, July to December 1954, Avon Papers.

79. Ambrose, *The President, 1952–1969*, 231; in a Memorandum of Conversation, Department of State, Washington, January 20, 1955, with John Foster Dulles, Sir Roger Makins, Sir Robert Scott, Mr. Robertson, and Mr. Merchant, *FRUS, 1955–1957*, vol. 2, *China*, 88–89.

80. Dwight D. Eisenhower to Winston Churchill, January 25, 1955, Chur 2/217, The Sir Winston Churchill Archive Trust, Churchill Archives Centre, Churchill College, University of Cambridge. Editorial Note, during a meeting of National Security Council on August 5, 1954, *FRUS, 1952–1954*, vol. 14, *China and Japan*, pt. 1, 518–19: "The President recalled that the Navy was under an injunction to make periodic visits to this area, including going ashore from time to time. He said that if the Communists tried an invasion of Formosa by a fleet of junks this might make a good target for an atomic bomb."

81. Dwight D. Eisenhower to Winston Churchill on January 25, 1955, Chur 2/217, The Sir Winston Churchill Archive Trust, Churchill Archives Centre, Churchill College, University of Cambridge.

82. Ibid.

83. Memorandum from the British Embassy at Washington to the Department of State, Washington, January 28, 1955, Substance of Message from Mr. Trevelyan in Peking, January 28, 1955, *FRUS, 1955–1957*, vol. 2, *China*, 157–58; Anna Kasten Nelson, "John Foster Dulles and the Bipartisan Congress," *Political Science Quarterly* 102, no. 1 (Spring 1987): 55: "The skillful handling of the Formosa resolution gave the President, as well as his principal foreign policy advisor, an unprecedented blank check." See also Robert Accinelli, "Eisenhower, Congress, and the 1954–55 Offshore Island Crisis," *Presidential Studies Quarterly* 20, no. 2, Eisenhower Centennial Issue (Spring 1990): 335: "The Formosa Resolution was intended to serve multiple purposes. It removed any uncertainty about Eisenhower's congressional authority to use American armed forces as he saw fit in the Formosa Strait area. . . . Above all, it would signal the Chinese Communists (and their Soviet allies) that a united and resolute America was determined to uphold its interests in the Formosa Strait area." See *FRUS, 1955–1957*, vol. 2, *China*, 30–110; Ambrose, *The President, 1952–1969*, 235; and PM's Minute, from Winston Churchill to Anthony Eden, January 29, 1955, FO 800/787, Far East, 1955, Avon Papers.

84. PM's Minute, from Winston Churchill to Anthony Eden, January 29, 1955, FO 800/787, Far East, 1955, Avon Papers.

85. Acting Secretary of State [Herbert Hoover Jr.] to the Embassy in the Republic of China, telegram, Washington, January 31, 1955, *FRUS, 1955–1957*, vol. 2, *China*, 182–83.

86. Anthony Eden to Winston Churchill, February 10, 1955, FO 800/787, Far East, 1955, Avon Papers.

87. Dwight D. Eisenhower to Winston Churchill, February 10, 1955, Chur 6/3B, The Sir Winston Churchill Archive Trust, Churchill Archives Centre, Churchill College, University of Cambridge; Memorandum of Discussion at the 234th Meeting of the National Security Council, Washington, January 27, 1955, *FRUS, 1955–1957*, vol. 2, *China*, 137. See NSC 505 paragraph 4-c, which the Joint Chiefs wanted deleted, but Eisenhower wanted retained.

88. Dwight D. Eisenhower to Winston Churchill, February 10, 1955, Chur 6/3B, The Sir Winston Churchill Archive Trust, Churchill Archives Centre, Churchill College, University of Cambridge.

89. Roger Makins to Anthony Eden, February 14, 1955, CAB/129/73, National Archives, Kew, London, United Kingdom: "The President, for all the moderating influence which he has so skillfully exercised to calm American public opinion, is pretty firm, and will be influenced by the 'psychological factors' which Dulles mentioned recently: the reluctance to go

on retreating in the face of Communist threats, and the need to maintain the morale of the Nationalists. . . . I have the impression that the President may be rather firmer in his attitude about the off-shore islands than Dulles."

90. Winston Churchill to Dwight D. Eisenhower, February 15, 1955, Chur 6/3A, The Sir Winston Churchill Archive Trust, Churchill Archives Centre, Churchill College, University of Cambridge; Winston Churchill to Dwight D. Eisenhower on February 15, 1955, CAB/129/73, National Archives, Kew, London, United Kingdom. See also Anthony Eden, Juridical Aspects of the Formosa Situation, February 7, 1955, ibid.

91. Gilbert, *Never Despair*, 1092.

92. Dwight D. Eisenhower to Winston Churchill on February 19, 1955, Chur 6/3B, The Sir Winston Churchill Archive Trust, Churchill Archives Centre, Churchill College, University of Cambridge.

93. Ibid.; Conclusions of a Meeting of the Cabinet, Formosa, February 22, 1955, CAB/128/28, National Archives, Kew, London, United Kingdom: "The Cabinet were impressed by the firmness with which the President had stated the considerations underlying the policy of the United States Administration in respect of the islands off the China coast."

94. Winston Churchill to Anthony Eden on February 19, 1955, FO 800/787, Far East, 1955, Avon Papers; Chang and Di, "The Absence of War in the U.S.-China Confrontation over Quemoy and Matsu in 1954–1955," 1516: "Since the United States did not pose a genuine threat to China in Mao's eyes, Beijing could continue to keep pressure on to split the allied camp and weaken the main enemy, the United States, without risking widespread conflict. As a Central Committee comment on British-Chinese relations put it, maintaining the campaign against Taiwan would 'enlarge the contradiction between England and the United States.'"

95. Klaus Larres, "The Road to Geneva 1955: Churchill's Summit Diplomacy and Anglo-American Tension after Stalin's Death," in *The Cold War after Stalin's Death: A Missed Opportunity for Peace?*, ed. Klaus Larres and Kenneth Osgood (New York: Rowman and Littlefield, 2006), 151.

96. Memorandum of a Conversation between the President and the Secretary of State, Washington, March 6, 1955, *FRUS, 1952–1954*, vol. 2, *China*, 336–37.

97. Memorandum of Discussion at the 240th Meeting of the National Security Council, Washington, March 10, 1955, *FRUS, 1952–1954*, vol. 2, *China*, 347–49.

98. Ambrose, *The President, 1952–1969*, 239; Gordon H. Chang, "To the Nuclear Brink: Eisenhower, Dulles, and the Quemoy and Matsu Crisis," *International Security* 12, no. 4 (Spring 1988): 108. See also Memorandum of the Secretary of State for Foreign Affairs and the Minister of Defence on "Distinction between Large and Tactical Weapons," April 5, 1955, CAB/129/74, National Archives, Kew, London, United Kingdom: "It is not possible to draw any definite dividing line between small and large nuclear weapons." Roger Makins to the Foreign Office, Atomic Weapons, March 16, 1955, ibid.

99. Secretary of Defense (Wilson) to the Joint Chiefs of Staff, memorandum, March 22, 1955, *FRUS, 1955–1957*, vol. 2, *China*, 385; Editorial Note, Presidential Press Secretary James Hagerty's Diary, March 28, 1955, ibid., 408–9.

100. Brands, "The Age of Vulnerability," 983.

101. Dwight D. Eisenhower to Winston Churchill on March 29, 1955, Chur 2/217, Sir

Winston Churchill Archive Trust, Churchill Archives Centre, Churchill College, University of Cambridge.

102. Dwight D. Eisenhower to Lewis Williams Douglas, March 29, 1955 EM, AWF, Administration Series, *The Presidency: The Middle Way,* vol. 16 of *The Papers of Dwight David Eisenhower,* 1643; J. Smith, *Eisenhower: In War and Peace,* 660–61.

103. Dwight D. Eisenhower to Winston Churchill on March 29, 1955, Chur 2/217, Sir Winston Churchill Archive Trust, Churchill Archives Centre, Churchill College, University of Cambridge.

CHAPTER FIVE

1. Barry Rubin, *Paved with Good Intentions: The American Experience and Iran* (Oxford: Oxford University Press, 1980), 54, 59.

2. Ervand Abrahamian, *Iran between Two Revolutions* (Princeton, N.J.: Princeton University Press, 1982), 323; Chaqueri Cosroe, "Did the Soviets Play a Role in Founding the Tudeh Party in Iran?" *Cahiers du Monde* 40, no. 3 (July–September 1999): 525: "The biggest challenge the Tudeh faced was when it opposed Iran's national democratic movement under Mossadegh for the nationalization of Iranian petroleum industry, which had been in the hands of the British since the beginning of the century. The Tudeh's ferocious opposition to Mossadegh and labeling him an 'American stooge'—no doubt a line recommended by its Soviet mentor—cost the party an enormous price, identifying it increasingly with Soviet interests in Iran."

3. James A. Bill, "America, Iran, and the Politics of Intervention, 1951–1953," in *Mussadiq, Iranian Nationalism and Oil,* ed. James A. Bill and Wm. Roger Louis (Austin: University of Texas Press, 1988), 280.

4. Richard W. Cottam, *Nationalism in Iran* (Pittsburgh, Pa.: University of Pittsburgh Press, 1979), 215.

5. Ambassador Henderson to Dulles and Byroade, February 23, 1953, *FRUS, 1952–1954,* vol. 10, *Iran 1951–1954,* 677; Nikki R. Keddie, *Roots of Revolution: An Interpretive History of Modern Iran* (New Haven, Conn.: Yale University Press, 1981), 138.

6. Memorandum of Discussion at the 135th Meeting of the National Security Council, Washington, March 4, 1953, *FRUS, 1952–1954,* vol. 10, *Iran 1951–1954,* 693.

7. Ibid., 698–99; Bill, "America, Iran, and the Politics of Intervention," 279: "American foreign policy makers were somewhat in awe of the British experience and expertise concerning Iran."

8. Eden, *Full Circle,* 234–36.

9. Anthony Eden to Winston Churchill, March 7, 1953, FO 800/814, Persia 1953–1955, Avon Papers.

10. Brands, "The Cairo-Tehran Connection in Anglo-American Rivalry in the Middle East, 1951–1953," 434.

11. Donald Newton Wilbur, *Clandestine Service History: Overthrow of Premier Mossadeq of Iran, November 1952–August 1953* (Washington, D.C.: Central Intelligence Agency, Clandestine Service, 1969), 2–3, iii–iv; Wm. Roger Louis, "Mussadiq and the Dilemmas of British

Imperialism," in *Mussadiq, Iranian Nationalism and Oil*, ed. Bill and Louis, 252, 253. Operation Boot was the British code name for Operation Ajax.

12. James A. Bill, *The Eagle and the Lion* (New Haven, Conn.: Yale University Press, 1988), 89–90.

13. Bill, "America, Iran, and the Politics of Intervention," 280; Selwyn Lloyd to Winston Churchill, May 5, 1953, FO 800/814, Persia 1953–1955, Avon Papers; Wilbur, *Clandestine Service History*, CIA, Appendix A, "Initial Operational Plan for TPAJAX as Cabled from Nicosia to Headquarters on June 1, 1953."

14. Cottam, *Nationalism in Iran*, 215.

15. Wilbur, *Clandestine Service History*, v–vi. The British government's reply may be seen in CIA, Appendix C, "Foreign Office Memorandum of 23 July 1953 from British Ambassador Makins to Assistant Under Secretary of State Smith."

16. Eisenhower, *Mandate for Change, 1953–1956*, 162.

17. See Bill, "America, Iran, and the Politics of Intervention," 282, on Allen Dulles, Kermit Roosevelt, and Frank Wisner: "All were gregarious, intrigued by possibilities, liked to do things, had three bright ideas a day, shared the optimism of the stock market plungers, and were convinced that the CIA could find a way to reach it. They also tended to be white, Anglo-Saxon patricians from old families with old money, at least in the beginning, and they somehow inherited traditional British attitudes toward the colored races of the world—not the pukka sahib arrogance of the Indian Raj, but the mixed fascination and condescension of men like T. E. Lawrence, who were enthusiastic partisans of the alien cultures into which they dipped for a time and rarely doubted their ability to help, until it was too late." Ambrose, *The President, 1952–1969*, 111; Wilbur, *Clandestine Service History*, vi.

18. Ambrose, *The President, 1952–1969*, 112; Eisenhower, *Mandate for Change, 1953–1956*, 159–66.

19. Wilbur, *Clandestine Service History*, vii–viii; John Foster Dulles, Telephone Conversation with Allen W. Dulles, Washington, July 24, 1953–10:55 a.m., *FRUS, 1952–1954*, vol. 10, *Iran 1951–1954*, 738: "AWD said it is moving along reasonably well but the young man may pull out at the last minute, he is an unaccountable character but the sister has agreed to go."

20. Editorial Note, *FRUS, 1952–1954*, vol. 10, *Iran 1951–1954*, 740n3, 741.

21. British Memorandum, Persia: Political Review of the Recent Crisis, September 2, 1953, *FRUS, 1952–1954*, vol. 10, *Iran 1951–1954*, 781–82; The Ambassador (Berry) in Iraq to the Department of State, Baghdad, August, 17, 1953, ibid., 747.

22. Memorandum by the Under Secretary of State (Smith) to the President, Washington, August 18, 1953, *FRUS, 1952–1954*, vol. 10, *Iran 1951–1954*, 748.

23. British Memorandum, Persia: Political Review of the Recent Crisis, September 2, 1953, *FRUS, 1952–1954*, vol. 10, *Iran 1951–1954*, 783–86. The Ambassador in the United Kingdom (Aldrich) to the Department of State, London, August 25, 1953, ibid., 786. Aldrich had a message from Churchill to be delivered to the shah: "I salute and congratulate Your Majesty on your safe return to your country. May I express the sincere hope that success will now attend your efforts to guide Persia towards those better things which you have always so ardently desired for her." See also Conclusions of a Cabinet Meeting, Persia, August 25, 1953, CAB/128/26, National Archives, Kew, London, United Kingdom.

24. British Memorandum, Persia: Political Review of the Recent Crisis, September 2, 1953, *FRUS, 1952–1954*, vol. 10, *Iran 1951–1954*, 786.

25. Wilbur, *Clandestine Service History*, 81–82; Memo from C. A. E. Shuckburgh to Lord Salisbury, Sir J. Bowker, Mr. Nutting, Mr. Gandy, August 29, 1953, FO 800/814, Persia 1953–1955, Avon Papers.

26. Stephen G. Rabe, *Eisenhower and Latin America: The Foreign Policy of Anticommunism* (Chapel Hill: University of North Carolina, 1988), 26–27.

27. Selwyn Lloyd to Winston Churchill on May 9, 1953, FO 800/802, Latin America 1952–1954, Avon Papers; National Intelligence Estimate, Probable Developments in Guatemala, Washington, May 19, 1953, *FRUS, 1952–1954*, vol. 4, *The American Republics*, 1061–71.

28. Rabe, *Eisenhower and Latin America*, 33, 39, 40–41; see also Richard H. Immerman, "Guatemala as Cold War History," *Political Science Quarterly* 95, no. 4 (Winter 1980–81): 629–30n1.

29. Richard H. Immerman, *The CIA in Guatemala: The Foreign Policy of Intervention* (Austin: University of Texas Press, 1982), 133–34.

30. Stephen G. Rabe, *The Killing Zone: The United States Wages Cold War in Latin America* (New York: Oxford University Press, 2012), 44: "On August 12, 1953, Eisenhower's NSC authorized the overthrow of President Arbenz." Piero Gleijeses, *Shattered Hope: The Guatemalan Revolution and the United States, 1944–1954* (Princeton, N.J.: Princeton University Press, 1991), 243, 247; Draft Policy Paper Prepared in the Bureau of Inter-American Affairs, NSC Guatemala, Washington, August 19, 1953, *FRUS, 1952–1954*, vol. 4, *The American Republics*, 1074–78.

31. Memorandum for the Record, Briefing of John E. Peurifoy re Guatemala by Mr. Frank Wisner, September 1, 1953, *FRUS, 1952–1954, Guatemala*, 93–94; John W. Young, "Great Britain's Latin American Dilemma: The Foreign Office and the Overthrow of 'Communist' Guatemala, June 1954," *International History Review* 8, no. 4 (November 1986): 575; Ambassador to Guatemala (Peurifoy) to the Assistant Secretary of State for Inter-American Affairs (Cabot), Guatemala City, December 28, 1953, *FRUS, 1952–1954, Guatemala*, 159; Immerman, *The CIA in Guatemala*, 138.

32. Immerman, *The CIA in Guatemala*, 145.

33. Ambrose, *The President, 1952–1969*, 197.

34. Statement by Secretary of State John Foster Dulles Chairman of the United States Delegation to the Tenth Inter-American Conference, Caracas, Venezuela, March 5, 1954, File of Caracas Tenth Inter-American Conference, March 1954, Box 79, John Foster Dulles Papers, Seeley G. Mudd Manuscript Library, Princeton University. Immerman, "Guatemala as Cold War History," 644: "Existing treaties referred implicitly to the 1947 Rio Pact, which called for a Meeting of Consultation of the Foreign Ministers of the Organization of American States to determine acceptable measures for the common defense in the event of aggression. The State Department began to solicit support for such a meeting." Memorandum for the Record, Washington, April 21, 1954, Synthesis of Ambassador Peurifoy's Remarks Relevant to PBSUCCESS Made at a Meeting, April 21, 1954, Present, Ambassador Peurifoy (5 names not declassified), *FRUS, 1952–1954, Guatemala*, 244; Young, "Great Britain's Latin American Dilemma," 575.

35. Immerman, "Guatemala as Cold War History," 636–37: "The prime illustration of this principle of guilt by association was the well-known 'duck test.' In 1950 Richard C. Patterson,

Jr., then ambassador to Guatemala but already declared persona non grata by the Arevalo government and recalled to Washington, explained in a speech how to uncover communists. . . . 'Many times it is impossible to prove legally that a certain individual is a communist; but for cases of this sort I recommend a practical method of detection—the "duck test." The duck test works this way: suppose you see a bird walking around in a farm yard. This bird wears no label that says "duck." But the bird certainly looks like a duck. Also, he goes to the pond and you notice he swims like a duck. Well, by this time you have probably reached the conclusion that the bird is a duck, whether he's wearing a label or not.'"

36. Young, "Great Britain's Latin American Dilemma," 575–76.

37. Memorandum by the Assistant Secretary of State for Inter-American Affairs (Holland) to the Secretary of State on Action to Prevent Delivery of Czech Arms to Guatemala, Washington, May 18, 1954, *FRUS, 1952–1954*, vol. 4, *The American Republics*, 1111–12; Memorandum of Conversation with the President, by the Secretary of State, Washington, May 19, 1954, ibid., 1116–17; Richard H. Immerman, "Psychology," *Journal of American History* 77, no. 1 (June 1990): 178; Young, "Great Britain's Latin American Dilemma," 577.

38. Young, "Great Britain's Latin American Dilemma," 578.

39. Ibid.; Editorial Note on the Caracas Resolution, June 2, 1954, *FRUS, 1952–1954*, vol. 4, *The American Republics*, 1154.

40. For Rumbold from Duff, June 9, 1954, FO 800/802, Latin America 1952–1954, Avon Papers. For Duff from Rumbold, June 10, 1954, ibid.

41. Young, "Great Britain's Latin American Dilemma," 579; Excerpt from the Diary of James C. Hagerty, Press Secretary to the President, Washington, June 19, 1954, *FRUS, 1952–1954*, vol. 4, *The American Republics*, 1173: "I think the State Department made a very bad mistake, particularly with the British, in attempting to search ships going to Guatemala."

42. Memorandum of Telephone Conversation between the Assistant Secretary of State for Inter-American Affairs (Holland) and Secretary of State Dulles, Washington, June 17, 1954, 5:15 p.m., *FRUS, 1952–1954*, Guatemala: "He said Sec. Anderson just told him that he has a military telegram from Honduras that Armas (?) 'is moving.' The Sec. said he didn't know what that means, but he supposes it means something. H. said A. is revolutionary individual lurking in the forest." Editorial Note, *FRUS, 1952–1954*, vol. 4, *The American Republics*, 1177; Dwight D. Eisenhower, *Mandate for Change, 1953–1956*, 425–26; Rabe, *The Killing Zone*, 40; Immerman, "Psychology," 168; Jim Newton, *Eisenhower: The White House Years* (New York: Doubleday, 2011), 168.

43. Rabe, *Eisenhower and Latin America*, 60: "The president recalled that he warned his closest advisors that 'if you at any time take the route of violence or support of violence . . . then you commit yourself to carry it through, and it's too late to have second thoughts, not facing up to the possible consequences, when your midway in an operation."

44. Young, "Great Britain's Latin American Dilemma," 583–84.

45. Memo for Record: Phone Conversation between Secretary of State John Foster Dulles and UN Ambassador Henry Cabot Lodge on June 24, 1954 at 9:55 AM, John Foster Dulles File June 1954 (1), Dulles-Herter Series Box No. 3, Ann Whitman File, Papers of Dwight D. Eisenhower, 1953–61.

46. Young, "Great Britain's Latin American Dilemma," 584.

47. Memorandum by the Assistant Secretary of State for United Nations Affairs (Key) of Meeting of Secretary of State Dulles and Foreign Secretary Eden at the Department of State on the Morning of June 25, 1954, *FRUS, 1952–1954*, vol. 6, *Western Europe and Canada*, pt. 1, 1075–76: "Mr. Eden stated that he shared our views as to the desirability of having the OAS act on the Guatemalan complaint and that likewise he did not wish this matter to be acted upon in the Security Council." Young, "Great Britain's Latin American Dilemma," 584.

48. Charles McMoran Wilson, *Winston Churchill: The Struggle for Survival* (Boston: Houghton Mifflin, 1966), 603–4, 585–86.

49. Memorandum of Conversation between Prime Minister Winston Churchill and Ambassador Henry Cabot Lodge, Jr. on June 26, 1954, Churchill-Eden Visit June 25–29, 1954 (1) File, Series Box No. 5, John Foster Dulles Papers, 1951–59, Dwight D. Eisenhower Library; Memorandum of Conversation by the United States Representative at the United Nations, Washington, June 26, 1954, *FRUS, 1952–1954*, vol. 6, *Western Europe and Canada*, pt. 1, 1107–10; Young, "Great Britain's Latin American Dilemma," 90; in a Memorandum of Conversation summarizing the Secretary of State's staff meeting held on July 7, 1954, *FRUS, 1952–1954*, vol. 4, *The American Republics*, 1208: "Mr. Holland reported the British are preparing a 'White Paper' on our actions in the United Nations on the Guatemalan incident."

50. Rabe, *Eisenhower and Latin America*, 60–61.

51. Fred I. Greenstein and Richard H. Immerman, "What Did Eisenhower Tell Kennedy about Indochina? The Politics of Misperception," *Journal of American History* 79, no. 2 (September 1992): 568–87; Rabe, *Eisenhower and Latin America*, 68.

52. Nick Cullather, *Secret History: The CIA's Classified Account of Its Operations in Guatemala, 1952–1954* (Stanford, Calif.: Stanford University Press, 2006).

CHAPTER SIX

1. See Gamal Abdel Nasser, *Egypt's Liberation: The Philosophy of the Revolution* (Washington: Public Affairs Press, 1955).

2. See Stephen Dorril, *MI6: Inside the Covert World of Her Majesty's Secret Intelligence Service* (New York: Free Press, 2000).

3. Anthony Eden to Dwight D. Eisenhower, January 16, 1956, AP 20/27/37, Avon Papers.

4. Dooley, "Great Britain's 'Last Battle' in the Middle East," 487.

5. Dorril, *MI6*, 610: "Indeed, the French intelligence service, SDECE, already had a special operations action branch in Egypt, code named Rap 700, supervised by Capt. Paul Leger. As early as 1954 a paid hitman from the action branch had organized an attempt on Nasser with an agent, Jean-Marie Pellay, who just missed his target."

6. John Colville, *The Fringes of Power: 10 Downing Street Diaries* (New York: Norton, 1985), 708; Paul Addison, "The Political Beliefs of Winston Churchill," *Transactions of the Royal Historical Society*, 5th ser., 30 (1980): 23–47; Stuart Ball, "Churchill and the Conservative Party," *Transactions of the Royal Historical Society*, 6th ser., 11 (2001): 307–30; Moran, *Winston Churchill: The Struggle for Survival*, 594.

7. David Carlton, *Anthony Eden: A Biography* (London: Penguin, 1981), 300; Diary, Janu-

ary 10, 1956 EM, AWF, DDE Diaries Series, *The Presidency: The Middle Way*, vol. 16 of *The Papers of Dwight David Eisenhower*, 1948; Editorial Note, *FRUS, 1955–1957*, vol. 12, *Near East Region; Iran; Iraq*, 214.

8. Visit of the Prime Minister and the Secretary of State to Washington, January 30–February 3, 1956, Meeting at the White House, January 30, 1956, AP 20/29/2, Avon Papers, 2–3; Eden, *Full Circle*, 484; Prime Minister Eden to Amman, March 1, 1956, AP 20/32/64, Avon Papers; Prime Minister Eden to Amman, March 2, 1956, AP 20/32/67, ibid.; Eden, *Full Circle*, 484.

9. Eden, *Full Circle*, 484; Anthony Eden to Dwight D. Eisenhower, March 5, 1956, AP 20/27/47, Avon Papers.

10. Evelyn Shuckburgh and John Charmley, *Descent to Suez: Diaries, 1951–1956* (New York: Norton, 1987), 12–3–56; Dorril, *MI6*, 612–13; Diary, March 19, 1956 EM, AWF, Ann Whitman Diary Series, *The Presidency: The Middle Way*, vol. 16 of *The Papers of Dwight David Eisenhower*, 2077n1: "According to the British Prime Minister, agreement had been reached at the January Conference of Egyptian Ambassadors and Ministers to the Arab States that an organization of United Arab States was to be created. The organization would eliminate custom barriers, establish common educational and economic systems, and create an Arab currency bank to control the financial affairs of all Arab states. Egypt's long-term policy was to isolate Saudi Arabia as the only remaining monarchy in the region and then to remove King Saud. The Soviet Union was supporting these anti-monarchical policies, the report stated, and was helping to organize intelligence activities throughout the Arab world." Donald Neff, *Warriors at Suez: Eisenhower Takes America into the Middle East* (New York: Linden Press/Simon and Schuster, 1981), 316.

11. Anthony Nutting, *No End of a Lesson: The Story of Suez* (London: Constable, 1967), 26.

12. Ibid., 34–35. In the book, Nutting used the word "removed" rather than what Eden actually said, which Nutting later claimed was "murdered." Dorril, *MI6*, 613.

13. Dorril, *MI6*, 613.

14. Dwight D. Eisenhower to Anthony Eden, March 9, 1956, AP 20/27/50, Avon Papers; Department of State to the Embassy in the United Kingdom, telegram, Washington, March 9, 1956, *FRUS, 1955–1957*, vol. 15, *The Arab-Israeli Dispute, January 1–July 26, 1956*, 337; Dorril, *MI6*, 614; Eden to Eisenhower, March 15, 1956, in *The Eden-Eisenhower Correspondence, 1955–1957*, ed. Peter G. Boyle (Chapel Hill: University of North Carolina Press, 2005), 123–24; Dooley, "Great Britain's 'Last Battle' in the Middle East," 488–90: "Playing the themes of pan-Arab unity, anti-imperialism, and neutralism brought Nasser formidable influence throughout the region, and raised the specter that Egypt, commanding a union of Arab states, could someday fill the vacuum left by the waning of British power." "Great Britain had taken its first strategic decision on the road to Suez: to topple the governments of Egypt and Syria, and re-group the Middle Eastern states around Iraq." Dwight D. Eisenhower to Anthony Eden, March 20, 1956, AP 20/27/54, Avon Papers. Selwyn Lloyd's memo on this British policy change with Egypt can be seen in Note from the British Ambassador (Makins) to Secretary of State Dulles, Washington, March 21, 1956, *FRUS, 1955–1957*, vol. 15, *The Arab-Israeli Dispute, January 1–July 26, 1956*, 383–87.

15. Memorandum from the Secretary of State to the President, Washington, March 28, 1956, *FRUS, 1955–1957*, vol. 15, *The Arab-Israeli Dispute, January 1–July, 26, 1956*, 419–21; Chris-

topher M. Andrew, *For the President's Eyes Only: Secret Intelligence and the American Presidency from Washington to Bush* (New York: HarperCollins, 1995), 224–25; Mohamed Hasanein Heikel, *The Cairo Documents; The Inside Story of Nasser and His Relationship with World Leaders, Rebels, and Statesmen* (Garden City, N.Y.: Doubleday, 1973), 116. For Operation Omega and Douglas MacArthur II as coordinator of the program, see *FRUS, 1955–1957*, vol. 15, *Arab-Israeli Dispute, January 1–July 26, 1956*, 435, 461–62.

16. Andrew, *For the President's Eyes Only*, 225. See also Dooley, "Great Britain's 'Last Battle' in the Middle East," 490–91: "Behind the scenes, officials in Whitehall began talking of 'when war comes' rather than 'if war comes.' By the end of March 1956, an apocalyptic mood pervaded MI6. The deputy director, George Kennedy Young, told an American intelligence colleague, Wilbur Crane Eveland of the CIA, that 'Britain is now prepared to fight its last battle; 'no matter what the cost, we will win'; and 'we have to face the possibility that Nasser might close the canal.'" Ibid., 491: "The code-name given to the coup planned for the autumn of 1956 in Syria was Straggle. Although most Public Record Office files for Syria and Iraq in 1956 remains classified, trials held in Damascus between December 1956 and February 1957, and later in Baghdad after the 1958 revolution, exposed a labyrinthine conspiracy involving the Iraqis, the British and the Americans. A note in the Foreign Secretary's private files, dated 2 May, also records that 'covert action to diminish Nasser's influence in other Arab states is being actively prepared,' while the agenda for a Foreign Office meeting scheduled for 30 May contains the cryptic notation: 'Syria, Straggle.'"

17. James E. Doughtery, "The Aswan Decision in Perspective," *Political Science Quarterly* 74, no. 1 (March 1959): 22.

18. Selwyn Lloyd, *Suez 1956: A Personal Account* (New York: Mayflower, 1978), 33–34, 70–71; Egypt, High Dam at Aswan, Conclusions of a Meeting of the Cabinet, July 17, 1956, CAB/128/30, National Archives, Kew, London, United Kingdom; Dooley, "Great Britain's 'Last Battle' in the Middle East," 493; Embassy in Egypt to the Department of State, telegram, Cairo, June 16, 1956, *FRUS, 1955–1957*, vol. 15, *Arab-Israeli Dispute, January 1–July 26, 1956*, 731–34; ibid., 861–74.

19. See Nigel John Ashton, "The Hijacking of a Pact: The Formation of the Baghdad Pact and Anglo-American Tensions in the Middle East, 1955–1958," *Review of International Studies* (1993): 19, 133; Lloyd, *Suez 1956*, 78.

20. Terence Robertson, *Crisis: The Inside Story of the Suez Conspiracy* (New York: Atheneum, 1965), 50

21. Lloyd, *Suez 1956*, 90–91.

22. Dorril, *MI6*, 627; Harold Macmillan, *Riding the Storm 1956–1959* (New York: Harper and Row, 1971), 111–12.

23. Dooley, "Great Britain's 'Last Battle' in the Middle East," 495.

24. Dorril, *MI6*, 633.

25. Ibid., 633–34: "The French and the Israelis, too, organized a number of assassination plots. The head of the SDECE and former socialist resister Pierre Boursicot, who supervised the various meetings that worked out the plan for the Suez expedition, Musketeer, was an important go-between with the British and Israeli secret services. SDECE had a special operations action branch in Egypt which scheduled one attempt for September 1, the original

date for Musketeer. A French commando team was to cross the West bank of the Nile from the French embassy, in rubber boats, and destroy Nasser's Revolutionary Command Council building at the northern tip of Gezira Island. When the date was changed, the plan was aborted. An Israeli assassination attempt employed a Greek waiter from one of the famous catering companies, who was to slip a poison pill in to Nasser's coffee. It probably would've succeeded 'but his hand shook so much when it came time to the point that he gave up and confessed.' CIA operative Miles Copeland claimed to have knowledge of the MI6 assassination plans. He joked with Nasser: 'Turn your head, Gamal, and let me see if I can put this poison in your coffee.' Nasser, pointing to his nearby bodyguards, said it would not work."

26. Andrew, *For the President's Eyes Only*, 225–26.

27. Anthony Eden, Suez Canal Company (Expropriation), *Hansard, House of Commons Debates*, vol. 557, July 27, 1956, 777–80; Eden, *Full Circle*, 473–74; Embassy in the United Kingdom (Andrew Foster) to the Department of State, telegram, London, July 27, 1956, *FRUS, 1955–1957*, vol. 16, *The Suez Crisis, July 26–December 31, 1956*, 3–5; Khosrow Mostofi, "The Suez Dispute: A Case Study of a Treaty," *Western Political Quarterly* 10, no. 1 (March 1957): 1; Convention between Great Britain, Germany, Austria-Hungary, Spain, France, Italy, the Netherlands, Russia, and Turkey, respecting the Free Navigation of the Suez Maritime Canal, Signed at Constantinople, October 29, 1888, DSND, 15/4, Duncan Sandys Papers, Churchill Archives Centre, Churchill College, University of Cambridge.

28. Eden, *Full Circle*, 473–74, 477; Prime Minister Eden to President Eisenhower, London, July 27, 1956, *FRUS, 1955–1957*, vol. 16, *The Suez Crisis, July 26–December 31, 1956*, 9–11; Prime Minister to President, July 27, 1956, AP 20/27/70, Avon Papers.

29. Memorandum of a Conference with the President, Secretary Hoover, and Colonel Goodpaster, White House, Washington, July 27, 1956, *FRUS, 1955–1957*, vol. 16, *The Suez Crisis, July 26–December 31, 1956*, 11; Ambrose, *The President, 1952–1969*, 331; Embassy in the United Kingdom to the Department of State, telegram, London, July 31, 1956, *FRUS, 1955–1957*, vol. 16, *Suez Crisis, July 26–December 31, 1956*, 60–61; Memorandum of a Conference with the President, White House, Washington, July 31, 1956, ibid., 62–68.

30. Ambrose, *The President, 1952–1969*, 331; Dwight D. Eisenhower to Robert Anthony Eden, July 31, 1956, EM, AWF, International Series: Eden, *The Presidency: The Middle Way*, vol. 17 of *The Papers of Dwight David Eisenhower*, 2222–23; Dwight D. Eisenhower to Anthony Eden, July 31, 1956, AP 20/27/73, Avon Papers.

31. Memorandum of Conversation, British Foreign Office, London, August 1, *FRUS, 1955–1957*, vol. 16, *The Suez Crisis, July 26–December 31, 1956*, 94–97; participants included Selwyn Lloyd, Harold Caccia, Mr. Ross, Mr. Fitzmaurice, Secretary Dulles, Ambassador Aldrich, Carl W. McCardle, Herman Phleger, and Robert Murphy. Eden, *Full Circle*, 487; Memorandum of Conversation between Prime Minister Eden and Secretary of State Dulles, 10 Downing Street, London, August 1, 1956, *FRUS, 1955–1957*, vol. 16, *The Suez Crisis, July 26–December 31, 1956*, 98–100; Dooley, "Great Britain's 'Last Battle' in the Middle East," 497–98: "There were four military plans. Three are known in some detail: the initial plan, conceived in the immediate aftermath of nationalization; Operation Musketeer, developed in early August; and modification, Musketeer Revise, the basis for Anglo-French operations between 30 October and 6 November. Declassification of the Suez documents open to inspection a

Winter Plan which would have gone into effect had the diplomatic standoff continued any longer."

32. Ambrose, *The President, 1952–1969*, 333; John Foster Dulles Statement upon returning from London on August 3, 1956, Anthony Eden file, Duplicate Correspondence Box 102, John Foster Dulles Papers, Seeley G. Mudd Library, Princeton University.

33. Lloyd, *Suez 1956*, 76; *FRUS, 1955–1957*, vol. 16, *The Suez Crisis, July 26, 1956–December 31, 1956*, 228–29, 249–85; Memorandum of Conversation between Secretary of State Dulles and Prime Minister Eden, 10 Downing Street, August 24, 1956, ibid., 285–86; Prime Minister Eden to President Eisenhower, London, August 27, 1956, ibid., 304–5; Prime Minister Eden to President Eisenhower, August 27, 1956, AP 20/27/77, Avon Papers; Memorandum of Conversation with the President, Dwight D. Eisenhower and John Foster Dulles, 9:30 AM on August 29, 1956, File Meetings with the President, Aug.–Dec. 1956 (6), White House Memoranda Series Box no. 4, A67–28, Papers of John Foster Dulles, Dwight D. Eisenhower Library; *FRUS, 1955–1957*, vol. 16, *The Suez Crisis, July 26, 1956–December 31, 1956*, 342–60.

34. Memorandum of Conversation with the President, Dwight D. Eisenhower, and John Foster Dulles, 4:30 PM, August 30, 1956, File Meetings with the President, Aug.–Dec. 1956 (6), White House Memoranda Series Box no. 4, A67–28, Papers of John Foster Dulles, Dwight D. Eisenhower Library.

35. Dwight D. Eisenhower to Anthony Eden, September 3, 1956, AP 20/27/78, Avon Papers; Dwight D. Eisenhower to Robert Anthony Eden, September 2, 1956, EM, AWF, International Series: Eden, *The Presidency: The Middle Way*, vol. 17 of *The Papers of Dwight David Eisenhower*, 2264; President Eisenhower to Prime Minister Eden, Washington, September 2, 1956, *FRUS, 1955–1957*, vol. 16, *The Suez Crisis, July 26–December 31, 1956*, 355–56.

36. Dwight D. Eisenhower to Anthony Eden, September 3, 1956, AP 20/27/78, Avon Papers; Dwight D. Eisenhower to Robert Anthony Eden, September 2, 1956, EM, AWF, International Series: Eden, *The Presidency: The Middle Way*, vol. 17 of *The Papers of Dwight David Eisenhower*, 2264; President Eisenhower to Prime Minister Eden, Washington, September 2, 1956, *FRUS, 1955–1957*, vol. 16, *The Suez Crisis, July 26–December 31, 1956*, 355–56.

37. Prime Minister Eden to President Eisenhower, September 6, 1956, AP 20/27/79, Avon Papers; Prime Minister Eden to President Eisenhower, London, September 6, 1956, *FRUS, 1955–1957*, vol. 16, *The Suez Crisis, July 26–December 31, 1956*, 400–403.

38. Memorandum of Conversation with the President, Dwight D. Eisenhower, John Foster Dulles, and Herbert Hoover Junior, September 6, 1956, File Meetings with the President, Aug.–Dec. 1956 (6), White House Memoranda Series Box no. 4, A67–28, Papers of John Foster Dulles, Dwight D. Eisenhower Library.

39. "Probable Repercussions of British-French Military Action in the Suez Crisis," Special National Intelligence Estimate, September 5, 1956, *FRUS, 1955–1957*, vol. 16, *The Suez Crisis, July 26–December 31, 1956*, 382–91; Dwight D. Eisenhower to Anthony Eden, AP 20/27/80, Avon Papers; Dwight D. Eisenhower to Robert Anthony Eden, September 8, 1956, EM, AWF, International Series: Eden, *The Presidency: The Middle Way*, vol. 17 of *The Papers of Dwight David Eisenhower*, 2275–76; President Eisenhower to Prime Minister Eden, Washington, September 8, 1956, *FRUS, 1955–1957*, vol. 16, *Suez Crisis, July 26–December 31, 1956*, 435–38.

40. President Nasser to the Chairman of the Suez Committee, September 9, 1956, SELO 6/64, Selwyn Lloyd Papers, Churchill Archives Centre, Churchill College, University of Cambridge; The President's News Conference of September 5, 1956, *Public Papers of the Presidents of the United States: Dwight D. Eisenhower, 1956* (Washington, D.C.: U.S. Government Printing Office, 1958), 732–45; Lloyd, *Suez 1956*, 129–30, 76: "Next morning, September 5, there were flaring headlines in the newspapers: Eisenhower, questioned at a press conference about the possible use of force, had rejected it completely and unconditionally. If Nasser rejected the present proposals, others would have to be worked out: 'We are committed to a peaceful settlement of this dispute, nothing else.' That destroyed any chance Menzies might have had of success and made the mission futile." For more on Ivone Kirkpatrick, see Memorandum from Carl W. McCardle of the Senior Staff of Advisors in the Delegation at the Suez Canal Conference to the Secretary of State, London, August 21, 1956, *FRUS, 1955–1957*, vol. 16, *The Suez Crisis, July 26–December 31, 1956*, 250.

41. The President's News Conference of September 11, 1956, *Public Papers of the Presidents of the United States: Dwight D. Eisenhower, 1956*, 756; Lloyd, *Suez 1956*, 130–31.

42. Eden, *Full Circle*, 535, 539.

43. Summary of Developments in Suez Situation, Washington, September 14, 1956, *FRUS, 1955–1957*, vol. 16, *The Suez Crisis, July 26, 1956–December 31, 1956*, 495–97; Embassy in the United Kingdom to the Department of State by John Foster Dulles, telegram, London, September 18, 1956, *FRUS, 1955–1957*, vol. 16, *The Suez Crisis, July 26–December 31, 1956*, 513–16.

44. Anthony Eden to Winston Churchill, September 21, 1956, Chur 2/216, The Sir Winston Churchill Archive Trust, Churchill Archives Centre, Churchill College, University of Cambridge; Andrew, *For the President's Eyes Only*, 226.

45. Macmillan, *Riding the Storm*, 134.

46. Ibid., 134–36, 155; Memorandum of a Conversation between Secretary of State Dulles and the Chancellor of the Exchequer Macmillan, Department of State, Washington, September 25, 1956, *FRUS, 1955–1957*, vol. 16, *The Suez Crisis, July 26–December 31, 1956*, 580–81.

47. Prime Minister Eden to President Eisenhower, October 1, 1956, AP 20/27/83, Avon Papers; Prime Minister Eden to President Eisenhower, London, October 1, 1956, *FRUS, 1955–1957*, vol. 16, *The Suez Crisis, July 26–December 31, 1956*, 618–19.

48. Secretary Dulles' News Conference, October 2, 1956, File: Suez Canal, United Nations, October 5–14, 1956, Box 110, Duplicate Correspondence, John Foster Dulles Papers, Seeley G. Mudd Manuscript Library, Princeton University; Eden, *Full Circle*, 556–57; *FRUS, 1955–1957*, vol. 16, *The Suez Crisis, July 26–December 31, 1956*, 560–640; Memorandum of Conversation, H. C. Lodge's Notes on Conversation between John Foster Dulles, Selwyn Lloyd, and Christian Pineau, Secretary Dulles' Suite, Waldorf Astoria, New York, October 5, 1956, ibid., 639–45; Secretary of State to the President, New York, October 5, 1956, ibid., 648: "Both Pineau and Lloyd said in effect that they did not believe there was any peaceful way of solution and they argued that only the use of force against Nasser would restore Western prestige in Africa and the Middle East."

49. Memorandum of Conversation, Dwight D. Eisenhower and John Foster Dulles, on October 2, 1956, File Meetings with the President, Aug.–Dec. 1956 (5), White House Memoranda Series Box no. 4, A67–28, Papers of John Foster Dulles, Dwight D. Eisenhower Library.

50. Ambrose, *The President, 1952–1969*, 351; Dorril, *MI6*, 638–39: "Eden had a 'toothy grin' when Young laughingly said that 'thuggery is not on the agenda.' Dick White claimed that he expressly told the Prime Minister that he would not sanction MI6's further involvement in Nasser's assassination. He 'made it clear that MI6 was a hostile service, but not a collection of hit men.' Officers of the time smile at the denial. Everyone, it appears, was knowingly playing the deniability game. By then MI6 no longer had any assets in Cairo and it was decided that a three-man hit team would be sent by the SPA [Special Political Actions] Group from London as 'a Special Service to assassinate Nasser.' They apparently did enter Egypt but got 'cold feet and left.' At the same time, the Egyptian security service had been tipped off about the presence in Cairo of a German mercenary who had been hired by MI6 for a 'wet job.' He disappeared before the security net was closed and was believed to have been smuggled out of the country under diplomatic cover. There was also a British plan to use SIS troops in the run-up to the invasion to kill or capture Nasser. Senior SIS officers gave an assurance that 'any evidence of their involvement would be removed so smartly as to be deniable.'"

51. Kennett Love, *Suez—The Twice-Fought War: A History* (New York: McGraw-Hill, 1969), 444.

52. "The People Ask the President," October 12, 1956, *Public Papers of the Presidents of the United States: Dwight D. Eisenhower, 1956*, 903; Lloyd, *Suez 1956*, 160.

53. Ambrose, *The President, 1952–1969*, 353.

54. Editorial Note, telephone call from John Foster Dulles to Allen Dulles on October 18, 1956, *FRUS, 1955–1957*, vol. 16, *The Suez Crisis, July 26–December 31, 1956*, 754: "The Secretary said he is quite worried about what may be going on in the Near East. He does not think we have really any clear picture as to what the British and French are up to there. He thinks they are deliberately keeping us in the dark." Lloyd, *Suez 1956*, 168.

55. Richard Austen Butler, *The Art of the Possible: The Memoirs of Lord Butler* (Boston: Gambit, 1972), 193; Moshe Dayan, *Moshe Dayan: Story of My Life* (New York: Morrow, 1976), 218.

56. Dayan, *Story of My Life*, 218; Avi Shlaim, "The Protocol of Sevres, 1956: Anatomy of a War Plot," *International Affairs* 73, no. 3 (1997): 509–30; Patrick Dean, The Dean Memorandum, FCO 73/ 205, National Archives, Kew, London, United Kingdom; British Cabinet agrees to possible Anglo-French Intervention in Egypt, Conclusions of a Meeting of the Cabinet, October 25,1956, CAB/128/30, National Archives, Kew, London, United Kingdom; Translation of the Third Chapter of the Third Part of *1956 Suez* by Christian Pineau, The Sevres Protocol, SELO 6/65, Selwyn Lloyd Papers, Churchill Archives Centre, Churchill College, University of Cambridge.

57. Andrew, *For the President's Eyes Only*, 231; Confidential Annex on Suez Canal, Conclusions of a Meeting of the Cabinet, October 23, 1956, CAB/128/30, National Archives, Kew, London, United Kingdom.

58. Andrew, *For the President's Eyes Only*, 232–33; Memorandum of a Conference with the President, Secretary Dulles, Mr. Coulson, Colonel Goodpaster, White House, Washington, October 29, 1956, *FRUS, 1955–1957*, vol. 16, *The Suez Crisis, July 26–December 31, 1956*, 839–40.

59. Tripartite Declaration Regarding Security in the Near East," *U.S. Department of State Bulletin* 22, no. 570 (June 5, 1950): 886; Andrew, *For the President's Eyes Only,* 232–33; Dwight D. Eisenhower to Robert Anthony Eden, October 30, 1956, EM, AWF, International Series: Eden, *The Presidency: The Middle Way,* vol. 17 of *The Papers of Dwight David Eisenhower,* 2341; Editorial Note, *FRUS, 1955–1957,* vol. 16, *The Suez Crisis, July 26–December 31, 1956,* 840–42; President Dwight D. Eisenhower to Prime Minister Anthony Eden, October 30, 1956, AP 20/27/86, Avon Papers.

60. President to Prime Minister, October 30, 1956, AP 20/27/92, Avon Papers; Dwight D. Eisenhower to Robert Anthony Eden, October 30, 1956, EM, AWF, International Series: Eden, *The Presidency: The Middle Way,* vol. 17 of *The Papers of Dwight David Eisenhower,* 2343–44.

61. Andrew, *For the President's Eyes Only,* 234.

62. Ibid., 234–35.

63. Dooley, "Great Britain's 'Last Battle' in the Middle East," 515.

64. Ibid., 595–96; Dwight D. Eisenhower to John Foster Dulles, November 1, 1956, EM, AWF, International Series: Eden, *The Presidency: The Middle Way,* vol. 17 of *The Papers of Dwight David Eisenhower,* 2347n5: "Eisenhower would slow shipments of petroleum to Western Europe, allowing only the minimum to maintain NATO reserves. When Under Secretary Hoover commented that in the event of a cut off of oil from the Middle East, 'the British may be estimating that we would have no choice but to take extraordinary means to get oil to them.' Eisenhower had replied that 'he did not see much value in an unworthy and unreliable ally and that the necessity to support them might not be as great as they believed.'" See Peter J. Hahn, *The United States, Great Britain, and Egypt, 1945–1956: Strategy and Diplomacy in the Early Cold War* (Chapel Hill: University of North Carolina Press, 1991), 231–34.

65. National Security Meeting, November 1, 1956, NSC Series Box No. 8, Ann Whitman File, Papers of Dwight D. Eisenhower, 1953–61; Memorandum of Discussion at the 302d Meeting of the National Security Council, Washington, November 1, 1956, *FRUS, 1955–1957,* vol. 16, *The Suez Crisis, July 26–December 31, 1956,* 902–16.

66. Andrew, *For the President's Eyes Only,* 236; Editorial Note, *FRUS, 1955–1957,* vol. 16, *The Suez Crisis, July 26, 1956–December 31, 1956,* 932–33.

67. Eden, *Full Circle,* 604; Conclusions of a Meeting of the Cabinet, November 2, 1956, CAB/128/30, National Archives, Kew, London, United Kingdom.

68. Lloyd, *Suez 1956,* 202; Ambrose, *The President, 1952–1969,* 365.

69. Ambrose, *The President, 1952–1969,* 367.

70. Report by the Joint Middle East Planning Committee to the Joint Chiefs of Staff: Analysis of Possible Soviet Courses of Action in the Middle East, Washington, November 3, 1956, *FRUS, 1955–1957,* vol. 16, *The Suez Crisis, July 26–December 31, 1956,* 970.

71. Andrew, *For the President's Eyes Only,* 236; Eisenhower, *Waging Peace,* 88–89.

72. Memorandum of Conference with the President with Gov. Adams, Sec. Hoover, Mr. Phleger, Mr. Hegarty, Emmet Hughes, and Colonel Goodpaster on November 5, 1956, Memorandum by Goodpaster on November 7, 1956, File Meetings with the President, Aug.– Dec. 1956 (3), White House Memoranda Series Box no. 4, A67–28, Papers of John Foster Dulles, Dwight D. Eisenhower Library. See also Prime Minister Eden to President Eisenhower, November 5, 1956, AP 20/27/96, Avon Papers.

73. Ambrose, *The President, 1952–1969*, 368; Emmet John Hughes, *The Ordeal of Power: A Political Memoir of the Eisenhower Years* (New York: Atheneum, 1963), 222–23; Brian Mc-Cauley, "Hungary and Suez, 1956: The Limits of Soviet and American Power," *Journal of Contemporary History* 16, no. 4 (October 1981): 795: "Geography, then, played a central role in determining the response of the Soviet Union to the Suez Crisis and the United States to the Hungarian Revolution. The belligerent calls for 'rollback' and 'liberation' on the American side and the ardent support for 'anti-colonial' wars and 'wars of national liberation' on the Soviet side proved to be nothing but empty rhetoric in the autumn of 1956." E. Thomas, *Ike's Bluff*, 229.

74. Ambrose, *The President, 1952–1969*, 368.

75. Dwight D. Eisenhower to Anthony Eden, letter confirming the cease-fire, November 6, 1956, AP 20/27/97, Avon Papers; Prime Minister to President Eisenhower, November 6, 1956, AP 20/27/98, Avon Papers; Gilbert, *Never Despair*, 1224–25; British Cabinet Agrees to UN Ceasefire, Conclusions of a Meeting of the Cabinet, November 6, 1956, CAB/128/30, National Archives, Kew, London, United Kingdom; Record of a Conversation between the Secretary of State [Lloyd] and Sir Winston Churchill, June 25, 1958, SELO 6/70, Selwyn Lloyd Papers, Churchill Archives Centre, Churchill College, University of Cambridge: "He [Churchill] confirmed the remark that he would not have been brave enough to go in but, if he had gone in, he would not have been brave enough to come out. He said he thought we ought to have pushed on and taken Cairo."

CHAPTER SEVEN

1. Nichols, *Eisenhower 1956*, 264; James M. Boughton, "Northwest of Suez: The 1956 Crisis and the IMF," *IMF Staff Papers* 48, no. 3 (2001): 435; Randolph S. Churchill, *The Rise and Fall of Sir Anthony Eden* (New York: Putnam, 1959), 288–89.

2. Nichols, *Eisenhower 1956*, 263; Consulate General in Dharan to the Department of State from Ambassador Wadsworth, telegram, November 26, 1956, *FRUS, 1955–1957*, vol. 16, *The Suez Crisis, July 26–December 31, 1956*, 1200.

3. Adam Klug and Gregor W. Smith, "Suez and Sterling, 1956," Queen's Economics Department Working Paper No. 1256, Department of Economics, Queen's University, Kingston, Ontario, Canada, 1999, 17–18.

4. Memorandum of Conversation with President, Secretary of State, Mr. Hoover Junior and Mr. Macomber at Walter Reed Hospital on November 7, 1956, File Meetings with the President, Aug. thru Dec. 1956 (3), White House Memoranda Series Box No. 4, A67–28, Papers of John Foster Dulles, Dwight D. Eisenhower Library; Victor Rothwell, *Anthony Eden*, 236: "Eisenhower was building up resentment against Eden which exploded from 7 November as reports reached him from French sources of the three-power collusion, confirming the suspicions which he already entertained. From 'trying to understand' Eden his attitude became hostile to the point of vindictiveness." Prime Minister to President, November 7, 1956, AP 20/27/99, Avon Papers: "When you told me of your pre-occupations with Congress during the next two days I did not feel able to press my suggestion for an immediate meeting."

5. Winthrop W. Aldrich, "The Suez Crisis: A Footnote to History," *Foreign Affairs* 45, no. 3 (April 1967): 548.

6. Keith Kyle, *Suez* (New York: St. Martin's, 1991), 493, 497: "Ben Gurion was told by the head of Mossad on 1 December that 'the Americans will not make up with the English until Eden goes.'" Memorandum of Telephone Conversation between the President and the Acting Secretary of State, Washington, November 13, 1956, *FRUS, 1955–1957*, vol. 16, *The Suez Crisis, July 26–December 31, 1956*, 1122: "Secy. Hoover mentioned Selwyn Lloyd in N.Y. & suppose he should want to come see the President. State's reaction is that it would be almost as bad as Eden coming."

7. Memorandum of Conversation between the President, Secretary of State, and Mr. Macomber at Walter Reed Hospital on November 12, 1956, File Meetings with the President, Aug-Dec. 1956 (3), White House Memoranda Series Box no. 4, A67-28, Papers of John Foster Dulles, Dwight D. Eisenhower Library: "Returning to the Suez Crisis the President said he now believed that the British had not been in on the Israeli-French planning until the very last stages and they had no choice but to come into the operation. He had felt when the British originally denied collusion with the French and the Israelis that they were misleading us, but he had now come to the conclusion that they were telling the truth. One of the arguments President cited to support this view was the long delay that took place between the time the British declared their intent to go into Egypt and the time they actually went in."

8. Winthrop Aldrich to Herbert Hoover Junior, telegram, November 12, 1956, Foster Dulles Nov. 1956 (2), Dulles-Herter Series Box No. 8, Ann Whitman File, Papers of Dwight D. Eisenhower, 1953–61; Embassy in the United Kingdom to the Department of State, telegram, London, November 12, 1956, *FRUS, 1955–1957*, vol. 16, *Suez Crisis, July 26–December 31, 1956*, 1115–17.

9. Memorandum by the Director of Central Intelligence, Washington, November 6, 1956, *FRUS, 1955–1957*, vol. 16, *The Suez Crisis, July 26–December 31, 1956*, 1136; Lloyd, *Suez 1956*, 219.

10. Herman Finer, *Dulles over Suez: The Theory and Practice of His Diplomacy* (Chicago: Quadrangle, 1964), 446: "The British Foreign Minister could not get to see the President. He could not at first even get to see Herbert Hoover Jr." Memorandum of Conversation between Dwight D. Eisenhower and John Foster Dulles, and Mr. Macomber at Walter Reed Hospital on November 17, 1956, File Meetings with the President, Aug.–Dec. 1956 (3), White House Memoranda Series Box no. 4, A67-28, Papers of John Foster Dulles, Dwight D. Eisenhower Library.

11. Winthrop Aldrich to Dwight D. Eisenhower, John Foster Dulles, and Herbert Hoover Junior, telegram, Dulles, JF, November 19, 1956, Nov. 56 (1), Dulles-Herter Series Box No. 8, Ann Whitman File, Papers of Dwight D. Eisenhower, 1953–61.

12. Phone Conversation between Dwight D. Eisenhower and Ambassador Winthrop Aldrich on November 20, 1956, File November 56 Phone Calls, DDE Diary Box 19, Ann Whitman File, Papers of Dwight D. Eisenhower, 1953–61.

13. Goodpaster Memorandum of Conference, November 21, 1956, Ann Whitman File, *The Presidency: The Middle Way*, vol. 17 of *The Papers of Dwight David Eisenhower*, 2403n1: "As soon as things happen that we anticipate, we can furnish 'a lot of fig leaves.'"

14. Dorril, *MI6*, 649; letter of 6 December 1956: Churchill Papers, 2/143. See also Gilbert, *Never Despair*, 1224n3: "Randolph Churchill earned Eden's life-long opprobrium for writing to the *Manchester Guardian* that the disastrous position of Britain at Suez was like that of the Germans at Stalingrad. 'But even Hitler did not winter in Jamaica.'"

15. Dayan, *Story of My Life*, 450–51.

16. Eisenhower, *Waging Peace, 1956–1961*, 681; Dwight D. Eisenhower to Winston Spencer Churchill, November 27, 1956, EM, AWF, International Series: Churchill, *The Presidency: The Middle Way*, vol. 17 of *The Papers of Dwight David Eisenhower*, 2412–15.

17. Ronald Reagan, *The Notes: Ronald Reagan's Private Collection of Stories and Wisdom*, ed. David Brinkley (New York: HarperCollins, 2011), 69.

18. Dorril, *MI6*, 649; Dutton, *Anthony Eden*, 448: "The American aim seems to have been to keep a Conservative government in power, but one probably not headed by Eden. Not surprisingly, it was the Chancellor who took the lead. Despite the impression given in his memoirs, Macmillan now believed that Eden 'could never return and remain Prime Minister for long.'"

19. Dooley, "Great Britain's 'Last Battle' in the Middle East," 516: "On 20 November, at the same time oil rationing had to be introduced, the Cabinet was informed by Macmillan of the depth of the financial crisis. In the first of a series of reports recorded in confidential annexes to the Cabinet minutes, Macmillan reported that the loss of gold and dollars during the month could run as high as $300 million and that 'sterling might cease to be an international currency.'" Finer, *Dulles over Suez*, 454; National Security Council Meeting, November 30, 1956, NSC Series Box No. 8, Ann Whitman File, Papers of Dwight D. Eisenhower, 1953–61.

20. Dooley, "Great Britain's 'Last Battle' in the Middle East," 517.

21. Jonathan Pearson, *Sir Anthony Eden and the Suez Crisis: Reluctant Gamble* (Basingstoke, England: Palgrave Macmillan, 2003), 168; Memorandum of a Conversation on 'Unconditional' Suez Withdrawal between Selwyn Lloyd and John Foster Dulles, Ambassador Dillon's Residence, Paris, December 10, 1956, *FRUS, 1955–1957*, vol. 16, *The Suez Crisis, July 26–December 31, 1956*, 1278: "Mr. Lloyd opened the conversation by saying that his Government had done an "extraordinary thing" in that it had agreed "because the U.S. demanded it" to come out unconditionally from Egypt. He added parenthetically that as the Secretary knew the sterling area also had a good deal to do with this decision." Prime Minister Eden to Dame Irene Ward, December 28, 1956, AP 20/33/CA, Avon Papers: "Yet so many seem to fail to see this and give Nasser as much trust as others gave Hitler years ago."

22. Pearson, *Sir Anthony Eden and the Suez Crisis*, 168; Lloyd, *Suez 1956*, 236.

23. Lloyd, *Suez 1956*, 236; Sir Anthony Eden, Resignation, Conclusions of a Meeting of the Cabinet, January 9, 1957, CAB/128/30, National Archives, Kew, London; A.E.'s note on meeting with Queen Elizabeth II on January 9, 1957, AP 20/30/10A, Avon Papers; Manchester and Reid, *The Last Lion: Winston Spencer Churchill; Defender of the Realm, 1940–1965*, 1043: "Thus Churchill's audience with the Queen. He advised her to choose Macmillan, later telling friends he did so because Macmillan was the older and more experienced man."

24. Eden to Eisenhower, January 17, 1957, in *The Eden-Eisenhower Correspondence, 1955–1957*, ed. Boyle, 190.

CHAPTER EIGHT

1. Will Herberg, *Protestant, Catholic, Jew: An Essay in American Religious Sociology* (Chicago: University of Chicago Press, 1955), 79: "The American way of life is individualistic, dynamic, and pragmatic. It affirms the supreme value and dignity of the individual, it stresses incessant activity on his part, for he is never to rest but is always to be striving to 'get ahead,' it defines an ethic of self-reliance, merit, and character, and judges by achievement: 'deeds, not creeds' are what count. The 'American Way of Life' is humanitarian, 'forward looking,' optimistic. Americans are easily the most generous and philanthropic people in the world, in terms of their ready and unstinting response to suffering anywhere on the globe. The American believes in progress, in self-improvement, and quite fanatically in education. But above all, the American is idealistic."

2. John W. Young, *Winston Churchill's Last Campaign: Britain and the Cold War 1951–5* (Oxford: Clarendon, 1996); Larres, *Churchill's Cold War*; David Carlton, "Churchill and the Two 'Evil Empires,'" *Transactions of the Royal Historical Society*, 6th ser., 11 (2001): 331–51.

3. Gilbert, *Churchill: A Life*.

4. Eisenhower, *Mandate for Change 1953–1956*, 180; Douglas MacArthur, *Reminiscences* (New York: McGraw-Hill, 1964); Brands, "The Dwight D. Eisenhower Administration, Syngman Rhee, and the 'Other Geneva' Conference of 1954," 59–85.

5. Global Firepower: 2011 World Military Strength Ranking," www.globalfirepower.com.

6. Historians praising Eisenhower for restraining Dulles include Chalmer Roberts, Townsend Hoopes, Arthur Krock, R. Gordon Hoxie, Donald Neff, Burton Kaufman, Warren I. Cohen, Elmo Richardson, Stephen E. Ambrose, Stephen G. Rabe, Fred I. Greenstein, Gregory J. Pemberton, Arthur Larson, Bernard B. Fall, Richard M. Saunders, David L. Anderson, Richard Immerman, Melanie Billings-Yun, and John Prados.

7. Rabe, "Eisenhower Revisionism," 109.

8. Dwight D. Eisenhower, "Special Message to the Congress on the Situation in the Middle East," January 5, 1957, www.presidency.ucsb.edu/ws/index.php?pid=11007&st=&st1=.

9. Ibid.

10. Robert Dallek, "The Untold Story of the Bay of Pigs," *Newsweek*, August 22 and 29, 2011, 26–28.

11. Nassir Ghaemi, *A First-Rate Madness: Uncovering the Links between Leadership and Mental Illness* (New York: Penguin, 2011), 177.

12. Ambrose, *The President, 1952–1969*, 660, 664.

BIBLIOGRAPHY

PRIMARY SOURCES

Archival Material

Acheson, Dean G., Papers. Harry S. Truman Presidential Library, Independence, Missouri, United States.

Attlee, Clement R., Papers. Churchill Archives Centre, Churchill College, University of Cambridge, Cambridge, United Kingdom.

Avon, Anthony Eden, 1st Earl of Avon, Papers. Special Collections, University of Birmingham Library, Birmingham, United Kingdom.

Butler, R. A., Papers. Wren Library, Trinity College, University of Cambridge, Cambridge, United Kingdom.

Churchill, Randolph, Papers. Churchill Archives Centre, Churchill College, University of Cambridge, Cambridge, United Kingdom.

Churchill, Winston, Papers. Churchill Archives Centre, Churchill College, University of Cambridge, Cambridge, United Kingdom.

Churchill, Winston, Cabinet Papers. National Archives, Kew, Surrey, United Kingdom.

Colville, John, Papers. Churchill Archives Centre, Churchill College, University of Cambridge, Cambridge, United Kingdom.

Dulles, Allen W., Papers. Seeley G. Mudd Manuscript Library, Princeton University, Princeton, New Jersey, United States.

Dulles, John Foster, Papers. Seeley G. Mudd Manuscript Library, Princeton University, Princeton, New Jersey, United States; and Dwight D. Eisenhower Presidential Library, Abilene, Kansas, United States.

Duncan-Sandys, Duncan Edwin, Papers. Churchill Archives Centre, Churchill College, University of Cambridge, Cambridge, United Kingdom.

Eden, Anthony, Cabinet Papers. National Archives, Kew, Surrey, United Kingdom.

Eisenhower, Dwight David, Papers. Dwight D. Eisenhower Presidential Library, Abilene, Kansas, United States.

Hailsham, Baron, Quintin Hogg, Papers. Churchill Archives Centre, Churchill College, University of Cambridge, Cambridge, United Kingdom.

Hoover, Herbert, Papers. Herbert Hoover Presidential Library, West Branch, Iowa, United States.

Johnson, Lyndon Baines, Papers. Lyndon B. Johnson Presidential Library, Austin, Texas, United States.

Kennan, George F., Papers. Seeley G. Mudd Manuscript Library, Princeton University, Princeton, New Jersey, United States.

Selwyn-Lloyd, Baron, John Selwyn Lloyd, Papers. Churchill Archives Centre, Churchill College, University of Cambridge, Cambridge, United Kingdom.

Sherfield, Baron, Sir Roger Makins, Papers. Bodleian Library, University of Oxford, Oxford, United Kingdom.

Soames, Baron, Christopher Soames, Papers. Churchill Archives Centre, Churchill College, University of Cambridge, Cambridge, United Kingdom.

Stevenson, Adlai, Papers. Seeley G. Mudd Manuscript Library, Princeton University, Princeton, New Jersey, United States.

Truman, Harry S., Papers. Harry S. Truman Presidential Library, Independence, Missouri, United States.

Published Documents and Records

Foreign Relations of the United States (FRUS). Washington, D.C., 1984–90.

   1952–1954, vol. 2: *China*

   1952–1954, vol. 2: *National Security Affairs*, pt. 2

   1952–1954, vol. 4: *The American Republics*

   1952–1954, vol. 5: *Western European Security*

   1952–1954, vol. 6: *Western Europe and Canada*, pt. 1

   1952–1954, vol. 8: *Eastern Europe, Soviet Union, Eastern Mediterranean*

   1952–1954, vol. 10: *Iran, 1951–1954*

   1952–1954, vol. 13: pt. 2, *Indochina*

   1952–1954, vol. 14: pt. 1, *China and Japan*

   1952–1954, vol. 15: *Korea*, pt. 1

   1952–1954, vol. 15: *Korea*, pt. 2

   1952–1954, vol. 16: *The Geneva Conference*

   1952–1954, *Guatemala*

   1955–1957, vol. 2: *China*

   1955–1957, vol. 12: *Near East Region; Iran; Iraq*

1955–1957, vol. 15: *The Arab-Israeli Dispute, January 1–July 26, 1956*

1955–1957, vol. 16: *The Suez Crisis, July 26–December 31, 1956*

Hansard, House of Commons Debates, 1950–1957.

Published Works

Acheson, Dean. *A Democrat Looks at His Party.* New York: Harper, 1955.

———. *Papers of Dean Acheson: Princeton Seminars.* Independence, Mo: Harry S. Truman Library, 1975.

———. *Power and Diplomacy.* The William L. Clayton Lectures on International Economic Affairs and Foreign Policy. Cambridge: Harvard University Press, 1958.

———. *Present at the Creation: My Years.* New York: Norton, 1969.

———. *Sketches from Life of Men I Have Known.* New York: Harper, 1961.

Adams, Sherman. *First-Hand Report: The Inside Story of the Eisenhower Administration.* New York: Harper, 1961.

Attlee, C. R. *As It Happened.* New York: Viking, 1954.

Bevin, Ernest. *The Balance Sheet of the Future.* New York: McBride, 1941.

———. *Ernest Bevin's Work in Wartime (1940–1945).* N.p: Labour Party, 1945.

Bevin, Ernest, and C. R. Attlee. *Britain's Foreign Policy.* London: Labour Party, 1946.

Bidault, Georges. *Resistance: The Political Autobiography of Georges Bidault.* Translated by Marianne Sinclair. New York: Praeger, 1965.

Boyle, Peter G., ed. *The Churchill–Eisenhower Correspondence, 1953–1955.* Chapel Hill: University of North Carolina Press, 1990.

———. *The Eden–Eisenhower Correspondence, 1955–1957.* Chapel Hill: University of North Carolina Press, 2005.

Bradley, Omar Nelson, and Clay Blair. *A General's Life: An Autobiography.* New York: Simon and Schuster, 1983.

Bundy, McGeorge. *Danger and Survival: Choices about the Bomb in the First Fifty Years.* New York: Random House, 1988.

Butler of Saffron Walden, Richard Austen Butler. *The Art of the Possible: The Memoirs of Lord Butler.* Boston: Gambit, 1972.

Butler, Susan, ed. *My Dear Mr. Stalin: The Complete Correspondence between Franklin D. Roosevelt and Joseph V. Stalin.* New Haven, Conn.: Yale University Press, 2005.

Churchill, Randolph Frederick Edward Spencer. *The Rise and Fall of Sir Anthony Eden.* London: MacGibbon and Kee, 1959.

Churchill, Winston. *Blood, Toil, Tears, and Sweat: The Speeches of Winston Churchill.* Edited by David Cannadine. Boston: Houghton Mifflin, 1989.

———. *The Churchill War Papers.* Edited by Martin Gilbert. New York: Norton, 1993.

———. *The Gathering Storm.* Boston: Houghton Mifflin, 1948.

———. *The Grand Alliance.* Boston: Houghton Mifflin, 1950.

———. *Great Contemporaries.* New York: Putnam, 1937.

———. *The Hinge of Fate.* Boston: Houghton Mifflin, 1950.

———. *Their Finest Hour.* Boston: Houghton Mifflin, 1949.

———. *Triumph and Tragedy.* Boston: Houghton Mifflin, 1953.

———. *Winston S. Churchill: His Complete Speeches, 1897–1963.* Edited by Robert Rhodes James. New York: Chelsea House, 1974.

———. *The World Crisis.* New York: Scribner, 1931.

Churchill, Winston, and Randolph S. Churchill. *While England Slept: A Survey of World Affairs, 1932–1938.* New York: Putnam, 1938.

Colville, John Rupert. *The Fringes of Power: 10 Downing Street Diaries, 1939–1955.* New York: Norton, 1985.

Dayan, Moshe. *Moshe Dayan: Story of My Life.* New York: Morrow, 1976.

Dulles, Allen Welsh. *The Craft of Intelligence.* New York: Harper and Row, 1963.

———. *Germany's Underground.* New York: Macmillan, 1947.

Dulles, John Foster. *The Papers of John Foster Dulles.* Wilmington, Del.: Scholarly Resources, 1993.

———. *War or Peace.* New York: Macmillan, 1950.

Eden, Anthony. *Facing the Dictators: The Memoirs of Anthony Eden, Earl of Avon.* Boston: Houghton Mifflin, 1962.

———. *Full Circle; The Memoirs of Anthony Eden.* Boston: Houghton Mifflin, 1960.

———. *The Reckoning; The Memoirs of Anthony Eden, Earl of Avon.* Boston: Houghton Mifflin, 1965.

———. *Toward Peace in Indochina.* Boston: Houghton Mifflin, 1966.

Eisenhower, Dwight D. *At Ease: Stories I Tell to Friends.* Garden City, N.Y.: Doubleday, 1967.

———. *Crusade in Europe.* Garden City, N.Y.: Doubleday, 1948.

———. *The Eisenhower Diaries.* Edited by Robert H. Ferrell. New York: Norton, 1981.

———. *Mandate for Change, 1953–1956.* Vol. 1 of *The White House Years.* Garden City, N.Y.: Doubleday, 1963.

———. *The Papers of Dwight David Eisenhower.* Edited by Alfred D. Chandler, Louis Galambos, and Duan Van Ee. Baltimore: Johns Hopkins University Press, 1970.

———. *Public Papers of the Presidents of the United States: Dwight D. Eisenhower, 1953–1957.* Washington, D.C.: Government Printing Office, 1958–60.

———. *Waging Peace, 1956–1961.* Vol. 2 of *The White House Years.* Garden City, N.Y.: Doubleday, 1965.

Hagerty, James C. *The Diary of James C. Hagerty: Eisenhower in Mid-Course, 1954–1955.* Edited by Robert H. Ferrell. Bloomington: Indiana University Press, 1983.

Hoover, Herbert. *Addresses upon the American Road, 1945–1948.* New York: Van Nostrand, 1949.

———. *Addresses upon the American Road, 1950–1955.* Stanford, Calif.: Stanford University Press, 1955.

———. *Addresses upon the American Road, 1955–1960.* Caldwell, Idaho: Caxton Printers, 1961.

———. *American Individualism.* Garden City, N.Y.: Doubleday, Page, 1922.

———. *The Hoover Commission Report on Organization of the Executive Branch of the Government.* New York: McGraw-Hill, 1949.

———. *Memoirs.* New York: Macmillan, 1951.

———. *The Ordeal of Woodrow Wilson.* New York: McGraw-Hill, 1958.

Hoover, Herbert. *Herbert Hoover's Challenge to America; His Life and Words.* Edited by Robert L. Polley. Waukesha. Wisc.: Country Beautiful Foundation, 1965.

Hughes, Emmet John. *The Ordeal of Power: A Political Memoir of the Eisenhower Years.* New York: Atheneum, 1963.

Kennan, George F. *American Diplomacy, 1900–1950.* Charles R. Walgreen Foundation Lectures. Chicago: University of Chicago Press, 1951.

———. *Memoirs.* Boston: Little, Brown, 1967.

———. *Realities of American Foreign Policy.* Princeton, N.J.: Princeton University Press, 1954.

———. *Russia, the Atom and the West.* New York: Harper, 1958.

———. *Russia and the West under Lenin and Stalin.* Boston: Little, Brown, 1961.

Kennan, George F., and John Lukacs. *George F. Kennan and the Origins of Containment, 1944–1946: The Kennan-Lukacs Correspondence.* Columbia: University of Missouri Press, 1997.

Kennedy, John F. *Profiles in Courage.* New York: Harper and Row, 1964.

———. *The Strategy of Peace.* New York: Harper, 1960.

———. *Why England Slept.* New York: Funk, 1940.

Khrushchev, Nikita Sergeevich. *The Anti-Stalin Campaign and International Communism: A Selection of Documents.* New York: Columbia University Press, 1956.

———. *Conquest without War: An Analytical Anthology of the Speeches, Interviews, and Remarks of Nikita Sergeyevich Khrushchev.* Edited by N. H. Mager and Jacques Katel. New York: Simon and Schuster, 1961.

———. *Khrushchev Remembers.* With introduction, commentary, and notes by Edward Crankshaw. Translated by Strobe Talbott. Boston: Little, Brown, 1970.

———. *Khrushchev Speaks; Selected Speeches, Articles, and Press Conferences, 1949–1961.* Edited by Thomas P. Whitney. Ann Arbor: University of Michigan Press, 1963.

———. *The National Liberation Movement: Selected Passages, 1956–63.* Moscow: Foreign Languages Pub. House, 1963.

Kimball, Warren F., ed. *Churchill and Roosevelt: The Complete Correspondence.* Princeton, N.J.: Princeton University Press, 1984.

Kissinger, Henry. *Nuclear Weapons and Foreign Policy*. New York: Published for the Council on Foreign Relations by Harper, 1957.

——. *On China*. New York: Penguin, 2011.

Krock, Arthur. *Memoirs: 60 Years on the Firing Line*. New York: Funk and Wagnall, 1968.

Lippmann, Walter. *The Cold War: A Study in U.S. Foreign Policy*. New York: Harper, 1947.

——. *Isolation and Alliances; An American Speaks to the British*. Boston: Little, Brown, 1952.

——. *U.S. Foreign Policy: Shield of the Republic*. Boston: Little, Brown, 1943.

——. *Western Unity and the Common Market*. Boston: Little, Brown, 1962.

Lloyd, Selwyn. *Suez 1956: A Personal Account*. New York: Mayflower, 1978.

MacArthur, Douglas. *Reminiscences*. New York: McGraw-Hill, 1964.

——. *Revitalizing a Nation: A Statement of Beliefs, Opinions, and Policies Embodied in the Public Pronouncements of Douglas MacArthur*. Chicago: Heritage Foundation, 1952. Distributed by Garden City Books, Garden City, N.Y., 1952.

Macmillan, Harold. *Riding the Storm, 1956–1959*. New York: Harper and Row, 1971.

——. *Tides of Fortune, 1945–1955*. New York: Harper and Row, 1969.

Marshall, George Catlett. *The Papers of George Catlett Marshall*. Edited by Larry I. Bland and Sharon Ritenour Stevens. Baltimore: Johns Hopkins University Press, 1981.

Moran, Lord, (Charles McMoran Wilson). *Churchill: The Struggle for Survival, 1940–1965*. Boston: Houghton Mifflin, 1966.

Murray, John Courtney. *Morality and Modern War*. New York: Council on Religion and International Affairs, 1959.

——. *St. Robert Bellarmine on the Indirect Power*. N.p., 1950.

Murray, John Courtney, and William Clancy. *The Moral Dilemma of Nuclear Weapons: Essays from "Worldview."* New York: Council on Religion and International Affairs, 1961.

Murphy, Robert D. *Diplomat among Warriors*. Garden City, N.Y.: Doubleday, 1964.

Niebuhr, Reinhold. *The Children of Light and the Children of Darkness: A Vindication of Democracy and a Critique of Its Traditional Defence*. New York: Scribner, 1944.

——. *Christian Realism and Political Problems*. New York: Scribner, 1953.

——. *The Irony of American History*. New York: Scribner, 1952.

——. *Moral Man and Immoral Society: A Study in Ethics and Politics*. New York: Scribner, 1960.

——. *The Structure of Nations and Empires; A Study of the Recurring Patterns and Problems of the Political Order in Relation to the Unique Problems of the Nuclear Age*. New York: Scribner, 1959.

Nitze, Paul H. *The Recovery of Ethics.* New York: Council on Religion and International Affairs, 1960.

Nixon, Richard M. *In the Arena: A Memoir of Victory, Defeat, and Renewal.* New York: Simon and Schuster, 1990.

———. *Leaders.* New York: Warner, 1982.

———. *The Real War.* New York: Warner, 1980; distributed in the United States by Random House.

———. *RN: The Memoirs of Richard Nixon.* New York: Grosset and Dunlap, 1978.

———. *Six Crises.* Garden City, N.Y.: Doubleday, 1962.

Nutting, Anthony. *Nasser.* New York: Dutton, 1972.

———. *No End of a Lesson: The Story of Suez.* London: Constable, 1967.

Philby, Kim. *My Silent War: The Soviet Master Spy's Own Story.* New York: Grove, 1968.

Radford, Arthur William. *From Pearl Harbor to Vietnam: The Memoirs of Admiral Arthur W. Radford.* Edited by Stephen Jurika. Stanford, Calif.: Hoover Institution Press, 1980.

Reagan, Ronald. *The Notes: Ronald Reagan's Private Collection of Stories and Wisdom.* Edited by David Brinkley. New York: Harper, 2011.

Ridgway, Matthew B. *The Korean War: How We Met the Challenge: How All-Out Asian War Was Averted: Why MacArthur Was Dismissed: Why Today's War Objectives Must Be Limited.* Garden City, N.Y.: Doubleday, 1967.

Roberts, Chalmers M. *First Rough Draft: A Journalist's Journal of Our Times.* New York: Praeger, 1973.

Roosevelt, Kermit. *Countercoup: The Struggle for the Control of Iran.* New York: McGraw-Hill, 1979.

Shuckburgh, Evelyn, and John Charmley. *Descent to Suez: Diaries, 1951–56.* New York: Norton, 1987.

Stalin, Joseph. *Foundations of Leninism.* New York: International, 1939.

———. *Works.* Moscow: Foreign Languages Publishing House, 1952.

Stevenson, Adlai E. *Call to Greatness.* New York: Harper, 1954.

———. *Major Campaign Speeches of Adlai E. Stevenson, 1952.* New York: Random House, 1953.

———. *The Papers of Adlai E. Stevenson.* Edited by Walter Johnson. Boston: Little, Brown, 1972.

———. *Putting First Things First: A Democratic View.* New York: Random House, 1960.

Taft, Robert A. *A Foreign Policy for Americans.* Garden City, N.Y.: Doubleday, 1951.

———. *The Papers of Robert A. Taft.* Edited by Clarence E. Wunderelin. Kent, Ohio: Kent State University Press, 1997.

Truman, Harry S. *Memoirs.* Garden City, N.Y.: Doubleday, 1955.

———. *Mr. Citizen.* New York: Geis Associates; 1960; distributed by Random House.

———. *Off the Record: The Private Papers of Harry S. Truman.* Edited by Robert H. Ferrell. New York: Harper and Row, 1980.

Truman, Margaret, ed. *Where the Buck Stops: The Personal and Private Writings of Harry S. Truman.* New York: Warner, 1989.

Vandenberg, Arthur H. *Arthur H. Vandenberg Correspondence.* Bowling Green, Ohio: Jerome Library, Center for Archival Collections, 1991.

———. *The Private Papers of Senator Vandenberg.* Edited by Joe Alex Morris. Boston: Houghton Mifflin, 1952.

Woodhouse, C. M. *Something Ventured.* London: Granada, 1982.

Zedong, Mao. *Selected Works.* New York: International, 1954.

Vital Speeches

Bulganin, Nikolai A. "Relaxation of International Tension: Collective Security System for Europe." *Vital Speeches* 21, no. 20 (1955): 1384–87.

Churchill, Winston. "British Foreign Policy: Statement on Washington Talks." *Vital Speeches* 20, no. 20 (1954): 610–13.

———. "Defense through Deterrents: Free World Should Retain Superiority in Nuclear Weapons." *Vital Speeches* 21, no. 11 (1955): 1090–94.

———. "Peace through Strength: The London Agreement." *Vital Speeches* 21, no. 3 (1954): 836–38.

———. "Survey of the World Scene: Change of Attitude and Mood in the Kremlin." *Vital Speeches* 19, no. 17 (1953): 522–26.

Dulles, John Foster. "Creating a Strong and Peaceful Europe: European Army Only 'Good Solution.'" *Vital Speeches* 19, no. 15 (1953): 456–57.

———. "Enlightened Self-Interest: Encirclement a Deadly Threat to United States." *Vital Speeches* 19, no. 9 (1953): 264–67.

———. "Human Equality versus Class Rule: The Struggle for Power by Communist Party." *Vital Speeches* 21, no. 10 (1955): 1061–64.

———. "The Peace We Seek: The Desperate Struggle against the War System." *Vital Speeches* 21, no. 8 (1955): 999–1001.

———. "The Power of the United Nations: An Era of Peaceful Change." *Vital Speeches* 22, no. 1 (1955): 2–6.

———. "Report from Asia: We Will Meet Force with Greater Force." *Vital Speeches* 21, no. 12 (1955): 1122–25.

———. "The Struggle for Justice: The Spirit in Which Our Nation Was Conceived." *Vital Speeches* 22, no. 6 (1956): 162–65.

———. "The Ultimate Weapon Is Moral Principle: Conference Gave Post-Stalin Knowledge of Soviet Intentions." *Vital Speeches* 20, no. 11 (1954): 322–25.

———. "Unity Must Be Achieved Soon: It May Never Be Possible for Integration to Occur in Freedom." *Vital Speeches* 20, no. 6 (1954): 165–66.

Eden, Anthony. "Principles of British Foreign Policy: To Preserve Our Way of Life and to Live in Peace." *Vital Speeches* 21, no. 3 (1954): 834–36.

Eisenhower, Dwight D. "An Atomic Stockpile for Peace: Dedicated to Serve the Needs Rather Than the Fears of Mankind." *Vital Speeches* 20, no. 6 (1954): 162–65.

———. "Defense of Our Country and Its Cost: Budget and Tax Recommendations." *Vital Speeches* 19, no 16 (1953): 482–85.

———. "The New Tax Program: Economic Conditions Do Not Warrant Additional Tax Reductions." *Vital Speeches* 20, no. 12 (1954): 364–66.

———. "Peace in the World: Acts, Not Rhetoric, Needed." *Vital Speeches* 19, no. 14 (1953): 418–21.

———. "The Search for Peace: International Trade A Step on the Road to Universal Peace." *Vital Speeches* 21, no. 15 (1955): 1218–20.

———. "The State of the Union: Building a Stronger America." *Vital Speeches* 20, no. 8 (1954): 226–31.

———. "The State of the Union: Three Main Purposes of our Federal Government." *Vital Speeches* 21, no. 7 (1955): 962–68.

———. "World Freedom and Peace: The Responsibilities of Leadership." *Vital Speeches* 19, no. 8 (1953): 252–54.

Kennedy, John F. "The War in Indochina: The Wholehearted Support of the Peoples of the Associated States Is Necessary for Victory." *Vital Speeches* 20, no. 14 (1954): 418–24.

MacArthur, Douglas. "The Abolition of War: Triumph of Scientific Annihilation." *Vital Speeches* 21, no. 9 (1955): 1040–43.

Macmillan, Harold. "Diplomacy's Long Haul: The New Phase in East-West Relations." *Vital Speeches* 22, no. 1 (1955): 11–14.

Makins, Roger. "The Balance of Power: Anglo-American Unity Vitally Necessary to World Peace." *Vital Speeches* 21, no. 12 (1955): 1131–35.

Martin, Joseph W., Jr. "Liberty, Intelligence, Our Nation's Safety: 'Coexistence' with Communism Impossible." *Vital Speeches* 20, no. 20 (1954): 613–15.

Oliver, Robert T. "American Foreign Policy in a World Adrift: We Must Assert Leadership Not Partnership." *Vital Speeches* 21, no. 1 (1954): 776–81.

Ridgway, Matthew B. "The Statesman and the Soldier: Foreign Policy Has a Military Aspect as Well as Peaceful Aspect." *Vital Speeches* 20, no. 22 (1954): 674–76.

Stevenson, Adlai E. "China Policy: Condemns Force in Formosa Strait." *Vital Speeches* 32, no.14 (1955): 1188–91.

Taft, Robert A. "United States Foreign Policy: Forget United Nations in Korea and Far East." *Vital Speeches* 19, no.17 (1953): 529–31.

SECONDARY SOURCES

Books

Abrahamian, Ervand. *Iran between Two Revolutions*. Princeton, N.J.: Princeton University Press, 1982.

Aldrich, Richard J. *The Hidden Hand: Britain, America and Cold War Secret Intelligence*. London: Murray, 2001.

Allen, H. C. *Great Britain and the United States; A History of Anglo-American Relations (1783–1952)*. New York: St. Martin's, 1955.

Ambrose, Stephen E. *Eisenhower*. New York: Simon and Schuster, 1983.

———. *Nixon*. New York: Simon and Schuster, 1987.

———. *The President, 1952–1969*. Vol. 2 of *Eisenhower*. New York: Simon and Schuster, 1984.

Ambrose, Stephen E., and Douglas Brinkley. *Rise to Globalism: American Foreign Policy since 1938*. New York: Penguin, 1997.

Anderson, David L. *Trapped by Success: The Eisenhower Administration and Vietnam, 1953–1961*. New York: Columbia University Press, 1991.

Anderson, Terry H. *The United States, Great Britain, and the Cold War, 1944–1947*. Columbia: University of Missouri Press, 1981.

Andrew, Christopher M. *For the President's Eyes Only: Secret Intelligence and the American Presidency from Washington to Bush*. New York: HarperCollins, 1995.

Arnold, James R. *The First Domino: Eisenhower, the Military, and America's Intervention in Vietnam*. New York: Morrow, 1991.

Aster, Sidney. *Anthony Eden*. New York: St. Martin's, 1976.

Barnet, Richard J. *Intervention and Revolution: The United States in the Third World*. New York: World, 1968.

Bartlett, C. J. *"The Special Relationship": A Political History of Anglo-American Relations since 1945*. Postwar World series. London: Longman, 1992.

Baylis, John. *Anglo-American Defence Relations, 1939–1984: The Special Relationship*. London: Macmillan, 1984.

Beisner, Robert L. *Dean Acheson: A Life in the Cold War*. Oxford: Oxford University Press, 2006.

Beschloss, Michael R. *The Crisis Years: Kennedy and Khrushchev, 1960–1963*. New York: Edward Burlingame, 1991.

———. *Mayday: Eisenhower, Khrushchev, and the U-2 Affair*. New York: Harper and Row, 1986.

Best, Richard A. *Co-Operation with Like-Minded Peoples: British Influences on American Security Policy, 1945–1949*. Contributions in American History, no. 116. New York: Greenwood, 1986.

Betts, Richard K. *Nuclear Blackmail and Nuclear Balance.* Washington, D.C.: Brookings Institution, 1987.

Bill, James A. *The Eagle and the Lion: The Tragedy of American-Iranian Relations.* New Haven, Conn.: Yale University Press, 1988.

Bill, James A., and William Roger Louis. *Musadiq, Iranian Nationalism, and Oil.* Austin: University of Texas Press, 1988.

Billings-Yun, Melanie. *Decision against War: Eisenhower and Dien Bien Phu, 1954.* New York: Columbia University Press, 1988.

Blair, Clay. *The Forgotten War: America in Korea, 1950–1953.* New York: Times Books, 1987.

Blasier, Cole. *The Hovering Giant: U.S. Responses to Revolutionary Change in Latin America.* New York: University of Pittsburgh Press, 1976.

Botti, Timothy J. *The Long Wait: The Forging of the Anglo-American Nuclear Alliance, 1945–1958.* Contributions in Military Studies, no. 64. New York: Greenwood, 1987.

Brinkley, Douglas. *Dean Acheson: The Cold War Years, 1953–71.* New Haven, Conn.: Yale University Press, 1992.

———. *Dean Acheson and the Making of U.S. Foreign Policy.* New York: St. Martin's, 1993.

Brown, Seyom. *The Faces of Power: Constancy and Change in United States Foreign Policy from Truman to Johnson.* New York: Columbia University Press, 1968.

Burk, Robert Fredrick. *Dwight D. Eisenhower, Hero and Politician.* Boston: Twayne, 1986.

Campbell-Johnson, Alan. *Eden: The Making of a Statesman.* Westport, Conn.: Greenwood, 1976.

Carlton, David. *Anthony Eden, a Biography.* London: Penguin, 1981.

Chang, Gordon H. *Friends and Enemies: The United States, China, and the Soviet Union, 1948–1972.* Stanford, Calif.: Stanford University Press, 1990.

Chang, Jung, and Jon Halliday. *Mao: The Unknown Story.* New York: Knopf, 2005.

Charmley, John. *Churchill's Grand Alliance: The Anglo-American Special Relationship, 1940–57.* New York: Harcourt Brace, 1995.

Chen, Jian. *Mao's China and the Cold War.* Chapel Hill: University of North Carolina Press, 2001.

Chernus, Ira. *Apocalypse Management: Eisenhower and the Discourse of National Insecurity.* Stanford, Calif.: Stanford University Press, 2008.

———. *Eisenhower's Atoms for Peace.* College Station: Texas A&M University Press, 2002.

———. *General Eisenhower: Ideology and Discourse.* East Lansing: Michigan State University Press, 2002.

Churchill, Randolph S. *The Rise and Fall of Sir Anthony Eden.* New York: Putnam, 1959.

Churchill, Randolph S., and Martin Gilbert. *Winston S. Churchill*. Boston: Houghton Mifflin, 1966.

Clark, Ian. *Nuclear Diplomacy and the Special Relationship: Britain's Deterrent and America, 1957–1962*. Oxford: Clarendon, 1994.

Cohen, Warren I. *America in the Age of Soviet Power, 1945–1991*. Vol. 4 of *The Cambridge History of American Foreign Relations*. Cambridge: University of Cambridge, 1993.

———, ed. *New Frontiers in American–East Asian Relations: Essays Presented to Dorothy Borg*. New York: Columbia University Press, 1983.

Cohen, Warren I., and Akira Iriye. *The Great Powers in East Asia, 1953–1960*. New York: Columbia University Press, 1990.

Cottam, Richard W. *Nationalism in Iran*. Pittsburgh, Pa.: University of Pittsburgh Press, 1979.

Crabb, Cecil Van Meter. *Bipartisan Foreign Policy: Myth or Reality?* Evanston, Ill.: Row, Peterson, 1957.

Cullather, Nick, and Piero Gleijeses. *Secret History: The CIA's Classified Account of Its Operations in Guatemala, 1952–1954*. Stanford, Calif.: Stanford University Press, 1999.

Cumings, Bruce. *Child of Conflict: The Korean-American Relationship, 1943–1953*. Seattle: University of Washington Press, 1983.

Damms, Richard V. *The Eisenhower Presidency, 1953–1961*. London: Pearson Education, 2002.

Dean, Robert D. *Imperial Brotherhood: Gender and the Making of Cold War Foreign Policy*. Culture, Politics, and the Cold War series. Amherst: University of Massachusetts Press, 2001.

Dickie, John. *"Special" No More: Anglo-American Relations: Rhetoric and Reality*. London: Weidenfeld and Nicolson, 1994.

Divine, Robert A. *Eisenhower and the Cold War*. New York: Oxford University Press, 1981.

Dixon, Pierson. *Double Diploma: The Life of Sir Pierson Dixon, Don and Diplomat*: London: Hutchinson, 1968.

Dobson, Alan P. *Anglo-American Relations in the Twentieth Century: Of Friendship, Conflict, and the Rise and Decline of Superpowers*. London: Routledge, 2002.

———. *The Politics of the Anglo-American Economic Special Relationship, 1940–1987*. Brighton, Sussex, England: Wheatsheaf, 1988.

Dockrill, M. L., and John W. Young. *British Foreign Policy, 1945–56*. New York: St. Martin's, 1989.

Doenecke, Justus D. *Anti-Intervention: A Bibliographical Introduction to Isolationism and Pacifism from World War I to the Early Cold War*. New York: Garland, 1987.

———. *Not to the Swift: The Old Isolationists in the Cold War Era*. Lewisburg, Pa.: Bucknell University Press, 1979.

Donovan, Robert J. *Conflict and Crisis: The Presidency of Harry S. Truman, 1945–1948.* New York: Norton, 1977.

———. *Eisenhower: The Inside Story.* New York: Harper, 1956.

———. *Tumultuous Years: The Presidency of Harry S. Truman, 1949–1953.* New York: Norton, 1982.

Dorril, Stephen. *MI6: Inside the Covert World of Her Majesty's Secret Intelligence Service.* New York: Free Press, 2000.

Drummond, Roscoe, and Gaston Coblentz. *Duel at the Brink: John Foster Dulles' Command of American Power.* Garden City, N.Y.: Doubleday, 1960.

Duffield, John S. *Power Rules: The Evolution of NATO's Conventional Force Posture.* Stanford, Calif.: Stanford University Press, 1995.

Duiker, William J. *Ho Chi Minh.* New York: Hyperion, 2000.

Dutton, David. *Anthony Eden: A Life and Reputation.* New York: St. Martin's, 1997.

Edmonds, Robin. *Setting the Mould: The United States and Britain, 1945–1950.* New York: Norton, 1986.

Engel, Jeffrey A. *Cold War at 30,000 Feet: The Anglo-American Fight for Aviation Supremacy.* Cambridge: Harvard University Press, 2007.

Eubank, Keith. *The Summit Conferences, 1919–1960.* Norman: University of Oklahoma Press, 1966.

Fall, Bernard B. *Hell in a Very Small Place: The Siege of Dien Bien Phu.* New York: Da Capo, 1985.

Finer, Herman. *Dulles over Suez: The Theory and Practice of His Diplomacy.* Chicago: Quadrangle, 1964.

Fontaine, André. *History of the Cold War.* New York: Pantheon, 1968.

Freeman, J. P. G. *Britain's Nuclear Arms Control Policy in the Context of Anglo-American Relations, 1957–68.* New York: St. Martin's, 1986.

Fursdon, Edward. *The European Defence Community: A History.* New York: St. Martin's, 1980.

Fursenko, A. A., and Timothy J. Naftali. *Khrushchev's Cold War: The Inside Story of an American Adversary.* New York: Norton, 2006.

Gaddis, John Lewis. *The Cold War: A New History.* New York: Penguin, 2005.

———. *The Long Peace: Inquiries into the History of the Cold War.* New York: Oxford University Press, 1987.

———. *Strategies of Containment: A Critical Appraisal of Postwar American National Security Policy.* New York: Oxford University Press, 1982.

———. *The United States and the Origins of the Cold War, 1941–1947.* New York: Columbia University Press, 1972.

Gardner, Lloyd C. *Approaching Vietnam: From World War II through Dienbienphu, 1941–1954.* New York: Norton 1988.

Gasiorowski, Mark J., and Malcolm Byrne. *Mohammad Mosaddeq and the 1953 Coup in Iran*. Syracuse, N.Y.: Syracuse University Press, 2004.

George, Alexander L., and Richard Smoke. *Deterrence in American Foreign Policy: Theory and Practice*. New York: Columbia University Press, 1974.

Ghaemi, Nassir. *A First-Rate Madness: Uncovering the Links between Leadership and Mental Illness*. New York: Penguin, 2011.

Gibbons, William Conrad. *The U.S. Government and the Vietnam War: Executive and Legislative Roles and Relationships*. Princeton, N.J.: Princeton University Press, 1986.

Gilbert, Martin. *Churchill: A Life*. New York: Holt, 1991.

———. *Churchill and America*. New York: Free Press, 2005.

———. *Never Despair: Winston S. Churchill, 1945–1965*. London: Heinemann, 1988.

Gleijeses, Piero. *Shattered Hope: The Guatemalan Revolution and the United States, 1944–1954*. Princeton, N.J.: Princeton University Press, 1991.

Goold-Adams, Richard. *John Foster Dulles; A Reappraisal*. Westport, Conn.: Greenwood, 1974.

Grayling, Christopher, and Christopher Langdon. *Just Another Star? Anglo-American Relations since 1945*. London: Harrap, 1988.

Greenstein, Fred I. *The Hidden-Hand Presidency: Eisenhower as Leader*. New York: Basic, 1982.

Gunther, John, and Carl Howard Pforzheimer. *The Riddle of MacArthur: Japan, Korea, and the Far East*. New York: Harper, 1951.

Harbutt, Fraser J. *The Iron Curtain: Churchill, America, and the Origins of the Cold War*. New York: Oxford University Press, 1986.

Harding, Harry, and Ming Yuan. *Sino-American Relations, 1945–1955: A Joint Reassessment of a Critical Decade*. Wilmington, Del.: SR, 1989.

Harnsberger, Caroline Thomas. *A Man of Courage: Robert A. Taft*. Chicago: Wilcox and Follett, 1952.

Hathaway, Robert M. *Ambiguous Partnership: Britain and America, 1944–1947*. Contemporary American History Series. New York: Columbia University Press, 1981.

———. *Great Britain and the United States: Special Relations since World War II*. Twayne's International History Series, no. 4. Boston: Twayne, 1990.

Haykal, Muḥammad Ḥasanayn. *Cutting the Lion's Tail: Suez through Egyptian Eyes*. London: Deutsch, 1986.

Heikel, Mohamed Ḥasanein. *The Cairo Documents; The Inside Story of Nasser and His Relationship with World Leaders, Rebels, and Statesmen*. Garden City, N.Y.: Doubleday, 1973.

Herberg, Will. *Protestant, Catholic, Jew: An Essay in American Religious Sociology*. Chicago: University of Chicago Press, 1955.

Hermes, Walter G. *Truce Tent and Fighting Front*. Washington, D.C.: Office of Military History, United States Army, 1966.

Higgins, Trumbull. *Korea and the Fall of MacArthur: A Précis in Limited War*. New York: Oxford University Press, 1960.

Hoopes, Townsend. *The Devil and John Foster Dulles*. Boston: Little, Brown, 1973.

Horowitz, David. *The Free World Colossus; A Critique of American Foreign Policy in the Cold War*. New York: Hill and Wang, 1965.

Huth, Paul K. *Extended Deterrence and the Prevention of War*. New Haven, Conn.: Yale University Press, 1988.

Immerman, Richard H. *The CIA in Guatemala: The Foreign Policy of Intervention*. Austin: University of Texas Press, 1982.

———. *John Foster Dulles and the Diplomacy of the Cold War*. Princeton, N.J.: Princeton University Press, 1990.

Jackson, Robert. *Suez: The Forgotten Invasion*. Shrewsbury, England: Airlife, 1996.

James, D. Clayton. *The Years of MacArthur*. Boston: Houghton Mifflin, 1970.

James, Laura M. *Nasser at War: Arab Images of the Enemy*. Basingstoke, England: Palgrave Macmillan, 2006.

James, Robert Rhodes. *Anthony Eden*. New York: McGraw-Hill, 1987.

Jankowski, James P. *Nasser's Egypt, Arab Nationalism, and the United Arab Republic*. Boulder, Colo.: Rienner, 2002.

Jenkins, Roy. *Churchill: A Biography*. New York: Penguin, 2002.

Jones, Peter. *America and the British Labour Party: The Special Relationship at Work*. London: Tauris, 1997.

Jordan, Robert S. *Generals in International Politics: NATO's Supreme Allied Commander, Europe*. Lexington: University Press of Kentucky, 1987.

Kahin, George McTurnan. *Intervention: How America Became Involved in Vietnam*. New York: Knopf, 1986.

Kalicki, J. H. *The Pattern of Sino-American Crises: Political-Military Interactions in the 1950s*. London: Cambridge University Press, 1975.

Kaplan, Lawrence S. *The Long Entanglement: NATO's First Fifty Years*. Westport, Conn.: Praeger, 1999.

———. *NATO and the United States: The Enduring Alliance*. Twayne's International History Series, no. 1. Boston: Twayne, 1988.

———. *The United States and NATO: The Formative Years*. Lexington: University Press of Kentucky, 1984.

Kapstein, Ethan B. *The Insecure Alliance: Energy Crises and Western Politics since 1944*. New York: Oxford University Press, 1990.

Kaufman, Burton Ira. *Trade and Aid: Eisenhower's Foreign Economic Policy, 1953–1961*. Johns Hopkins University Studies in Historical and Political Science, 100th ser., 1. Baltimore: Johns Hopkins University Press, 1982.

Keddie, Nikki R., and Yann Richard. *Roots of Revolution: An Interpretive History of Modern Iran*. New Haven, Conn.: Yale University Press, 1981.

Keegan, John. *Churchill.* London: Weidenfeld and Nicolson, 2002.

Kenneally, James J. *A Compassionate Conservative: A Political Biography of Joseph W. Martin Jr., Speaker of the U.S. House of Representatives.* Lanham, Md.: Lexington, 2003.

Kinzer, Stephen. *All the Shah's Men: An American Coup and the Roots of Middle East Terror.* Hoboken, N.J.: Wiley, 2003.

Kirby, William C., Robert S. Ross, and Li Gong. *Normalization of U.S.-China Relations: An International History.* Cambridge: Harvard University Asia Center, 2005.

Kirk, Russell, and James McClellan. *The Political Principles of Robert A. Taft.* New York: Fleet, 1967.

Klein, Christina. *Cold War Orientalism: Asia in the Middlebrow Imagination, 1945–1961.* Berkeley: University of California Press, 2003.

Kolko, Joyce, and Gabriel Kolko. *The Limits of Power: The World and United States Foreign Policy, 1945–1954.* New York: Harper and Row, 1972.

Kuniholm, Bruce Robellet. *The Origins of the Cold War in the Near East: Great Power Conflict and Diplomacy in Iran, Turkey, and Greece.* Princeton, N.J.: Princeton University Press, 1980.

Kunz, Diane B. *Butter and Guns: America's Cold War Economic Diplomacy.* New York: Free Press, 1997.

———. *The Economic Diplomacy of the Suez Crisis.* Chapel Hill: University of North Carolina Press, 1991.

Kyle, Keith. *Suez.* New York: St. Martin's, 1991.

Larres, Klaus. *Churchill's Cold War: The Politics of Personal Diplomacy.* New Haven, Conn.: Yale University Press, 2002.

Larres, Klaus, and Kenneth Alan Osgood. *The Cold War after Stalin's Death: A Missed Opportunity for Peace?* New York: Rowman and Littlefield, 2006.

Larson, Arthur. *Eisenhower: The President Nobody Knew.* New York: Scribner, 1968.

Larson, Deborah Welch. *Origins of Containment: A Psychological Explanation.* Princeton, N.J.: Princeton University Press, 1985.

Leaming, Barbara. *Churchill Defiant: Fighting On, 1945–1955.* New York: Harper, 2010.

LeFeber, Walter. *America, Russia, and the Cold War, 1945–1975.* New York: Wiley, 1976.

Leffler, Melvyn P. *A Preponderance of Power: National Security, the Truman Administration, and the Cold War.* Stanford Nuclear Age Series. Stanford, Calif.: Stanford University Press, 1992.

Leigh-Phippard, Helen. *Congress and US Military Aid to Britain: Interdependence and Dependence, 1949–56.* Southampton Studies in International Policy. New York: St. Martin's Press in association with the Mountbatten Centre for International Studies, University of Southampton, 1995.

Leventhal, F. M., and Roland E. Quinault. *Anglo-American Attitudes: From Revolution to Partnership.* Burlington, Vt.: Ashgate, 1988.

Louis, William Roger. *The British Empire in the Middle East 1945–1951: Arab Nationalism, the United States, and Postwar Imperialism.* Oxford: Clarendon, 1985.

Louis, William Roger, and Hedley Bull. *The "Special Relationship": Anglo-American
Relations since 1945.* Oxford [Oxfordshire]: Clarendon, 1986.

Louis, William Roger, and Roger Owen. *Suez 1956: The Crisis and Its Consequences.*
Oxford: Clarendon, 1989.

Love, Kennett. *Suez—the Twice-Fought War: A History.* New York: McGraw-Hill, 1969.

Lucas, W. Scott. *Divided We Stand: Britain, the US, and the Suez Crisis.* London: Hod-
der and Stoughton, 1991.

Lukacs, John. *The Duel: 10 May–31 July 1940 : The Eighty-Day Struggle between Churchill
and Hitler.* New York: Ticknor and Fields, 1991.

———. *Five Days in London, May 1940.* New Haven, Conn.: Yale University Press,
1999.

Lytle, Mark H. *The Origins of the Iranian-American Alliance, 1941–1953.* New York:
Holmes and Meier, 1987.

Manchester, William Raymond. *American Caesar: Douglas MacArthur, 1880–1964.* Boston: Little, Brown, 1978.

———. *The Last Lion: Winston Spencer Churchill; Alone, 1932–1940.* New York: Dell,
1988.

———. *The Last Lion: Winston Spencer Churchill; Visions of Glory 1874–1932.* New York:
Dell, 1989.

Manchester, William, and Paul Reid. *The Last Lion: Winston Spencer Churchill; Defender of the Realm, 1940–1965.* New York: Little, Brown, 2012.

Manderson-Jones, R. B. *The Special Relationship; Anglo-American Relations and Western European Unity 1947–56.* London: London School of Economics and Political
Science, 1972.

Mark, Chi-Kwan. *Hong Kong and the Cold War: Anglo-American Relations 1949–1957.*
Oxford: Clarendon, 2004.

Martin, Edwin W. *Divided Counsel: The Anglo-American Response to Communist Victory
in China.* Lexington: University Press of Kentucky, 1986.

Mawby, Spencer. *Containing Germany: Britain and the Arming of the Federal Republic.*
Contemporary History in Context Series. Houndmills, Basingstoke, Hampshire,
England: Macmillan, 1999.

Mayers, David Allan. *Cracking the Monolith: U.S. Policy against the Sino-Soviet Alliance,
1949–1955.* Baton Rouge: Louisiana State University Press, 1986.

McCullough, David G. *Truman.* New York: Simon and Schuster, 1992.

Medhurst, Martin J., ed. *Eisenhower's War of Words: Rhetoric and Leadership.* East Lansing: Michigan State University Press, 1994.

Melanson, Richard A., and David Allan Mayers. *Reevaluating Eisenhower: American
Foreign Policy in the 1950s.* Urbana: University of Illinois Press, 1987.

Melissen, Jan. *The Struggle for Nuclear Partnership: Britain, the United States, and the Making of an Ambiguous Alliance, 1952–1959*. Groningen: Styx, 1993.

Mikdadi, Faysal. *Gamal Abdel Nasser: A Bibliography*. New York: Greenwood, 1991.

Miller, Merle. *Plain Speaking: An Oral Biography of Harry S. Truman*. New York: Berkley, 1974.

Millis, Walter. *Arms and Men: A Study in American Military History*. New York: Putnam, 1956.

Neff, Donald. *Warriors at Suez*. New York: Linden Press/Simon and Schuster, 1981.

Newton, Jim. *Eisenhower: The White House Years*. New York: Doubleday, 2011.

Nichols, David A. *Eisenhower 1956: The President's Year of Crisis: Suez and the Brink of War*. New York: Simon and Schuster, 2011.

Ovendale, Ritchie. *The English-Speaking Alliance: Britain, the United States, the Dominions, and the Cold War, 1945–1951*. London: Allen and Unwin, 1985.

Painter, David S. *Oil and the American Century: The Political Economy of U.S. Foreign Oil Policy, 1941–1954*. Baltimore: Johns Hopkins University Press, 1986.

Patterson, James T. *Mr. Republican: A Biography of Robert A. Taft*. Boston: Houghton Mifflin, 1972.

Pearson, Jonathan. *Sir Anthony Eden and the Suez Crisis: Reluctant Gamble*. Basingstoke, England: Palgrave Macmillan, 2003.

Pelling, Henry. *Britain and the Marshall Plan*. New York: St. Martin's, 1988.

———. *Winston Churchill*. New York: Dutton, 1974.

Perret, Geoffrey. *Eisenhower*. New York: Random House, 1999.

———. *Jack: A Life Like No Other*. New York: Random House, 2001.

———. *Old Soldiers Never Die: The Life of Douglas MacArthur*. New York: Random House, 1996.

Petersen, Tore T. *The Middle East between the Great Powers: Anglo-American Conflict and Cooperation, 1952–7*. New York: St. Martin's, 2000.

Pilat, Joseph F., Robert E. Pendley, and Charles K. Ebinger. *Atoms for Peace: An Analysis after Thirty Years*. Westview Special Studies in International Relations. Boulder, Colo.: Westview, 1985.

Podeh, Elie. *The Decline of Arab Unity: The Rise and Fall of the United Arab Republic*. Brighton, England: Sussex Academic, 1999.

Pogue, Forrest C. *George C. Marshall*. New York: Viking, 1963.

Powaski, Ronald E. *The Entangling Alliance: The United States and European Security, 1950–1993*. Contributions to the Study of World History, no. 42. Westport, Conn.: Greenwood, 1994.

Prados, John. *Presidents' Secret Wars: CIA and Pentagon Covert Operations since World War II*. New York: Morrow, 1986.

———. *Safe for Democracy: The Secret Wars of the CIA*. Chicago: Dee, 2006.

———. *The Sky Would Fall: Operation Vulture: The U.S. Bombing Mission in Indochina, 1954.* New York: Dial, 1983.

———. *Vietnam: The History of an Unwinnable War, 1945–1975.* Lawrence: University Press of Kansas, 2009.

Pressman, Jeremy. *Warring Friends: Alliance Restraint in International Politics.* Ithaca: Cornell University Press, 2008.

Rabe, Stephen G. *Eisenhower and Latin America: The Foreign Policy of Anticommunism.* Chapel Hill: University of North Carolina Press, 1988.

———. *The Killing Zone: The United States Wages Cold War in Latin America.* New York: Oxford University Press, 2012.

Ranelagh, John. *The Agency: The Rise and Decline of the CIA.* New York: Simon and Schuster, 1986.

Rees, G. Wyn. *The Western European Union at the Crossroads: Between Trans-Atlantic Solidarity and European Integration.* Boulder, Colo.: Westview, 1998.

Renwick, Robin. *Fighting with Allies: America and Britain in Peace and at War.* New York: Times Books, 1996.

Richardson, Elmo. *The Presidency of Dwight D. Eisenhower.* Lawrence: Regents Press of Kansas, 1979.

Robertson, Terence. *Crisis: The Inside Story of the Suez Conspiracy.* New York: Atheneum, 1965.

Rodgers, Judith. *Winston Churchill.* World Leaders Past & Present. New York: Chelsea House, 1986.

Ross, Robert S., and Changbin Jiang. *Re-Examining the Cold War: U.S.-China Diplomacy, 1954–1973.* Cambridge: Harvard University Asia Center, 2001.

Rostow, W. W. *Open Skies: Eisenhower's Proposal of July 21, 1955.* Austin: University of Texas Press, 1982.

Rothwell, Victor. *Anthony Eden: A Political Biography, 1931–57.* New York: Manchester University Press, 1992.

Rovere, Richard Halworth, and Arthur M. Schlesinger. *The General and the President, and the Future of American Foreign Policy.* New York: Farrar, Straus and Young, 1951.

Ruane, Kevin. *The Rise and Fall of the European Defence Community: Anglo-American Relations and the Crisis of European Defence, 1950–55.* Cold War History Series. Houndmills, Basingstoke, Hampshire, England: Macmillan, 2000.

Rubin, Barry M. *Paved with Good Intentions: The American Experience and Iran.* New York: Oxford University Press, 1980.

Schaller, Michael. *Douglas MacArthur: The Far Eastern General.* New York: Oxford University Press, 1989.

Schneider, Ronald M. *Communism in Guatemala, 1944–1954.* New York: Praeger, 1958.

Smith, Jean Edward. *Eisenhower: In War and Peace.* New York: Random House, 2012.

Smith, Richard Norton. *Thomas E. Dewey and His Times.* New York: Simon and Schuster, 1982.

Sokolsky, Joel J. *Seapower in the Nuclear Age: The United States Navy and NATO 1949–80.* London: Routledge, 1991.

Spanier, John W. *The Truman-MacArthur Controversy and the Korean War.* Cambridge: Belknap Press of Harvard University Press, 1959.

Statler, Kathryn C., and Andrew L. Johns. *The Eisenhower Administration, the Third World, and the Globalization of the Cold War.* Harvard Cold War Studies Series. Lanham, Md.: Rowman and Littlefield, 2006.

Stephens, Robert. *Nasser: A Political Biography.* New York: Simon and Schuster, 1971.

Stoler, Mark A. *George C. Marshall: Soldier-Statesman of the American Century.* Twayne's Twentieth-Century American Biography Series, no. 10. Boston: Twayne, 1989.

Stolper, Thomas E. *China, Taiwan, and the Offshore Islands: Together with an Implication for Outer Mongolia and Sino-Soviet Relations.* Armonk, N.Y.: Sharpe, 1985.

Stone, I. F. *The Hidden History of the Korean War.* New York: Monthly Review Press, 1969.

Swaine, Michael D., Tuosheng Zhang, and Danielle F. S. Cohen. *Managing Sino-American Crises: Case Studies and Analysis.* Washington, D.C.: Carnegie Endowment for International Peace, 2006.

Thomas, Evan. *Ike's Bluff: President Eisenhower's Secret Battle to Save the World.* New York: Little, Brown, 2012.

Thomas, Hugh. *Suez.* New York: Harper and Row, 1967.

Thorpe, D. R. *Eden: The Life and Times of Anthony Eden, First Earl of Avon, 1897–1977.* London: Chatto and Windus, 2003.

Tompkins, C. David. *Senator Arthur H. Vandenberg: the Evolution of a Modern Republican, 1884–1945.* Lansing: Michigan State University Press, 1970.

Trachtenberg, Marc. *A Constructed Peace: The Making of the European Settlement, 1945–1963.* Princeton Studies in International History and Politics. Princeton, N.J.: Princeton University Press, 1999.

Troen, S. Ilan, and Moshe Shemesh. *The Suez-Sinai Crisis, 1956: Retrospective and Reappraisal.* New York: Columbia University Press, 1990.

Tudda, Chris. *The Truth Is Our Weapon: The Rhetorical Diplomacy of Dwight D. Eisenhower and John Foster Dulles.* Baton Rouge: Louisiana State University Press, 2006.

Whitfield, Stephen J. *The Culture of the Cold War.* The American Moment series. Baltimore: Johns Hopkins University Press, 1991.

Wicker, Tom. *Dwight D. Eisenhower.* New York: Times Books, 2002.

———. *One of Us: Richard Nixon and the American Dream.* New York: Random House, 1991.

Wilber, Donald Newton. *Clandestine Service History: Overthrow of Premier Mossadeq of Iran, November 1952–August 1953.* Washington, D.C.: Central Intelligence Agency, Clandestine Service, 1969.

Williams, William Appleman. *The Tragedy of American Diplomacy.* New York: Dell, 1962.

Wise, David, and Thomas B. Ross. *The Invisible Government.* New York: Vantage, 1964.

Woods, Randall Bennett, and Howard Jones. *Dawning of the Cold War: The United States' Quest for Order.* Athens: University of Georgia Press, 1991.

Wunderlin, Clarence E. *Robert A. Taft: Ideas, Tradition, and Party in U.S. Foreign Policy.* Biographies in American Foreign Policy, no. 12. Lanham, Md.: SR, 2005.

Xia, Yafeng. *Negotiating with the Enemy U.S.-China Talks during the Cold War, 1949–1972.* Bloomington: Indiana University Press, 2006.

Yaqub, Salim. *Containing Arab Nationalism: The Eisenhower Doctrine and the Middle East.* Chapel Hill: University of North Carolina Press, 2004.

Young, John W. *Winston Churchill's Last Campaign: Britain and the Cold War, 1951–55.* Oxford: Clarendon, 1996.

Zabih, Sepehr. *The Mossadegh Era: Roots of the Iranian Revolution.* Chicago: Lake View Press, 1982.

Zubok, V. M., and Konstantin Pleshakov. *Inside the Kremlin's Cold War: From Stalin to Khrushchev.* Cambridge: Harvard University Press, 1996.

Journal Articles

Adamthwaite, Anthony. "Overstretched and Overstrung: Eden, the Foreign Office and the Making of Policy, 1951–5." *International Affairs (Royal Institute of International Affairs 1944–)* 64, no. 2 (1988): 241–59.

Addison, Paul. "The Political Beliefs of Winston Churchill." *Transactions of the Royal Historical Society* 30 (1980): 23–47.

Aldrich, Winthrop W. "The Suez Crisis: A Footnote to History." *Foreign Affairs* 45, no. 3 (1967): 541–52.

Anderson, David L. "Eisenhower, Dienbienphu, and the Origins of United States Military Intervention in Vietnam." *Mid-America* 71 (1989): 101–17.

Ashton, Nigel John. "The Hijacking of a Pact: The Formation of the Baghdad Pact and Anglo-American Tensions in the Middle East, 1955–1958." *Review of International Studies* 19 (1993): 123–37.

Ball, S. J. "Military Nuclear Relations between the United States and Great Britain under the Terms of the McMahon Act, 1946–1958." *Historical Journal* 38, no. 2 (1995): 439–54.

Ball, Stuart. "Churchill and the Conservative Party." *Transactions of the Royal Historical Society* 11, no. 1 (2001): 307–30.

Bentley, Michael. "Liberal Toryism in the Twentieth Century." *Transactions of the Royal Historical Society* 4 (1994): 177–201.

Bernstein, Barton J. "The Origins of America's Commitments in Korea." *Foreign Service Journal* 55 (1978): 10–13.

Boughton, James M. "Northwest of Suez: The 1956 Crisis and the IMF." *International Monetary Fund, Secretary's Dept.* (2001): 425–46.

Brands, H. W. "The Age of Vulnerability: Eisenhower and the National Insecurity State." *American Historical Review* 94, no. 4 (1989): 963–89.

———. "The Cairo-Tehran Connection in Anglo-American Rivalry in the Middle East, 1951–1953." *International History Review* 11, no. 3 (1989): 434–56.

———. "A Cold War Foreign Legion? The Eisenhower Administration and the Volunteer Freedom Corps." *Military Affairs: The Journal of Military History, Including Theory and Technology* 52, no. 1 (1988): 7–11.

———. "The Dwight D. Eisenhower Administration, Syngman Rhee, and the 'Other Geneva' Conference of 1954." *Pacific Historical Review* 56, no. 1 (1987): 59–85.

———. "Testing Massive Retaliation: Credibility and Crisis Management in the Taiwan Strait." *International Security* 12, no. 4 (1988): 124–51.

Brinkley, Douglas. "Dean Acheson and the 'Special Relationship': The West Point Speech of December 1962." *Historical Journal* 33, no. 3 (1990): 599–608.

Bundy, McGeorge. "Atomic Diplomacy Reconsidered." *Bulletin of the American Academy of Arts and Sciences* 38, no. 1 (1984): 25–44.

Buzenberg, Bill. "A Half Century Later, Another Warning in Eisenhower's Address Rings True." Center for Public Integrity, January 17, 2011.

Calhoun, Ricky-Dale. "The Art of Strategic Counterintelligence, The Musketeer's Cloak: Strategic Deception during the Suez Crisis of 1956." Central Intelligence Agency, June 20, 2007. www.cia.gov./library/center-for-the-study=of-intelligence/csi-publications/csi-studies/studies/vol51no2/the-art-of-strategic-count.

Carey, Roger. "The British Nuclear Force: Deterrent or Economy Measure?" *Military Affairs: The Journal of Military History, Including Theory and Technology* 36, no. 4 (1972): 133–38.

Carlton, David. "Churchill and the Two Evil Empires." *Transactions of the Royal Historical Society* 6, no. 1 (2004): 165–85.

Chang, Gordon H., and He Di. "The Absence of War in the U.S.–China Confrontation over Quemoy and Matsu in 1954–1955: Contingency, Luck, Deterrence." *American Historical Review* 98, no. 5 (1993): 1500–524.

Charmley, John. "Churchill and the American Alliance." *Transactions of the Royal Historical Society* 11, no. 1 (2001): 353–71.

Clubb, O. Edmund. "Formosa and the Offshore Islands in American Policy, 1950–1955." *Political Science Quarterly* 74, no. 4 (1959): 517–31.

Connelly, Matthew. "Rethinking the Cold War and Decolonization: The Grand Strategy of the Algerian War for Independence." *International Journal of Middle East Studies* 33, no. 2 (2001): 221–45.

Cosroe, Chaqueri. "Did the Soviets Play a Role in Founding the Tudeh Party in Iran?" *Cahiers du Monde* 40, no. 3 (1999): 497–528.

Dallek, Robert. "The Untold Story of the Bay of Pigs." *Newsweek*, August 22 and 29, 2011, 26–28.

Devereux, David R. "Britain, the Commonwealth and the Defence of the Middle East 1948–56." *Journal of Contemporary History* 24, no. 2 (1989): 327–45.

Dingman, Roger. "John Foster Dulles and the Creation of the South-East Asia Treaty Organization in 1954." *International History Review* 11, no. 3 (1989): 457–77.

Dobson, Alan P. "Labour or Conservative: Does It Matter in Anglo-American Relations?" *Journal of Contemporary History* 25, no. 4 (1990): 387–407.

Dooley, Howard. "Great Britain's 'Last Battle' in the Middle East: Notes on Cabinet Planning during the Suez Crisis of 1956." *International History Review* 11, no. 3 (1989): 486–517.

Duchin, Brian R. "The 'Agonizing Reappraisal': Eisenhower, Dulles, and the European Defense Community." *Diplomatic History* 16, no. 2 (April 1992): 201–22.

Dulles, John Foster. "A Policy of Boldness." *Life*, May 19, 1952, 146–57.

Eisenhower, Dwight D. "I Shall Go to Korea" Speech. October 25, 1952. http://www.eisenhower.archives.gov/education/bsa/citizenship_merit_badge/speeches_national_historical_importance/i_shall_go_to_korea.pdf.

———. "Special Message to the Congress on the Situation in the Middle East." (1957). www.presidency.ucsb.edu/ws/index.php?pid=11007&st=&st1=.

Eisenhower, Susan. "50 Years Later, We're Still Ignoring Ike's Warning. *Washington Post*, January 16, 2011, B3.

Francis, Martin. "Tears, Tantrums, and Bared Teeth: The Emotional Economy of Three Conservative Prime Ministers, 1951–1963." *Journal of British Studies* 41, no. 3 (2002): 354–87.

Friedman, Edward. "Nuclear Blackmail and the End of the Korean War." *Modern China* 1, no. 1 (1975): 75–91.

Gallicchio, Marc. "The Kuriles Controversy: U.S. Diplomacy in the Soviet-Japan Border Dispute, 1941–1956." *Pacific Historical Review* 60, no. 1 (1991): 69–101.

Glickman, Harvey. "The Toryness of English Conservatism." *Journal of British Studies* 1, no. 1 (1961): 111–43.

"Global Firepower-2011 World Military Strength Ranking." www.globalfirepower.com.

Gordon, Leonard H. D. "United States Opposition to Use of Force in the Taiwan Strait, 1954–1962." *Journal of American History* 72, no. 3 (1985): 637–60.

Gordon, Max. "A Case History of U.S. Subversion: Guatemala, 1954." *Sciences and Society* 35 (1971): 129–55.

Greenstein, Fred I. "Eisenhower as an Activist President: A Look at New Evidence." *Political Science Quarterly* 94, no. 4 (1980): 575–99.

Greenstein, Fred I, and Richard H Immerman. "Effective National Security Advising: Recovering the Eisenhower Legacy." *Political Science Quarterly* 115, no. 3 (2000): 335–45.

———. "What Did Eisenhower Tell Kennedy about Indochina? The Politics of Misperception." *Journal of American History* 79, no. 2 (1992): 568–87.

Hahn, Peter L. "Securing the Middle East: The Eisenhower Doctrine of 1957." *Presidential Studies Quarterly* 36, no. 1 (2006): 38–47.

Halperin, Morton H., and Tang Tsou. "United States Policy toward the Offshore Islands." *Public Policy* 15 (1966): 119–38.

Hamburg, Roger. "Massive Retaliation Revisited." *Military Affairs: The Journal of Military History, Including Theory and Technology* 38, no. 1 (1974): 17–23.

Harkness, Richard, and Gladys Harkness. "America's Secret Agents: The Mysterious Doings of the CIA." *Saturday Evening Post*, November 6, 1954, 34–35.

Heiss, Mary Ann "The United States, Great Britain, and the Creation of the Iranian Oil Consortium, 1953–1954." *International History Review* 16, no. 3 (1994): 511–35.

Hennessy, Peter. "Churchill and the Premiership." *Transactions of the Royal Historical Society* 11, no. 1 (2001): 295–306.

Herring, George C., and Richard H. Immerman. "Eisenhower, Dulles, and Dienbienphu: 'The Day We Didn't Go to War' Revisited." *Journal of American History* 71, no. 2 (1984): 343–63.

Hoxie, R. Gordon. "Eisenhower and Presidential Leadership." *Presidential Studies Quarterly* 23 (1983): 589–612.

Immerman, Richard H. "Guatemala as Cold War History." *Political Science Quarterly* 95, no. 4 (1981): 629–53.

———. "Psychology." *Journal of American History* 77, no. 1 (1990): 169–80.

Jackson, Michael Gordon. "Beyond Brinkmanship: Eisenhower, Nuclear War Fighting, and Korea, 1953–1968." *Presidential Studies Quarterly* 35, no. 1 (2005): 52–75.

Jalal, Ayesha. "Towards the Baghdad Pact: South Asia and Middle East Defence in the Cold War, 1947–1955." *International History Review* 11, no. 3 (1989): 409–33.

Kaufman, Victor S. "'Chirep': The Anglo-American Dispute over Chinese Representation in the United Nations, 1950–71." *English Historical Review* 115, no. 461 (2000): 354–77.

Keefer, Edward C. "The Truman Administration and the South Korean Political Crisis of 1952: Democracy's Failure?" *Pacific Historical Review* 60, no. 2 (1991): 145–68.

Larres, Klaus. "Eisenhower and the First Forty Days after Stalin's Death: The Incompatibility of Détente and Political Warfare." *Diplomacy & Statecraft* 6, no. 2 (1995): 431–69.

Lukacs, John. "Ike, Winston, and the Russians." *New York Times*, February 10, 1991. http://www.nytimes.com/1991/02/10/books/ike-winston-and-the-russians.html ?pagewanted=all&src=pm.

Maddox, Robert James. "Atomic Diplomacy: A Study in Creative Writing." *Journal of American History* 59, no. 4 (1973): 925–34.

Marchio, James D. "Risking General War in Pursuit of Limited Objectives: U.S. Military Contingency Planning for Poland in the Wake of the 1956 Hungarian Uprising." *Journal of Military History* 66, no. 3 (2002): 783–812.

Mark, Chi-Kwan. "A Reward for Good Behaviour in the Cold War: Bargaining over the Defence of Hong Kong, 1949–1957." *International History Review* 22, no. 4 (2000): 837–61.

Marks, Frederick W. "The Real Hawk at Dienbienphu: Dulles or Eisenhower?" *Pacific Historical Review* 59, no. 3 (1990): 297–322.

Matray, James I. "Captive of the Cold War: The Decision to Divide Korea at the 38th Parallel." *Pacific Historical Review* 50, no. 2 (1981): 145–68.

May, Ernest R. "The Nature of Foreign Policy: The Calculated versus the Axiomatic." *Daedalus* 91, no. 4 (1962): 653–67.

Mayers, David. "Eisenhower's Containment Policy and the Major Communist Powers, 1953–1956." *International History Review* 5, no. 1 (1983): 59–83.

McCauley, Brian. "Hungary and Suez, 1956: The Limits of Soviet and American Power." *Journal of Contemporary History* 16, no. 4 (1981): 777–800.

McKibbin, Ross. "Why Was There No Marxism in Great Britain?" *English Historical Review* 99, no. 391 (1984): 297–331.

McMahon, Robert J. "Eisenhower and Third World Nationalism: A Critique of the Revisionists." *Political Science Quarterly* 101, no. 3 (1986): 453–73.

———. "The Illusion of Vulnerability: American Reassessments of the Soviet Threat, 1955–1956." *International History Review* 18, no. 3 (1996): 591–619.

Murray, Geoffrey. "Glimpses of Suez 1956." *International Journal* 29, no. 1 (1974): 46–66.

Nelson, Anna Kasten. "John Foster Dulles and the Bipartisan Congress." *Political Science Quarterly* 102, no. 1 (1987): 43–64.

"Nixon's Secret Report Warns: Don't Recognize Red Chinese." *Newsweek*, January 4, 1954, 17.

Norman, John. "MacArthur's Blockade Proposals against Red China." *Pacific Historical Review* 26, no. 2 (1957): 161–74.

Oren, Michael B. "Escalation to Suez: The Egypt-Israel Border War, 1949–56." *Journal of Contemporary History* 24, no. 2 (1989): 347–73.

Owen, Nicholas. "The Conservative Party and Indian Independence, 1945–1947." *Historical Journal* 46, no. 2 (2003): 403–36.

Parmentier, Guillaume. "The British Press in the Suez Crisis." *Historical Journal* 23, no. 2 (1980): 435–48.

Paterson, Thomas G. "Potsdam, the Atomic Bomb, and the Cold War: A Discussion with James F. Byrnes." *Pacific Historical Review* 41, no. 2 (1972): 225–30.

Pemberton, Gregory J. "Australia, the United States and the Indochina Crisis of 1954." *Diplomatic History* 13 (1989): 45–66.

Petersen, Tore Tingvold. "Anglo-American Rivalry in the Middle East: The Struggle for the Buraimi Oasis, 1952–1957." *International History Review* 14, no. 1 (1992): 71–91.

Rabe, S. G. "Eisenhower Revisionism: A Decade of Scholarship." *Diplomatic History* 17, no. 1 (1993): 97–115.

Ramsay, Kristopher W. "Politics at the Water's Edge: Crisis Bargaining and Electoral Competition." *Journal of Conflict Resolution* 48, no. 4 (2004): 459–86.

Rose, Norman. "The Resignation of Anthony Eden." *Historical Journal* 25, no. 4 (1982): 911–31.

Ruane, Kevin. "Anthony Eden, British Diplomacy and the Origins of the Geneva Conference of 1954." *Historical Journal* 37, no. 1 (1994): 153–72.

———. "Refusing to Pay the Price: British Foreign Policy and the Pursuit of Victory in Vietnam, 1952–4." *English Historical Review* 110, no. 435 (1995): 70–92.

Rubinstein, W. D. "Education and the Social Origins of British Élites 1880–1970." *Past and Present*, no. 112 (1986): 163–207.

Rushkoff, Bennett C. "Eisenhower, Dulles and the Quemoy-Matsu Crisis, 1954–1955." *Political Science Quarterly* 96, no. 3 (1981): 465–80.

Ryan, Henry B. "A New Look at Churchill's 'Iron Curtain' Speech." *Historical Journal* 22, no. 4 (1979): 895–920.

Saunders, Richard M. "Military Force in the Foreign Policy of the Eisenhower Presidency." *Political Science Quarterly* 100, no. 1 (1985): 97–116.

Schlesinger, Stephen. "How Dulles Worked the Coup d'Etat." *Nation*, October 28, 1978, 425.

Schmidt, Gustav. "Divided Europe—Divided Germany (1950–63)." *Contemporary European History* 3, no. 2 (1994): 155–92.

Shaw, Tony. "The Information Research Department of the British Foreign Office and the Korean War, 1950–53." *Journal of Contemporary History* 34, no. 2 (1999): 263–81.

Streeter, Stephen M. "Interpreting the 1954 U.S. Intervention in Guatemala: Realist, Revisionist, and Postrevisionist Perspectives." *History Teacher* 34, no. 1 (2000): 61–74.

Warnock, A. Timothy. "Air War Korea, 1950–1953." *Air Force-Magazine.com* 83, no. 10 (October 2000).

Weiler, Peter. "British Labour and the Cold War: The Foreign Policy of the Labour Governments, 1945–1951." *Journal of British Studies* 26, no. 1 (1987): 54–82.

Wiltz, John Edward. "The MacArthur Hearings of 1951: The Secret Testimony." *Military Affairs: The Journal of Military History, Including Theory and Technology* 39, no. 4 (1975): 167–73.

Young, John W. "Churchill and East-West Détente." *Transactions of the Royal Historical Society* 11, no. 1 (2001): 373–92.

———. "Churchill's 'No' to Europe: The 'Rejection' of European Union by Churchill's Post-War Government, 1951–1952." *Historical Journal* 28, no. 4 (1985): 923–37.

———. "Churchill, the Russians and the Western Alliance: The Three-Power Conference at Bermuda, December 1953." *English Historical Review* 101, no. 401 (1986): 889–912.

———. "Great Britain's Latin American Dilemma: The Foreign Office and the Overthrow of 'Communist' Guatemala, June 1954." *International History Review* 8, no. 4 (1986): 573–92.

INDEX

MacArthur, Douglas: atomic weapons and, 50, 51, 168n5; on collective security, 41; Indochina and, 68; influence on Eisenhower, 3; Korean War, plans for, 51, 150–51

Macmillan, Harold, *plates;* appointed prime minister, 147, 190n23; Eden removal and, 5, 112, 140–47, 190n18; Egypt Committee and, 120; on nuclear war, 47; sterling crisis and, 8; Suez Crisis and, 121–22, 127–28

Mahan, Alfred Thayer, 3

Makins, Roger, *plates;* on balance-of-power diplomacy, 26, 42–43; on British Commonwealth, 42–43; on colonialism, 35–36; Guatemala and, 105; Indochina and, 33, 73; Korean War and, 55–56, 58–59

Manderson-Jones, R. B., 6

Manila Pact, 76, 87

Mao Zedong, 46, 54, 77, 81

Mark, Chi-Kwan, 6

Martin, Joseph W., 37

Mattison, Gordon, 98

McCarthy, Joseph R., 74

Menzies, Robert, 125–26, 185n40

MI6, 111, 113, 116, 120, 144, 186n50

Middle East: British concerns in Iran and Egypt, 12; British protectorates in, 112–13; British sphere of interest in, 6–7; Communism and, 112, 134, 135, 147; Eisenhower Doctrine, 153–54; Soviet expansionism in, 90–91, 144–45. *See also* Iran; Nasser, Gamal Abdel; Suez Crisis

military alliances, regional, 15, 36–37

military-industrial complex, Brands on, 157n5

military spending reductions, 14, 15

Molotov, Vyacheslav, 37, 67

Monckton, Walter, 120

moral principles, 25–26, 83

Moran, Charles McMoran Wilson, Lord, 56, 113

Mossadegh, Mohammed, 5, 89, 91–99

Mossman, James, 120

Murphy, Robert, 121–22, 146

Mussolini, Benito, comparisons to, 114–15, 119, 128, 147

Mutual Defense Treaty with Formosa, 43

Nagy, Imre, 133

Nasiri, Nematollah, 98

Nasser, Gamal Abdel: British assassination plots against, 111, 113, 119–21, 129, 144, 186n50; British vs. U.S. views of, 111, 114, 116–17, 118–19, 127–29; China and Aswan Dam issues and, 117–18; covert overthrow plan against, 111, 129, 131; Eden's vehemence about, 116; France and, 118; French assassination plots against, 180n5, 182n25; Hitler or Mussolini, comparison to, 112, 114–15, 119, 124, 128, 147, 190n14; Islamic Empire idea of, 111, 118; Israeli assassination plot against, 183n25; oil and, 138–39; *The Philosophy of Revolution,* 111, 117; Suez Crisis and, 112, 118, 121–27, 131, 136; U.S. assassination plans against, 129

national interests, British colonialism and, 32

National Security Council (NSC): Guatemala and, 101; Iran and, 92–93; Suez Crisis and, 134, 140

NATO (North Atlantic Treaty Organization), 24

Nehru, Jawaharlal, 54, 60, 74

New Look defense policy: military alliances, dependence on, 15; military buildup replaced with, 2; nuclear weapons and, 80; Ridgway on, 39; Taft, Mahan, and, 3

Nixon, Richard M., *plates;* on China recognition, 24–25; détente and, 149; on independence from British and French colonialism, 135; on Indochina, 63; on Iran, 93; on nuclear weapons, 85; Vietnam War and, 156

North Atlantic Council, 24

North Atlantic Treaty Organization (NATO), 24

North Korea. *See* Korean War

nuclear energy, 23–24

nuclear weapons and atomic diplomacy: Eisenhower statements on, 44, 162n33; endorsements of, by Radford, Dulles, and Nixon, 85; Formosa Straits crisis, 43–46, 76–87; Indochina and, 63–75, 171n37; Korean War and, 21–23, 50–62, 150–51; MacArthur and, 50, 51, 168n5; Macmillan on, 47; Middle East and, 137; Soviet Union, U.S. plans for attack against, 137; Truman and, 50; U.S.-British disagreement on nature of, 23, 79–80

Nutting, Anthony, 77–78, 115–16

oil: Eisenhower deal with Saud on, 112, 153; embargo on Britain, fear of, 134; Iranian, 12, 91–96, 99–100; Soviets and, 135; Suez Crisis and, 112, 121, 138–39, 143–44, 187n64

Old Right, 3–4, 9, 62, 148

Oliver, Robert T., 39

Operation Ajax, 94–100

Operation Blue Bat, 155

Operation Boot, 95

Operation Everready, 49, 57–62

Operation Musketeer, 111, 119, 122, 183n31

Operation Omega, 111–12, 117, 119

Operation PBSUCCESS, 101–10

Operation Pluto, 155

Operation Straggle, 111, 117, 153

Operation Vulture, 63, 88, 151

Organization of American States (OAS), 103, 106, 109, 178n34

Pahlavi, Ashraf, 97

Pahlavi, Mohammad Reza, Shah of Iran, 94, 97, 99, 177n23

Pan-Arabism, 115, 181n14, 181n24

Patterson, Richard C., Jr., 178n35

"peaceful coexistence," 37–38, 46

Pellay, Jean-Marie, 180n5

People's Republic of China. *See* China, Communist

Peterson, Tore T., 20

Peurifoy, John E., 102–3

The Philosophy of Revolution (Nasser), 111, 116

Pineau, Christian, 138, 141

"A Policy of Boldness" (Dulles), 4

Quemoy and Matsu (Formosa Straits Crisis), 43–46, 76–88, 152, 166n35, 174n83

Quinn, Frank, 120

Radford, Arthur W.: on atomic weapons, 85; on Geneva Agreements, 74–75; Indochina and, 27, 30–31, 63, 64, 67, 68, 75, 88; in London, 29

Reagan, Ronald, 136, 149, 155

regional military alliances, 15, 36–37

Republican foreign policy agenda: Churchill on, 51; Eisenhower and Old Right ideas, 3–4, 9, 62, 148; Eisenhower-Dulles team and, 4–5

Rhee, Syngman, 4, 49, 57–62, 150–51, 169n21

Ridgway, Matthew B., 38–39, 165n28

Rio Pact, 178n34

Robertson, Walter S., 60, 61–62

Roosevelt, Kermit, 95, 96, 99, 177n17

Rubin, Barry, 90

Rusk, Dean, 28

Salisbury, Robert Gascoyne-Cecil, Lord, 15, 61, 99, 112, 144–45, 150, *plates*

Saud, King of Saudi Arabia, 112, 139, 181n10

Schwarzkopf, Norman, 97–98

SDECE (French intelligence service), 180n5, 182n25

SEATO. *See* Southeast Asia Treaty Organization

Seventh Fleet, 52, 76, 83, 86
Shah of Iran (Mohammad Reza Pahlavi),
94, 97, 99, 177n23
Shuckburgh, C. A. E. (Evelyn), 100, 115
Sinclair, John 'Sinbad,' 116
Sino-Soviet Treaty, 30–31, 82–83
Sixth Fleet, 133
Smith, Gregor W., 139
Smith, Walter Bedell: Indochina and, 33,
34, 67, 69, 73; Iran and, 96, 98; Korean
War and, 55–56
Snyder, Howard, 137
Southeast Asia Treaty Organization
(SEATO): clarification of role of, 87;
collective security and, 150; creation of,
76; Eden on, 40; Indochina and, 65–66,
70–71
South Korea, defense perimeter and, 50.
See also Korean War; Rhee, Syngman
Soviet Union: Bermuda Conference and,
22–23; Churchill's possible visit to,
14–15, 36, 160n13; Churchill vs. Eisenhower on, 149–50; compared to Hitler
by Eisenhower, 137; conciliatory speech
from Eisenhower (April 1953), 13–14;
Czechoslovakia, invasion of, 136; détente
vs. Cold War approach to, 12–16; Egypt
and, 111; Formosa Straits crisis and, 82;
Hungarian Revolution and, 133, 134–36;
Indochina, nuclear weapons, and, 68;
Iran and, 90–91, 93; Middle East and, 8,
90–91, 144–45; nuclear weapons, fear of,
82–83; Stalin, death of, 12–13, 93; Suez
Crisis and, 134, 136–37; U.S. nuclear
attack plans against, 137; U.S. nuclear
weapons and, 54
"special relationship" between U.S. and
Great Britain, 2–6, 11–12
Stalin, Joseph, 12–13, 93
sterling crisis in Great Britain, 8, 112,
138–39
Stevenson, Adlai, 45, 76
Strang, William, 14

Suez Canal Users Association (SCUA),
126–27
Suez Crisis: Aswan Dam as trigger for, 117–
18; British, French, and Israeli military
intervention, 6–7, 111, 122–23, 130–33,
136; economic blackmail of Britain and,
145–46; Eden's legalistic approach to,
121; Eisenhower's public statements on,
125–26, 130, 185n40; Eisenhower's reaction and sterling crisis, 7–8, 112, 132–33;
Kirkpatrick on, 126; London Conference
on, 123, 125; Menzies mission, 125–26,
185n40; Nasser's view of, 121; SCUA proposals, 126–27; Soviet response to, 136–
37; United Nations and, 127–28, 134, 137;
U.S.-British relationship and, 19–20, 24;
U.S. Sixth Fleet actions, 133; U.S. vs. British view of, 112, 118–20, 123–25, 127–29,
133–34, 153; world opinion and economic
pressure on, 121
Sun, Yi, 76–77
Sun Tzu, 145
superpower status, 36
Syria, 111, 117, 153

Taft, Robert A., 3, 17–18, 25, 150
Taiwan. *See* Formosa
Thomas, Evan, 57
Three Power meeting, 23, 36, 37
transatlantic Anglo-American alliance:
bridge metaphor for, 71; British weakness
and, 5–6; Cold War pressures and fracturing of, 20; Eden's lack of subservience
and Churchill's accommodation efforts,
5; Eisenhower-Churchill role reversal
and, 1–2; Formosa Straits crisis and,
78–79; Middle East, Suez Crisis, and,
6–8; military considerations in, 6; Republican foreign policy agenda and, 3–4;
"special relationship" between U.S. and
Great Britain, 2–6, 11–12. *See also specific
policy issues*
Tripartite Agreement of 1950, 130, 132